Suddenly Diverse

Suddenly Diverse

*How School Districts Manage
Race and Inequality*

ERICA O. TURNER

THE UNIVERSITY OF CHICAGO PRESS   CHICAGO AND LONDON

The University of Chicago Press, Chicago 60637
The University of Chicago Press, Ltd., London
© 2020 by The University of Chicago
All rights reserved. No part of this book may be used or reproduced in any manner whatsoever without written permission, except in the case of brief quotations in critical articles and reviews. For more information, contact the University of Chicago Press, 1427 E. 60th St., Chicago, IL 60637.
Published 2020
Printed in the United States of America

29 28 27 26 25 24 23 22 21 20   1 2 3 4 5

ISBN-13: 978-0-226-67522-0 (cloth)
ISBN-13: 978-0-226-67536-7 (paper)
ISBN-13: 978-0-226-67553-4 (e-book)
DOI: https://doi.org/10.7208/chicago/9780226675534.001.0001

Library of Congress Cataloging-in-Publication Data

Names: Turner, Erica O., author.
Title: Suddenly diverse : how school districts manage race and inequality / Erica O. Turner.
Description: Chicago : University of Chicago Press, [2020] | Includes bibliographical references and index.
Identifiers: LCCN 2019024371 | ISBN 9780226675220 (cloth) | ISBN 9780226675367 (paperback) | ISBN 9780226675534 (ebook)
Subjects: LCSH: Educational equalization—United States. | Multicultural education—United States. | School management and organization—United States.
Classification: LCC LC213.2 .T87 2020 | DDC 379.2/60973—dc23
LC record available at https://lccn.loc.gov/2019024371

♾ This paper meets the requirements of ANSI/NISO Z39.48-1992 (Permanence of Paper).

FOR

MY FATHER, CHARLES B. TURNER JR.,

THE CITY PLANNER,

AND

MY MOTHER, KATHLEEN OWYANG TURNER,

THE EDUCATION AND CIVIL RIGHTS ADVOCATE

Contents

Preface

This book is about two school districts, Milltown and Fairview, at a complex and precarious moment for the two public school systems and for public education more broadly. The economic resources and politics of the communities they served differed, but as their student populations were becoming more racially diverse and more unequal, both Milltown's and Fairview's school district leaders were trying to navigate inequity while under substantial pressures. They were expected to equip all students—irrespective of race, poverty, language, or legal status—with the knowledge and skills needed for democratic citizenship and success in an increasingly high-tech, globalizing, diverse, and economically inequitable world. Yet expectations for academic achievement and pressure to increase test scores were greater than ever, education budgets had been slashed, competition for students had grown, and the public schools were confronting political pressures from multiple directions.

The story I tell here is about school *district* officials: the school board members, superintendents, assistant superintendents, and central office managers who are responsible for leading public school systems. This book illuminates how they make sense of the challenges of poverty, racial diversity, and inequality; navigate complex pressures and equity issues; and come to respond with new managerial policies that, in practice, reinforce inequity.

I collected the data described and analyzed here in Wisconsin in 2009 and 2010 in two specific places. Milltown is more working-class and more conservative. Fairview is more middle-class and quite politically liberal. However, these two cases illuminate broader questions of relevance to people in school districts across the country: how public schools address greater diversity and inequality, economic anxiety, policy pressures, and challenges to their legitimacy, *and* how school district officials perpetuate inequity as they try to challenge it.

Wisconsin in 2009 and early 2010 was an instructive time and place to witness local school district leaders, these everyday managers of the state, dealing with the intersecting demographic, economic, and political pressures which are unfolding in communities across the country. Districts were grappling with the immense effects of state disinvestment, as well as school choice and test-based accountability policies put into place in the mid- to late 1990s and early 2000s. At the same time, the global financial crisis and the Great Recession were reaching their peak. The state's school district leaders were largely struggling on their own—in a relatively quiet manner—to respond to increased demands with less money. Just a year later, in early 2011 after this data was collected, the newly elected Republican Governor Scott Walker would sign into law Act 10, a budget bill which cut compensation and benefits for state workers and also weakened collective bargaining for teachers and some other public sector unions in the state. This move allowed school districts to balance budgets left depleted by state disinvestment by grabbing back benefits they had previously promised to teachers. The governor and the state of Wisconsin, in a sense, imposed a different solution to the same problems of rising costs and long-standing state disinvestment in public education. But this earlier time period, before Act 10, provides a window into how school district leaders deal with these challenges mostly on their own, as many across the country do today.

It might be tempting to think that the Milltown and Fairview school districts in 2009 and 2010 are cases with little relevance to the present moment. That would be a mistake. In those years Barack Obama was early in his tenure as the first Black president of the United States and the 2001 reauthorization of the Elementary and Secondary Education Act, also known as the No Child Left Behind Act (NCLB), was still the law of the land; but the issues of racial inequity and sustaining a commitment to public schools, which Milltown and Fairview district leaders confronted and which are examined in this book, are even more relevant today, as explicit white supremacy and nativism are resurgent and the privatization and erosion of public institutions like public schools have intensified in the intervening years.

In fact, there are considerable continuities between the Milltown and Fairview contexts in 2009 and 2010 and what has happened since. The school-aged population in the United States is now more racially diverse and more unequal than ever. American public schools now enroll more students identified as Native American, Asian, Black, and Latinx, than white (Maxwell 2014; US Department of Education 2013). More than half of US school children now qualify for federally subsidized meals (Suitts 2015). The trends contributing to rising economic inequality and financial pressures on these districts and families had begun earlier, and the consequences of the Great Recession continued for many years and even worsened. States made severe budget cuts in subsequent years, particularly in education, and many states still have not yet recovered (Leachman, Masterson, and Figueroa 2017).

In education policy, the Every Student Succeeds Act (ESSA) has replaced NCLB as a "friendlier," more flexible state-determined account-ability system, one that will still rely upon yearly high-stakes testing. Budget cuts and proposals to deregulate for-profit schooling or further privatize various aspects of education (e.g., scholarship tax credits, new vouchers initiatives) are simply a new phase in the longer-running pattern of disinvestment and injection of market competition into public education that has been in place since the 1980s. These earlier developments set the stage for what has followed.

When I started this research, the era of color-blind racism seemed firmly underfoot. The 1990s saw a dramatic rise in the notion that racism is a historical relic in US society, that people "no longer see race," and that racial inequality today is explained by individual effort or perceived cultural differences—what Bonilla-Silva (2003) has called color-blind racism. Despite talk of a "postracial" era, racism persisted in its many guises and overt white supremacy was lurking at the edges. I wasn't familiar with the vast world of white supremacist and nativist websites before I started this research, but in 2008 and 2009 I easily stumbled upon them when I searched online for information on anti-immigrant ordinances and "sanctuary" cities. Racism and white nationalism are more openly expressed, but purported "color blindness" has not gone away. Color-blind racism now persists alongside the resurgence of overt white supremacy in national discourse and in schools and communities. In fact, Glickman (2018) has argued that color-blind racism may have provided the fertile ground for the reemergence of explicit white supremacy, as color-blind language both reinforces and obscures the realities and dangers of racism that don't even register as such. It has become normalized. In other words, in analyzing the cases of Milltown and Fairview, this book helps us to understand how we got to this present moment.

In closely examining how school district leaders make sense of their complex contexts and try to act on inequity, and in assessing the consequences of their efforts, this book helps us to think critically about the intertwined issues of educational equity *and* sustaining public education, which are of concern to many people. It provides crucial insights into how and why these school districts tried to solve inequities with new managerial approaches, and the limits of such approaches for advancing educational equity. It also offers keys to how public school districts and their supporters might forge thoughtful ways forward amid pressures that are more explicit and heightened than before, but which otherwise remain much the same. We discount or ignore these stories to our detriment. Please read on.

Color-Blind Managerialism and the Contradictions of Public Schooling

In a busy bagel shop located at the end of a short shopping strip, Milltown[1] school board member Susan Leahy, a white woman, recalled organizing a successful school funding referendum in the mid-1990s, and described herself as a "thorn in the side of the school board" when her own children were young. When we talked in 2009, Susan had been a Milltown school board member for more than ten years, and was one of the school system's biggest advocates.

"The public schools experience the demographic changes before any other organized group in the community does. We educate anyone who comes to our door and so we get to see who's in our community," Susan observed. She said that she and her husband had sent their own children to their local elementary school because of the "diversity." "I appreciate the diversity," she said, referring to children of color. The growing numbers of Asian, Black and especially Latinx[2] families in the city were now becoming obvious to Milltown's white residents. Although Milltown was built on indigenous land and a Native American population that predated the city's founding continues to this day, the growing populations of people of color marked a significant change for Milltown's predominantly white residents.

Milltown was a solidly working-class city with a conservative political orientation. Milltown is a "very conservative community," Susan told me, adding: "I grew up in Milltown, so I can say this." By way of explanation, she said that "for a while, the county tried to make English the official language." She described this as the "fringe group efforts" of "people voicing their discontent."

Like many of her neighbors, Susan recalled a time when there were very few people of color in Milltown. Milltown had one prominent employer that historically recruited a substantially more racially diverse workforce than other local companies. "When I was growing up, if you saw someone of color on the street you assumed they were somehow affiliated with the Bright Star Corporation. Either a Bright Star employee, a Bright Star child, or a Bright Star wife." But, she added, "that has changed." In addition to a long-standing Native American population, the school district and the city now had growing numbers of Latinx, Asian, and Black families who had arrived for various reasons and were associated with a number of different organizations and companies in the city.

In the bagel shop, Susan chatted with a neighbor and her young child, who had stopped by the table to say hello. Sitting there as an outsider, it was easy for me to glimpse the small-town feel that many people in Milltown described. As a Milltown city council member told me, Milltown is the kind of place where the first question residents ask each other is, "Where did you go to high school?" The second question is, "Where did your grandparents go to high school?"

"It's a big district, but a small community," Susan explained. It wasn't uncommon for Milltown residents to stop her while she was out shopping or eating to ask questions or share opinions about the schools. Talking with these community members had shaped her insight on the challenges the Milltown school district was facing as it tried to better educate children of color, particularly Latinx immigrants.

Susan explained the concerns she heard as the product of resentment from economically anxious white residents. "The economy is such that people are resentful," she said. In a conservative manufacturing town where there were fewer and fewer well-paying manufacturing jobs, she described a perception among white residents that "their tax dollars are being spent to educate people who are here illegally, and people who aren't, in their perception, all that gung ho about learning English." These residents believed that Mexican immigrants "want everything in Spanish," Susan said. This was what she heard when she talked with constituents at school board meetings, in her volunteering, or at the supermarket. "They're trying to explain that in the produce section. It's a little challenging."

As she thought about the future of a more racially, culturally, and linguistically diverse school district, Susan said she would love to see more

Milltown schools offer a dual-language bilingual education program. She viewed the program, which allowed Spanish-speaking and English-speaking students to develop bilingualism in both languages while learning together in a single classroom, as promising for better serving Latinx students. "I think it would be a real benefit to kids in our district," she explained. "But it's a harder sell for some parts of the community." In Susan's experience, many Milltown residents viewed the city's growing racial, ethnic, and linguistic diversity as a threat rather than an opportunity.

I asked Susan if she thought the expansion of dual-language bilingual education programs was likely to happen. "It takes money," she said, noting—as others have—the limitations that current levels of school funding pose to serving all students well, particularly the nation's most marginalized children.

Historically, Milltown was a community that was very careful about public spending and conservative about taxation. With the Great Recession of 2008, the prospect of the school district securing additional resources from city residents seemed even more grim. Yet, with increased costs and state-imposed limits on school funding, money was exactly what Susan thought the Milltown school system needed to best serve all district students: English language learners and monolingual English speakers, Latinx and white. Meeting these needs would require contending with the reality that white Milltown residents seemed less and less interested in supporting the schools as economic pressures bore down on them, and as the schools became more racially diverse.

Susan concluded: "It's tough; I mean people are not real gung ho to raise their property taxes or support the schools. People are losing their jobs, their homes, and, as I say, people are circling their wagons." She paused for a moment before adding, in a weary tone, "And their wagons tend to be full of white people."

Though she might not have articulated it this way, talking with Susan about her school board work revealed the deep tensions or contradictions she faced as a school board member. To carry out the obligation of public schools to foster equality and democracy requires challenging inequities in the status quo. However, the public schools—like other institutions of government—are typically dependent upon and limited by dominant groups that want to maintain their advantages. These contradictions are inherent in US public schools, which espouse democratic and emancipatory ideals (and occasional fulfillment of these ideals) and a system that is nonetheless developed in and reflective of the intertwined capitalism and white supremacy that advantage those already advantaged under those systems (Apple 2006; Diamond 2018; Hochschild and Scovronick 2003; Labaree 1997; Ladson-Billings 2006; C. N. Stone 1993). The story Susan told in Milltown was not entirely unique.

More than a hundred miles away, school district leaders in Fairview—a more politically liberal and economically booming city—faced similar contradictions in educating a racially diverse and increasingly economically unequal student population.[3]

School superintendent Ben Sedlak sat at the corner of a dark wood conference table in the converted classroom that serves as his office. A social worker by training, this middle-aged white administrator had been in schools for more than thirty years, but had only just arrived in Fairview. Signs spring up from flower beds to welcome visitors to each of the city's neighborhoods and schools, and the city abounds with urban amenities—bicycle paths, coffee shops, and cultural institutions—that serve the city's predominantly white middle-class and upper-middle-class population. And increasingly, in low-income housing, city schools, supermarkets, thrift stores, and libraries, a more racially and ethnically diverse population of Fairview families lives near but also apart from the city's urban amenities, hoping that their children, too, will eventually share in the city's prosperity, social institutions, and famed quality of life.

On this day, late in November 2009, Ben was recovering from a cold as he reflected on his work in Fairview. Crossing and uncrossing his legs, he pulled out a cough drop and ruminated on the challenges of educating a student population that is rapidly shifting from predominantly white and middle-class to one that is increasingly Asian, Black, and Latinx; children who are living in poverty; and children whose first language is not English, many from immigrant and refugee families.

Ben laid out to me how he sees the situation. "Achievement gaps have probably existed forever," he said. "But the fact of the matter is they haven't been eliminated, and for this community to remain strong and for this nation to remain strong, it's probably, if you have to ask me, our number-one social justice issue."

"We have the highest graduation rate this country has ever had," he said. "We have an increasing graduation rate in the school district." But the district needed to do better, he added. "Ninety percent is not good enough."

Ben saw educational inequity or "achievement gaps" as being both a local and a national issue. He noted that young people represent fewer and fewer of the country's overall population at a time when the demand for their knowledge and skills is increasing. It was not just that schools need to ensure that all children will be proficient in reading and mathematics, irrespective of poverty, race, language, or identification of special needs. Schools are confronting the expectation from parents, employers, and state and federal policy makers that students complete more rigorous coursework and graduate from high school "college- and career-ready." To Ben, the decline of traditional manufacturing and the rise of a well-paid "knowledge" sector that requires educational credentials beyond high school has reinforced a sense that education is more important than ever. He recalled a time when having a 50-percent graduation rate was acceptable because students, whether or not they had graduated from high school, could find plentiful jobs in manufacturing. "That doesn't exist anymore. Those jobs are high-skill, high-demand kind of jobs, because they're technology-linked." With greater uncertainty about the future of work and the progress of the nation, Ben thought there was a mounting imperative that public schools address educational inequities and ensure that all children receive a good education.

As I sat talking with Ben in the brown brick school district offices where he works, he seemed quite committed to addressing inequities in schools, and described it as his responsibility as school superintendent to do so. Fairview appeared well positioned to educate a more diverse student population to the higher levels that Ben felt were required in a changing local, national, and global economy. Local leaders, including people of color, often celebrated the growing racial and ethnic diversity of the city. Just a few blocks from Ben's office, downtown Fairview was bustling with business and new construction. Health- and technology-based companies were growing or being attracted to the area, drawn in part by the relatively well educated population in Fairview and the talent associated with the local university.

In his office, Ben was not so certain. His hesitation spoke to the deep contradictions of his work as a leader of public schools. "This is a community that wants to do the right things," he said. Fairview residents were very generous, and they vocally espoused equity and inclusion. Nonetheless, Ben was concerned. He explained that "oftentimes, there can be some struggle about what those right things are."

For example, Ben told me that as he made his way around the city, talking with service groups and community organizations, he heard people react with astonishment and concern at the levels of poverty among schoolchildren. Despite the Great Recession, Fairview had a relatively strong local economy. And, despite the seemingly inclusive political orientation of city residents, many Fairview residents he spoke to also questioned the school district's ability to meet rising expectations for graduation and academic achievement. They asked Ben, "How well can we meet the needs of these kids?" Perhaps more concerning for him was that some Fairview residents also questioned whether the district was giving too many resources and too much attention to low-income students, who were often presumed to be children of color. At school board meetings and public forums they asked him, "Who are we focusing on?" and questioned how much district efforts to raise achievement and eliminate racial disparities were going to cost. While many of Fairview's predominantly white and middle-class residents viewed themselves as welcoming and inclusive, the questions Ben heard as he spoke with organizations around the city suggested a limited underlying commitment to the well-being of low-income students and students of color.

Ben had come to Fairview, he said, because he hoped that his experience in a demographically changing school district would contribute to the "conversation about how a community deals with the change in makeup of the student population in good, just ways." Yet, in conversations with members of this self-described "liberal" and inclusive city, Fairview's superintendent was also searching for ways to manage the contradictions between pursuing equity and maintaining support of local elites. He felt a need to inform people of the rising numbers of families living in poverty and the increase in students' basic needs, as well as the growing numbers of children of color and the new opportunities and richness of diversity that accompanied those changes. He had begun telling people, "It's now our reality, so the question really is: How well do we live the reality?" Despite Fairview's seeming advantages, both in terms of the relative economic prosperity and a local politics that vocally valorized inclusion, there were no easy answers to Ben's question. And, like Susan, Ben also did not feel he quite had the answer to these challenges.

I start here with Ben Sedlak and Susan Leahy because their stories, told in their own words, offer a rare glimpse into school district officials' views, contexts, and everyday struggles around race and equity. These vignettes highlight the profound shared concerns that these two school district leaders in different districts—one a superintendent and the other a school board member, one more conservative and more working-class and the other liberal and wealthier—grappled with as they attempted to manage their school districts. Despite their differences, both Ben and Susan were grappling with the contradictions inherent in the schools as places of both opportunity and maintenance of a raced and classed status quo.

The issues Ben, Susan, and their colleagues in Milltown and Fairview faced were much greater than choosing the right curriculum and instructional practices for an increasingly more racially diverse and less wealthy group of students. They faced sharp tensions, pervasive in district offices and board rooms, between imperatives to spur achievement and opportunity for working-class students of all races, and the desires of influential, predominantly white middle- and upper-middle-class teachers, families, and self-proclaimed "taxpayers" to maintain their own relatively privileged circumstances in these changing environments. In other words, in addition to education, these leaders' challenges were also about politics, resources, and questions of belonging, in a world where each of these is increasingly uncertain. Indeed, Ben and Susan worried about their school systems' viability. As some community residents' support of the schools seemed to be wavering, so did district leaders' ability to provide an equitable education for increasingly diverse and economically struggling students and families. Budget cuts, rising economic inequality and poverty, and greater racial diversity, as well as a turn toward market-based education policies by state and federal authorities, have exacerbated these contradictory pressures.

* * *

As leaders of school districts, school board members and school district administrators are the public officials charged with ensuring an educated, equitable, prosperous, and democratic society. Though often taken for granted or overlooked, school districts are necessary for educating the nation's young people to be contributing members of society, both as citizens and as workers, and school districts are expected to do so regardless of students' race, class, gender, immigration status, or creed (Hochschild and Scovronick 2003; Labaree 1997; C. N. Stone 1993). But public schools have never fully achieved these goals for minoritized peoples in the United States, nor were they intended to do so in the first place (Ladson-Billings 2006). School districts secure resources to support universal public education and serve as a mechanism for a more equitable distribution of educational opportunity across schools within districts, especially across students of different social classes (Katznelson and Weir 1985; Peterson 1981; Wheeler-Bell 2016). Yet they have also been enduring sites of exclusion for many children of color. The historic brutality against Native Americans in US boarding schools and the persistence of racially, economically, and linguistically segregated and unequal schools are just two examples (Adams 1995; Orfield et al. 2014; Orfield, Kuscera, and Siegel-Hawley 2012). As the public institutions with which people are most likely to interact, school districts also offer a site for political deliberation and mediate, however imperfectly, between unequal social groups (Berkman and Plutzer 2005; Marsh 2007). But in many cases their presence and responsiveness to the public—especially low-income communities of color—has been utterly lacking (e.g., Ewing 2018). Increasingly, school districts have also been among the central (and last) sites for addressing poverty, hunger, and the challenges of rising social diversity, even if they do so in ways that are not entirely adequate (e.g., A. Goldstein 2017; Hamann 2003). How school districts are run and how school board members and school district administrators do their work is a matter of great consequence. But it is rife with contradictions and challenges for governing in what Ben Sedlak has called "good, just ways."

School district leaders in urban, suburban, and rural school systems across the country face the need to educate a student population that is more racially, ethnically, and linguistically diverse and is more likely to be unequal and struggling in poverty. Big cities such as New York, Miami, Chicago, and Los Angeles have confronted such changes over the last century, but today new demographic and economic shifts are transforming schools and communities across the county. Thriving cities, both big and small, are gentrifying (Cucchiara 2013; Lipman 2011; Posey-Maddox 2014); suburbs across the country are becoming more racially and ethnically diverse (Frankenberg and Orfield 2012; Posey-Maddox 2017); Sunbelt and Mountain West cities are booming (Horsford and Sampson 2014; Horsford, Sampson, and Forletta 2013); and new patterns of Asian, African, and Latin American immigration are unfolding in destinations across the United States (Gonzales 2015; Lee and Hawkins 2015; Marrow 2005; Massey 2008; Wortham et al. 2002).

District leaders confront racial and ethnic change and growing pov-

erty at a time of rising economic anxiety and insecurity, increasing expectations for academic achievement, and policy currents that emphasize limiting public spending, adopting market-based approaches to
government, and dismantling social supports. School districts are under pressure to compete, to raise test scores, and to do so with stagnant,
shrinking, or insufficient funding.

This book examines how school districts are responding to these dramatic changes in their school environments and the persistence of racial
and class inequities in school districts through the comparative analysis
of two school systems, Milltown and Fairview, and the school district administrators and school board members who are charged with leading
them. These districts provide illustrative cases of how education leaders,
as everyday officials of "the state," are mediating or managing the contradictions and inequities endemic to their work.

The findings are based on my analysis of interviews, observations, and
documents collected primarily in the 2009–10 school year in two Wisconsin districts: the more conservative, change-resistant, working-class
Milltown—where Susan Leahy was a school board member—and the
wealthier, and more liberal and welcoming Fairview—where Ben Sedlak
had just started as superintendent. These were once both predominantly
white and middle-class school districts, but in recent years they have become more racially, ethnically, and linguistically diverse, and more socioeconomically unequal. I purposively selected these districts to provide contrasting political and economic contexts. In particular, previous
research suggested that fiscal scarcity and contentious racial politics or
community resistance to immigrant arrival pose significant barriers to
equitable and responsive school district reform (Dentler and Hafner
1997; Henig et al. 1999; C. N. Stone et al. 2001). Milltown provided a case
where greater fiscal scarcity and resistance to immigrants or people of
color might be expected to make equity-oriented school policy more difficult. For Fairview, were there was greater wealth and a more inclusionary rhetoric, we might expect the opposite.

Despite these differences, demographic changes and rising inequality have been part of longer-term political, economic and demographic
shifts in each city and across the country, and the two districts have both
been trending steadily toward deepening inequality and are moving toward a "majority-minority" demographic. Milltown and Fairview were
not "suddenly diverse." However, with accountability pressures, budget
cuts, and greater competition, all of which were more pressing concerns

for districts serving larger populations of minoritized and poor students, the changes certainly felt sudden to district leaders. These conditions make Milltown and Fairview prime sites for illuminating how school district leaders and the public officials on the ground navigate inequity. It also makes them like much of the country.

In 2009 and early 2010, Wisconsin proved a particularly illuminating opportunity to examine these issues. At the end of the first decade of the twenty-first century, this predominantly white state was becoming more racially diverse, but the pressures of state and federal policies set in place in the 1990s and early 2000s—like revenue caps, open-enrollment policy, and high-stakes accountability—were beginning to kick in while, as a result of long-term shifts in the economy and the Great Recession, people were becoming poorer and state and local budgets were hurting. But all of this was prior to the major political attack, known as Act 10, on Wisconsin public sector workers and public education budgets in 2011. In other words, this study captured a moment when district officials on the ground were maneuvering, mostly on their own accord, the enduring dilemmas and contradictions in public schooling under pressures that heightened those challenges.

I find that, amid major social change in their communities, Milltown and Fairview school district leaders—the administrators and board members officially charged with leading public schools—responded to student populations that were more racially and economically stratified by adopting remarkably similar "new managerial" policies and practices. Inspired by the notion that public institutions should be run like businesses, approaches like performance monitoring and marketing have become increasingly widespread throughout the United States. The businesslike logics of "new managerialism" emphasize entrepreneurialism, use of generic management skills, the quantitative measurement of outcomes for decision-making, market-based mechanisms, and the blurring of the lines between public and private as means for solving social problems and guiding public organizations like schools (Anderson and Cohen 2018; Clarke and Newman 1997). As such, new managerialism marks a distinct approach to governing and leading state institutions like public schools.

The new managerial or entrepreneurial policies and practices that Milltown and Fairview district leaders adopted have at times been touted by their proponents as efforts to better educate children of color, English language learners, and low-income children. District leaders like Ben and Susan expressed a similar hope that these efforts would do just that. Indeed, my analyses suggest that these approaches were a response to the race and class contradictions that were evident in Ben's and Susan's stories. The inherent contradictions of public schooling are being heightened by demographic change and rising inequality amid fiscal austerity, accountability policies, and competition that undermine public education and challenge the legitimacy of public schools.

As this book demonstrates, these approaches ultimately helped district leaders deal with the central dilemmas of equity in public schooling, and did so in ways that generally legitimated their actions and leadership. However, they did not fully address the inequity in the schools. These practices were inflected by economic, political, and sociocultural assumptions and structures that in practice advantaged wealthier and white populations. Managerial efforts typically were in lieu of acknowledging and confronting the racialized and classed structures, practices, and ideologies at the root of educational inequities. It is not surprising, then, that, though presented as efforts to address inequity, the managerial approaches school district leaders adopted as they attempted to balance contradictory imperatives continually fell short of upending inequity. Yet, through new and existing meanings of race, equity, and diversity, these approaches obscure the inequities of new managerialism and racial and class structures. Furthermore, this book shows that these new managerial policies and practices altered some aspects of schools, contributed to new norms, and offered new subjectivities for school district leaders in ways that repackaged race and class domination rather than upending them.

In this book I show that district leaders come to make sense of their conditions and respond in ways that frame entrepreneurial strategies and new managerialism as advancing racial equity. As I argue in this book, district leaders' policy making, policy enactment, decision processes, and practices can be thought of as racial projects that intertwine local school district officials' sense making and racial ideologies with particular policies and practices, school district governance, and race and class structures. In particular, color-blind ideology facilitates the uptake of new managerial approaches to education (i.e., performance monitoring, competition, and marketing), and in turn, new managerialism reinforces color-blind ideology. The linking of color-blind notions of equity with new managerial policies, practices, and structures, or what I call *color-blind managerialism*, normalizes managerial approaches and new color-blind understandings of inequity, including the notion that managerial approaches are equitable. Thus, color-blind managerialism contributes to the neglect of more emancipatory approaches for responding to race and class inequity, and is crucial to explaining the perpetuation of inequity in these school districts.

As this book shows, school district leaders in Milltown and Fairview used color-blind managerialism to navigate the contradictions of race in US schools and society amid increasing racial diversity and inequality, and the pressures of market-based policies from above. In many cases district leaders' sense of what was equitable and right was rearticulated and partially subsumed by a need to sustain white middle-class support. The "official antiracism" (Melamed 2011) of color blindness makes new managerialism seem equitable, and it does not alienate local elites. Furthermore, it positions policy makers, school district leaders, and others involved in educational governance as good people actively confronting racism or other inequities. This places them in a positive moral light and lends legitimacy to them and their work; but in furthering new managerialism, color-blind ideology undermines the democratic purposes of public schools and maintains or exacerbates existing race and class inequities. In this book, especially chapters 3 and 4, I give evidence of these consequences in Fairview and Milltown.

Researchers and practitioners frequently distinguish between school board members, district superintendents or executive-level administrators, and other midlevel district administrators. And for good reason. People in these roles often have different knowledge and resources and feel different pressures that can contribute to their responding to policy and people in different ways (Coburn, Bae, and Turner 2008; Honig 2006; Spillane 1998). Yet surprisingly, as I emphasize here and as my data suggests, there are broad similarities in how these different school district officials—almost all of whom were white and middle- or upper-middle-class—make sense of their conditions, their work, and their ways forward. My data show considerable convergence between roles and across districts. The Fairview and Milltown school districts faced remarkably similar challenges, and responded in strikingly similar ways. The differences between how people in these roles make sense of and act are important, of course, and I note important differences where they existed, but I believe that there is also much we can learn from understanding how and why school district people made sense of their conditions and responded in similar ways. In particular, the similarities reveal the pervasiveness of the ideologies and structures that drive educational policy and reinforce inequity in schools and communities. They reshape schools and race in ways that might be more or less equitable but are not predetermined.

Opening the Black Box: Understanding School District Policy and Inequity

Several exceptional books examine teachers, students, and families to explain how racial inequity persists in education. They show that school-level sorting and tracking mechanisms, school cultures and teachers' orientations toward students, relations with and between families, and pedagogical or disciplinary practices in classrooms and corridors are key mechanisms for the perpetuation of inequities in schools (e.g., Castagno 2014; Lee 2005; Lewis and Diamond 2015; Lewis-McCoy 2014; Oakes 1985; Pollock 2004; Valenzuela 1999). Others have shown how particular policies like tracking, "school choice," and high-stakes testing have contributed to greater segregation or have narrowed the curricular opportunities and pedagogical approaches to educating marginalized and minoritized students (e.g., Au 2007; McNeil 2000; Mickelson, Bottia, and Southworth 2012; Oakes 1985; Roda and Wells 2013; J. T. Scott 2005; Tienken and Zhao 2013; Tyson 2011). The findings from these studies are important and troubling. But they are not the full story.

This book places local school systems and school-district-level decision makers at the center of its analysis of race and class inequities in education. These public officials are often overlooked, ignored, or painted with a singular brush in scholarly accounts of US educational policy and practice. Yet the work of school system administrators and school board members—whether through the everyday operation of public school districts or in pursuit of public education's more lofty goals of equity and democracy—is consequential to the education of the more than fifty million students enrolled in US K–12 public schools (Gamson and Hodge 2016; Henig 2009; Honig 2008; National Center for Education Statistics n.d.; Spillane 1996).

I highlight how district-level leaders have made sense of and navigated the tensions around educational equity in public schools. Sense making—how individuals or communities draw on their experiences, knowledge, values, and pre-existing beliefs as well as on broader discourses and ideologies, to interpret and act on the social world—plays a sizeable role in district governance, including internal decision making and policy implementation (Binder 2002; Coburn, Toure, and Yamashita 2009; Coburn and Turner 2011; Dorner 2011; Honig 2006; Spillane 1998; Turner 2015; Turner and Spain 2016; Yanow 1996). In social interaction with others, and shaped by the broader contexts in which individuals and collectives are embedded, district leaders work out innumerable aspects of school governance, often without consciously doing so. They express, contest, and negotiate the nature and source of educational problems, the meanings of school district policy, and the implications and enactment of that policy. Through close analysis of interviews, observations, and documents, this book unveils how this sense making plays out in the decision making that occurs in the school board hearings, one-on-one conversations, and central office meetings of America's school districts. In opening up the "black boxes" of school districts, I offer a rare view into real people like Ben Sedlak and Susan Leahy, and their perspectives, pressing concerns, deliberations, discourses, everyday struggles, and actions, as well as the contexts and processes that explain how and why they responded in particular ways.

This book highlights district leaders' racial sense making—how they implicitly and explicitly make sense of racial inequity and the circumstances they face in highly racialized ways. I show that efforts to address racial equity were constantly intertwined with questions about predominantly white and middle-class residents' support of schools, and thus about key issues of school district legitimacy. Such questions are at the fore of district leaders' sense making and the ongoing contestation of what school districts do and why. While much of the research on school district leadership has not examined these concerns, this is an essential area of study.

Scholars studying school-level responses to demographic change have shown that school leaders' individual and shared meanings about race shape their responses, often in ways that do not fully respond to the needs of children of color or build on the resources in students' families and communities (Cooper 2009; Evans 2007a, 2007b). District-level studies have provided an overview of school district responses to demographic changes, and have begun to dig into the meanings they draw on (e.g., Frankenberg and Orfield 2012; Hamann 2003; Turner 2015; Welton, Diem, and Holme 2015). This book adds to that research by closely examining how district leaders make sense and respond across two policy trajectories as schools become more diverse and unequal. Significantly, this book reveals the multiple meanings that district leaders draw on in their decision making, their roles actively negotiating, creating, contesting, and often reproducing the inequitable predicaments in which they are embedded, and their rearticulation of meanings of inequity in the processes of adopting new managerial policies and practices.

Second, this book deeply situates school district decisions and inequities within the intertwined, race- and class-inflected demographic, economic, and political transformations shaping public schooling today. In paying attention to this broader macro-context and how it shapes local school district inequities, this book complements recent works like Lewis and Diamond's (2015) book *Despite the Best Intentions*, which reveal the school-level dynamics, organizational routines, micro-interactions, and pressures from privileged white parents that perpetuate race and class inequity in schooling. The story told here also complements earlier work, going back as far as the *Federalist Papers* in 1787, in which scholars have noted the excessive influence of local majorities and elites in perpetuating inequities in local governance (e.g., Boyd 1976; Hochschild 2005; Madison 1787; McDermott 1999; Peterson 1981; C. N. Stone, 1998). Like this prior scholarship, I have documented a persistent tension between democracy and equity that is particularly sharp in local government. This book brings that story into the current time period.

In attending to broader social, economic, and political shifts as they shape and undergird school district inequity, this book builds upon the vibrant and influential scholarship on the politics of contemporary education policy at the local level and political economy of urban education. Scholarship in the 1990s and early 2000s illuminated how school districts in many large postindustrial cities were shaped dramatically and inequitably not just by local majorities or elites, but also by the convergence of deindustrialization, suburbanization, federal policy, and demographic shifts in cities like Baltimore, Detroit, Newark, Oakland, and Washington (Anyon 1997; Henig et al. 1999; Noguera 2003; Rury and Mirel 1997). The interlocking social, economic, and political contexts of these large urban districts made equal educational opportunity and democratic decision making difficult, if not impossible. More recent scholarship has picked up where these earlier works left off, showing how changes in the political economy and social geography of cities have shaped schooling, and particularly the uptake of market-based or neoliberal policies in some of the country's largest urban school districts (S. E. Clarke et al. 2006; Cucchiara 2013; Lipman 2011; J. Scott and Holme 2016). While by no means ignoring school district leaders, these scholars have generally focused their attention on the business elites, philanthropists, and middle- and upper-middle-class families who have been major players in big-city school politics, and who have leveraged their class-based resources to shape school policy. In this book I center school district leaders and critically engage with race to understand school district inequities and the uptake of market-based policies in the ongoing social, political, and economic conditions of smaller urban school districts. I show that changing social, economic, and political conditions severely shape the tensions that school district leaders face, and thus the challenges and possibilities for equity and democracy in these school districts.

However, if we understand this as a case of just one place, or of just two places, we miss the bigger picture. Milltown and Fairview are part of a broader phenomenon, and in bringing its pieces together, this book helps us to understand it more deeply. A third contribution of this work, then, is that it provides a necessary conceptual and analytic perspective on the perpetuation of racial inequity in school districts. It highlights how public school district leadership and policy making can be seen as a racial project, or a contestation of racial projects, and it names and demonstrates analytically how and why one of these racial projects, colorblind managerialism, is advancing.

The similarities in Milltown and Fairview district leaders' pursuit of performance management and marketing strategies to address challenges of race and rising inequality are a key finding of this book, one that undergirds the theoretical argument about color-blind managerialism. To be sure, there were differences in the specific ideas, policies, and practices that took hold in each district. These differences, described in greater detail in chapters 3 and 4, reveal the unique characteristics of responses in each site and how economic and political conditions shape local experiences differently. Seen as racial projects of color-blind managerialism, the stories of these two cities inform our understanding of how schools and public institutions make sense of and navigate changing demographics, rising inequality, and new policy environments as well as the challenges and possibilities for educational equity across communities with different political and economic resources.

Suddenly Diverse in Milltown and Fairview

Like many school districts across the United States, both Milltown and Fairview were going through notable demographic changes that began in the 1980s and accelerated in the 1990s. School enrollment data from the 1995–96 school year, the earliest available, showed that 83 percent of Milltown students identified as white, and that 70 percent of Fairview students identified as such. These formerly predominantly white and middle-class school systems with some Native American students were increasingly enrolling Black, Asian (predominantly Hmong refugee families), and Latinx students. Milltown consisted of over 40 percent students of color in 2009, and approximately 60 percent white-identified students, while Fairview had a population of approximately 50 percent students of color in that same year and approximately the same percentage of white-identified students. About half of the students in each city were living in poverty, as measured by their eligibility for federally subsidized school meals. And, with growing numbers of immigrant families in each city, Milltown and Fairview student populations were also increasingly multilingual. Approximately a fifth of students in each district were identified as English language learners (ELLs) by 2009. The districts were experiencing similar demographic shifts, but in different political and economic contexts.

Milltown: A More Conservative and Working-Class City

Milltown, the more conservative working- and middle-class city with a manufacturing-based economy, was located in a metropolitan area of approximately one hundred thousand people. As Milltown's traditional manufacturing sector struggled to respond to rising global competition, there were fewer jobs that provided a family wage. And, while the city's private healthcare systems, finance sectors, and technology-intensive manufacturing prospered, jobs in these fields required additional credentials that many working-class people did not have. In 2009, at the height of the Great Recession, the median household income was approximately $42,899 averaged over the 2005–9 period (US Census Bureau 2017b), but homelessness was skyrocketing and Milltown residents were unemployed at a rate considerably higher (12 percent) than the state or nation's unemployment rate (US Bureau of Labor Statistics

2011). Per capita income for those who identified as white ($26,471) was much higher than for other races, and white-identified individuals had much lower unemployment (6.1 percent) and poverty rates (11.8 percent) than all other races (US Census Bureau 2009a).

Milltown's white residents were proud of their ethnic heritages, but the city was not so welcoming for recent immigrant arrivals, most of whom were Hmong, Mexican, or Somali. School district and community leaders described Milltown as a "conservative" community that was largely intolerant of difference from the white, middle-class norm. While the city's churches and aid organizations had sponsored refugees, offered free English lessons for many years, and hosted community diversity dialogues, there was substantial animosity toward the growing Latinx population, who were presumed to be immigrants without legal documentation. Susan had mentioned one controversial example of this, a county ordinance enacted in the 2000s that made English the official language in the county. In 2007 a Milltown ordinance followed that barred businesses with city licenses from hiring undocumented workers. The city council president was quoted as saying about the latter ordinance: "It's a message to the illegal alien community that says you are not welcome. Don't come here." Reflecting a broader wave of exclusionary state and local immigration policy activism that began in 2002 and accelerated thereafter (Varsanyi 2010), both ordinances were seen primarily as attacks directed at Latinx immigrants and sparked some local protest, but ultimately remained law.

Broader hostility and barriers for people of color in Milltown included a near absence of people of color holding elected office or positions in the Milltown police and fire departments. The city had only recently hired its first Black police officer. Furthermore, two local school leaders pointed to past conflicts over a nativity scene erected on government property. The nativity display was seen as an official demonstration and elevation of Christianity at a time when a small Somali population of practicing Muslims was growing in Milltown.

Fairview: A More Liberal and Economically Advantaged City

Fairview offered a far more inclusionary orientation toward immigrants and people of color than did Milltown. Often identified as a "sanctuary city," local officials had enacted laws prohibiting government employees from asking residents for proof of citizenship. A Fairview ordinance originally passed in 1963 called for equal opportunity in employment, housing, and use of city services irrespective of race, color, religion, or national origin. More recently, it had been amended to add additional protections, such as citizenship. African Americans, Latinx, and Hmong individuals served in various public services and in elected positions, and ran community organizations that advocated for the concerns of immigrant families and families of color, attesting to the city's more open political system and to a middle or professional class of people of color in Fairview. This relative inclusion extended to the schools; in 2006 a local newspaper editorial advocated that, in the midst of school budget cuts and the expenses associated with a "dramatic increase in the number of minority, immigrant and low-income students requiring extra services," a "high priority" be given to programs for those students.

While Fairview district leaders described their city as "progressive," and as a place where people cared about equity, local realities did not always reflect the officially espoused values. In 2008 a Fairview community organization issued a report highlighting racial disparities in employment, housing, incarceration, education, and health between African Americans and the broader population of Fairview County. Though many of the findings were not surprising to Fairview residents of color, taken together this visible report shattered many people's assumptions about how well the city (which prided itself on being a great place to live), was actually doing for its African American residents. At about the same time, the Fairview sheriff's office was defending its cooperation with Immigration and Customs Enforcement in carrying out raids in Latinx immigrant communities.

As a city, Fairview was wealthier than Milltown. The city population of over two hundred thousand people was growing, and the local economy was too. The median household income in Fairview was approximately $51,288, averaged over the five-year period from 2005 to 2009 (US Census Bureau 2017b). Fairview had a substantially lower unemployment rate (6 percent) than Milltown or the nation as a whole, even at the official end of the Great Recession in 2009 (US Census Bureau 2017b). The city's dominant economic sectors of education and government are typically less susceptible to changes in the economy, and technology-related industry was growing as well. However, there was still considerable rising poverty in Fairview. A local newspaper reported that the number of Fairview residents living below the poverty line increased almost 30 percent between 2000 and 2008. Per capita income for those who identified as white ($32,099) was much higher than for other races, and white-identified individuals had much lower unemployment (4.4 percent) and poverty rates (17.2 percent) than all other races with the exception of the relatively small group identified as "some other race" (US Census Bureau 2009a).

The changes that the Fairview and Milltown school districts were experiencing raise questions of racial and class inequity and how these two different school districts—one conservative and working-class, based in a more struggling manufacturing economy, and the other liberal and more wealthy, with a growing economy—would navigate these circumstances.

School District Leadership as a Racial Project

Over time, school district leadership has been carried out in different and contested ways (Gamson and Hodge 2016; Rigby 2014; Tyack 1974). These different forms of leadership and governance have not been race-neutral. Though it is not always acknowledged, struggles over racial inequity have been deeply intertwined with struggles over the governance of public schools. Race "saturates the entire schooling process" (Leonardo 2013, p. 3; see also Ladson-Billings and Tate 1995). However, too often, we have failed to view forms of governance and leadership as connected to and co-constituted by race, both historically and in the present.

Race is a multidimensional, sociopolitically constructed system of oppression. Based in part on perceived biological or phenotypic differences, race intersects with, reinforces, and co-constitutes other forms of oppression such as class, gender, and sexuality. It is a social construction that has real effects on our institutions and on people's lives (Bonilla-Silva 2003). Through an ever-evolving set of meanings and social, economic, and political structures, race has developed historically to classify, stratify, and dominate the people of color that it marks as inferior and to systematically advantage and exalt white-identified people (Bonilla-Silva 2003; Omi and Winant 2015). Race justifies inequity.

The ways in which educational leaders do their work (that is, how they make sense of their circumstances, negotiate the contradictory pressures they confront, navigate their everyday experiences, and shape these into particular policies and practices) can be thought of as racial projects of school governance. The sociologists Michael Omi and Howard

Winant (2015) identify a racial project as the linkage between particular racial meanings, identities or representations and social structures, institutions, or resources. They explain: *"A racial project is simultaneously an interpretation, representation, or explanation of racial identities and meanings, and an effort to organize and distribute resources (economic, political, cultural) along particular racial lines"* (2015, p. 125, italics in original). In a racial project, particular racial meanings are embedded within social structures. For instance, racialized representations of social groups contribute to racial segregation by influencing who is seen as likely to pay back a home loan, or what is deemed a "good" neighborhood. Racial projects may take many forms, including everyday interactions, organizational practices, or macro-level policies and collective action (Omi and Winant 2015).

School and district leaders' racial sense making and signification—the racial meanings, ideologies, and "common sense" that they use in their daily work—contribute to educational governance and policy decisions (Evans 2007; Turner 2015). In this way, their daily work can be seen as a racial project of school governance. However, school district administrators' and school board members' daily work is not solely of their own making. Racial sensemaking and signification are developed in social interaction with others and shaped by a wide range of people within and across organizations and the broader environments in which leaders are embedded. The contexts in which district leaders are embedded are themselves shaped by race and the larger political economy, in both past and present. The result may be decisions or action that promulgate racial equity or inequity in organizations, policies, everyday interactions or resources and contribute to new racial meanings and identities (Pollock 2004; Ray 2019). In this way, over time, as school and district officials make sense of their work, represent it, and translate it into policy and practice, their work can be understood as reinforcing or producing new racial projects.

Three Racial Projects of Educational Policy and Leadership

Surveying the field of education, one can roughly discern three central and contending racial projects of educational policy and leadership: a professional-bureaucratic approach, a social justice approach, and a new managerial approach. The new managerial approach is the focus of this book. While by no means exhaustive, each of these reflects a prominent view of how public schools should be governed and to what ends, as well as implicit or explicit notions of race, racism, and racial equity.

The Assimilationist Professional-Bureaucratic Racial Project

Beginning in the Progressive Era, an assimilationist professional-bureaucratic racial project has been the long prevailing approach to school governance in the United States, and much of the public sector has been guided by this ubiquitous set of beliefs. School district decision making reflects a mix of formal rules and bureaucratic procedures associated with scientific efficiency models of educational governance; professional educators' pedagogical, curricular, or child development expertise; and the decisions of elected school boards (Clarke and Newman 1997; Gamson and Hodge 2016; Tyack 1974). The specific practices and goals of educational governance have been somewhat flexible to meet school or "community" needs and values, but the structures of schooling have been firmly under the control of educational professionals who have organized schools to efficiently educate large numbers of students from diverse backgrounds through the "science" of IQ testing and other methods that sorted students into segregated and unequal schools or curricular options (Deschenes, Tyack, and Cuban 2001). Grounded in an ethos, if not always the reality, of universal public service,[4] school administrators who have been overwhelmingly white and middle-class have positioned themselves as authorities working for the public benefit, and as professionals to whom parents and communities should defer (Tyack 1974).

The professional-bureaucratic approach has typically been accompanied by an assimilationist view of school leadership. Such a view is based in explicit and implicit assumptions about the superiority of white-identified groups and the inferiority of immigrants and people of color. The knowledge, norms, and expectations of schools are not altered to reflect those valued by minoritized students and their families; rather, in an example of whiteness at work, schools have been seen as a way to inculcate white, middle-class, and Protestant values and manners into immigrant and minoritized youth who did not share those orientations (e.g., Tyack 1974). Whiteness, "the socially constructed and constantly reinforced power of white identifications and interests" (Leonardo 2013, p. 488) was evident in Progressive Era schools, and it continues to this day. White-identified people and institutions are commonly assumed to be right, good, or normal even by people of color. Predominantly white-identified schools are presumed to be good schools, and white-identified children are expected to be academically superior to children of color (e.g. Holme 2002; Oakes et al. 2007; Posey-Maddox 2014).

Today, in the professional-bureaucratic racial project, equity largely continues to be understood as "abstract equality," treating students the same despite their differing starting points, and without recognizing that racism and class inequality already permeate the values and structures in schools and society (Bonilla-Silva 2003). The ideals of liberalism, such as meritocracy, and neutrality, dominate educational decision making and undermine racial equity and social justice (Capper 2015; Castagno 2017; Khalifa, Gooden, and Davis 2016; Larson and Ovando 2001; Prier 2015; Welton et al. 2015). However, other views of school district leadership in relation to student diversity and equity have also emerged as part of a critique that professional-bureaucratic governance has been inefficient, ineffective, or unresponsive to marginalized communities (e.g., Meier 1995; Payne 2008).

The Social Justice Racial Project

The social justice approach to educational leadership is concerned with critiquing and confronting racist and otherwise inequitable policies and practices in schools and beyond (Khalifa et al. 2016; Theoharis 2007). Education leaders cultivate race-conscious, power-conscious, multiculturalist, culturally responsive, democratic approaches to their work. For example, they may actively promote access and achievement for marginalized students, culturally relevant and inclusive school curriculum and environments, and equitable family/school relations (Capper 2015; Cooper 2009; Khalifa et al. 2016). Policies and practices include challenging limiting beliefs individually and with colleagues through critical, reflective conversations or other forms of staff development; recognizing the impact of structural inequities in schools and society on students and families; and establishing equal relationships with parents and communities of color (Anderson 2009; Davis, Gooden, and Micheaux 2015; Khalifa et al. 2016; Theoharis 2007). Education leadership is seen as an inherently political act, and race and power are recognized as central to the work, given that schools are already inequitable institutions (e.g., Lopez 2003).

The social justice project is frequently framed in relation to race consciousness. Race consciousness itself has taken on different meanings over time (Omi and Winant 2015), but in the project of social justice leadership, race consciousness has been an emancipatory effort to recognize racial differences, racial identity, racial inequality, and racial hierarchy so as to address persistent and deeply entrenched racial inequity. Thus, while race and racism are often fraught topics, race and other deeply engrained inequities in schools and society must nevertheless be discussed and confronted. Furthermore, in this racial project, schooling is recognized as reproducing of social inequities, but it is also imagined as a potential means toward the achievement of antiracism and democracy, and the full flourishing of marginalized communities. In these ways, this racial project is a radical departure from the ubiquitous professional-bureaucratic model and the increasingly prominent color-blind managerial racial project.

The Color-Blind Managerialism Racial Project

The third racial project of school leadership, which I call color-blind managerialism, is central to this book. Color-blind managerialism emphasizes numerical accounting, entrepreneurialism, market-based mechanisms, and the blurring of the lines between public and private as means for guiding public organizations and solving social problems (Anderson 2009; Anderson and Kerr 2015; Clarke and Newman 1997; Trujillo 2014). We can think of managerialism, sometimes called "new managerialism," or new public management, as the organizational form of neoliberalism (Lynch 2014). It embeds and prioritizes market principles such as efficiency, productivity, competition, and privatization in the administration of organizations, particularly in public sector work. Leaders are expected to act flexibly and entrepreneurially to compete with other organizations, and to efficiently and effectively reach predetermined goals—typically, raising achievement or improving other measurable outcomes. Hallmark practices of color-blind managerialism include the use of performance metrics for monitoring, the setting up of markets and positioning of one's organization favorably in competition, service delivery orientations to the public, cost containment, and human capital development. As such, they mark a distinct way of governing public institutions like public schools in the United States.

Advocates of color-blind managerialism articulate a commitment to (racial) equity, but equity is understood in individualized terms: as raising achievement for a child or classroom of children, rather than as transforming structures, policies, or practices that systematically marginalize children and communities of color (Gewirtz 2002; Trujillo 2014). There is no attention to power or structural racism in this conception of equity; social change is accomplished through managerial mechanism (e.g., remedying inefficiencies or employing high-stakes testing) or through entrepreneurial means (e.g., competing and promoting one's school district). Thus, this racial project reflects a color-blind stance on race and racial inequity.

Color blindness is an ideology through which Americans increasingly understand race and racial inequity. Despite enduring whiteness and racialized social structures, color blindness holds that race is no longer a salient factor in US society. Racial inequity is said to have ended with the civil rights movement. Any racism that remains today is understood as the result of individual biases or prejudices that belong to a few aberrant individuals. Sociologist Eduardo Bonilla-Silva (2003) identifies several key frames which support the project of color blindness, or what he calls "color-blind racism." "Cultural racism" explains racial inequality as the result of differences in individual effort or perceived cultural differences, rather than as a consequence of the historical and contemporary imprint of racism. Like the professional-bureaucratic racial project, the color-blind project is also supported by notions of "abstract equality" (Bonilla-Silva 2003), such as effectiveness, rights, meritocracy, and neutrality, which are accepted as "objective" and "rational" descriptions of society, and which presume that the existing social terrain is fair. By obscuring the uneven playing field and the rigged rules that advantage white-identified people, these notions mask the continued salience of racism in society (Bonilla-Silva 2003; Harris 1995; Pollock 2004). Denying the privileges or advantages they enjoy from a system of racial oppression, white-identified people can claim any success they may have as their own. In other words, the assertion that that race does not matter today allows racism to persist and grow.

In the context of color-blind ideology, Castagno (2014) writes that "whiteness compels us to embrace diversity-related policy and practice uncritically and to praise any effort tagged with words like multicultural, diversity, and equality" (p. 4). Whether these actions actually reflect challenges to inequality or oppression is beside the point. Color blindness contributes to the investment of individuals and groups across partisan divides in constructing themselves as people who transcend racism (Burke 2017). Under color blindness, even when people and institutions adopt official antiracism, tolerance, or acceptance of racial and ethnic difference, they may nevertheless contribute to the perpetuation of inequity. Furthermore, color-blind notions of equity—such as cultural equality, abstract equality, market individualism, and the inclusion of "diverse" groups become "official antiracisms," which gesture at antiracism but do little to challenge or deconstruct existing systems of oppression (Melamed 2011). Entrepreneurial strategies and new managerial policies or practices are framed as advancing racial equity through these official antiracisms. However, calling or viewing them as equitable or antiracist obscures the systematic social inequities and race and class hierarchies which research evidence suggests they typically maintain or exacerbate (e.g., Au 2007; Diamond and Spillane 2004; Mickelson et al. 2012; Roda and Wells 2013). Thus, under the racial project of color-blind managerialism, the racism of managerialism comes to be seen as antiracism. For example, under the technocratic rationality of high-stakes testing and accountability, schools that are highly segregated and unequal by race, class, and language are measured and sanctioned as if all students have an equal opportunity to learn what is tested; these policies are billed as a means of ensuring that children of color, low-income children, and English learners are not "left behind" when the policy is actually doing just that.

Together, these three racial projects represent contested ways of governing American schools and public institutions more broadly. Yet, these racial projects are not static. "At any given moment, racial projects compete and overlap, evincing varying capacity either to maintain or to challenge the prevailing racial system" (Omi and Winant 2015, p. 126). Through people's experiences and social processes of representing, interpreting, and contesting what race means and how new social structures develop, racial projects are constantly made and remade. Over time, new racial projects develop and evolve (Omi and Winant 2015), as they are experienced differently from place to place, and are enacted anew in ways that overlap or blur, rearticulate prior projects, or chart new territory.

The Complications of Researching Race

This is not just a study about race inequity and racial politics; race and class permeate this research. As with all researchers, my identity and positionality shaped the research processes and findings described here. I identify as Black and Chinese American (Asian), though my racial identity is often ambiguous to people I meet. When I started this work, I was a newcomer of color to Wisconsin myself; however, as a US-born graduate student at a prestigious university who was raised in an upper-middle class family, I differed from many of the families of color arriving in these districts in terms of education, class, and legal status. I also differed from the majority of study participants.

The participants in this study—a school board member, school district administrators, and central office administrators—were overwhelmingly white. In a study about race, this raises some important considerations. First, race is a topic that people, especially white people, find difficult to discuss (DiAngelo 2011; Pollock 2004). This study is limited by what these predominantly white participants were willing to reveal to me, an outsider to their organization, an education researcher, and especially a woman of color. That I am a person of color likely influenced their responses in interviews. White participants may have responded to my questions in ways they felt showed that they were enlightened about race or ethnicity. Indeed, one of the points that I make in this book is that they viewed themselves as against racism and benefited from being seen as antiracist. In talking to an outside researcher interested in responses to demographic change, district leaders also had a stake in presenting themselves as "responding" to demographic change, in being seen as beyond racism, and in constructing others as responsible for inadequate district responses to demographic change.

At the same time, many of these district leaders were very frank with me, and invited me to attend their meetings, treating me as a mentee. Several district administrators saw me as a graduate student of educational leadership, as many of them had been in preparing to become administrators. They reminisced about their own experiences in graduate school, and gave me advice. Especially in Milltown, the administrators were generous in allowing me to observe their work. Thus, I also have reason to believe that these district leaders did not feel particularly threatened by me, and that, by virtue of my education and class background, I gained some measure of entry into their confidence.

In focusing on district leaders—or, more accurately, on officially elected school board members and district-level administrators—this study examines the perspectives of the predominantly white and middle-class district policy makers in Milltown and Fairview. Centering these individuals is crucial to this project, as I set out to learn how they make sense of things. However, centering them in this way can reinforce the views of people already in power (both the officeholders and those who hired or elected them) and obscure the realities of marginalized groups. In a society where whiteness is already normalized, this runs a double risk of reinforcing a dangerous status quo. Centering these officials' voices and perspectives can also give the impression that their views were the definitive way things were in these two places, rather than one set of perspectives among many others.

With that in mind, I have been careful to include the voices of people of color in each district, to illuminate alternative perspectives and experiences that may challenge the dominant discourses circulating among the predominantly white administrators and school board members who ran these districts. However, with the possible exception of one person, Milltown had no people of color in its district administration or on the school board at the time of my study. Fairview had a handful of current and former board members who identified as people of color. My data reflects that, although I did also interview some community members of color. The Black, Hmong, and Latinx participants I interviewed in each city may have felt more comfortable divulging their views to me, a person of color. Indeed, several asked me about my racial background, to confirm whether I held a shared set of meanings. They may also have responded to my questions in ways they felt would generate solidarity with me.

My identity has also shaped my research. As child growing up in 1980s and 1990s San Francisco, I attended three very different public schools, each distinctively shaped by policies infused with issues of race and class inequity (student assignment systems, desegregation, and selective admissions). The possibilities and the pitfalls of educational policy as an engine of equality were obvious, as was a question about how inequity emerges out of places that profess to want to do good. That continues to be a burning question, now that I am a parent of two young children in Madison, Wisconsin. For that reason, it has been a long and winding road to this book, one that has required much new reading, reexamination, and revision as I have grappled with the tensions, described in these pages, in what it takes to have a racially diverse and equitable public school system.

Looking Ahead

As Milltown and Fairview school board members and administrators sat in their offices or board rooms reading reports, examining data, sending emails, meeting with principals, working out marketing strategies, or trying to connect with local business leaders and community groups, their day-to-day work hardly seemed earth-shattering or even surprising. But it is vitally important at a moment when significant demographic, economic, and political changes are sweeping our country; inequality is growing, and schools are often the first institutions to see and respond to these shifts. The stories I tell here expand our understanding of district inequity through attention to district officials' sense making; the social, economic, and political contexts shaping their work; the policy trajectories of two issues; and some consequences of these processes. And the theorizing allowed to us by these two stories make them relevant far beyond these two districts.

Following the introduction of the districts and the argument and theory set forth in this chapter, chapters 1 and 2 take a deep dive into the structural and ideological contexts in which district leaders' work is situated: specifically, the broader contexts in which color-blind managerialism emerged. In chapter 1, I show how demographic changes, economic shifts, and new political realities emerging across the United States have intersected over time and are intertwined with racial, economic, and age-stratified inequities that heighten differences between residents and create a complex and challenging new context for district policy makers' work. These inequities are evolving in a new "color-blind" era, where the salience of structural or systemic racism is denied even as it persists and takes new forms. These shifts have stoked new uncertainties, fears, and confusions; they have sharpened contradictions and created challenges to which local officials in very different communities have responded with color-blind managerialism.

Chapter 2 illustrates the discursive foundations of color-blind managerialism in these two districts. It demonstrates how district policy makers came to understand the contradictions described in chapter 1 in terms of imagery and discourses of "the urban" that are common is US society. These discourses have captured the poverty, inequality, low academic achievement, and ongoing budgetary crisis that district leaders have confronted. However, discourses of the urban have also focused district leaders on white flight and the arrival of people of color as the root of their troubles, bypassing a more comprehensive political, economic, and social critique. Matters of power and race have often been understood as matters of culture and individual attitudes or choices, and have shaped what district leaders have understood as problems and possible solutions.

Chapters 3 and 4 examine two examples of color-blind managerialism, exploring how and why district leaders came to adopt them, and the ways in which they failed to disturb race and class inequities or created new ones. In chapter 3 I demonstrate that Milltown and Fairview policy makers embraced the use of data and performance monitoring to navigate "the achievement gap," accountability pressures, and teachers who objected to or ignored earlier initiatives to change their beliefs and classroom practices. Examining standardized test data and other measures caused district leaders to confront some inequities; but performance monitoring, while ostensibly an effort to address achievement gaps, catered to white teachers and legitimized schools and district leaders as enlightened, ethical, and rational actors without directly addressing the race and class inequities at the root of disparities in achievement and educational opportunity. Chapter 4 shows that district leaders use marketing to steer through negative perceptions of district schools, to heighten competition with other districts, and to attract predominantly white middle- or upper-middle class families who were seen as fleeing "urbanizing" schools and taking resources with them. Through the marketing of diversity, district leaders attempted to articulate an inclusive vision for schools; however, their discourses reflected a narrow vision of racial diversity, consistently centering on and privileging the concerns of white middle-class parents, and normalizing instrumental orientations toward racial diversity.

The concluding chapter considers the consequences of color-blind managerialism for racial inequity in education, for the work of district leaders, for racial formation, and for the future of public schooling. I review what we learn from this study, and take stock of the insights afforded by the concept of color-blind managerialism. Finally, I address ways forward from the color-blind managerialism approach that district leaders adopted. While district policymakers often saw color-blind managerialism as easing a necessary tradeoff between pursuing equity and maintaining public schools, I conclude by emphasizing that race equity and the future of *public* education are intimately linked and both depend upon moving beyond color-blind managerialism.

CHAPTER ONE

Globalization in the "Heartland": Changing Contexts of US School Districts

The Menominee and Winnebago were the first inhabitants of what would one day become the working-class and politically conservative city of Milltown (Bieder 1995). Their lives were violently upended over almost two hundred years of war, disease, and famine as well as cultural and land loss brought on by conflict with other indigenous groups, with European colonizers, and eventually with the US government and "American" settlers (Bieder 1995; Loew 2013). In the mid- to late-1800s, Milltown grew as Czech, Dutch, German, and many other European immigrants arrived. Today the city is dotted with mostly modest homes, libraries, schools, and factories. Those European immigrants' descendants, who make up the city majority, attend the "German church" or the "Belgian church" on Sundays, and serve their immigrant ancestors' dishes at the fund-raisers held for a family's unexpected health expense or a school choir's travel abroad.

As people have come from Mexico, Somalia, Southeast Asia, the Southwestern United States, or elsewhere in the Midwest, they too are making their mark on Milltown. Just beyond the downtown churches built by earlier European immigrants lie the neighborhoods around the meat processing plants where many of these recent arrivals, mostly Latinx immigrants, now live and work. Some have migrated from other parts of the United States, while others were recruited directly from Mexico by corporate managers of local industry. These immigrants have since built communities. Signs in Spanish advertise the groceries, restaurants, car lots, and other small businesses they have established to serve their neighbors. Just across the river, some Hmong families have started buying homes. In between, an African American church has moved into a former Episcopal church, a bigger building for a growing congregation and community.

Over the last thirty years, migration, immigration, and refugee resettlement have dramatically changed Milltown and other places in the American "heartland." A geographic area roughly synonymous with the Midwest, the word "heartland" evokes a set of ideas about the core or heart of "authentic" America. From the farms to the factories, that place is often imagined to be working-class or middle-class and, perhaps more importantly, white. But globalization has come to the heartland, and like many other parts of the United States, the heartland has been transformed. Milltown and Fairview now educate students from five racialized groups, who encompass numerous ethnic backgrounds and religions as well as various class distinctions and legal statuses, and who speak more than thirty-five home languages. The shifts affecting these cities and their school systems are not just demographic, but economic and political as well.

Three major shifts unfolded across much of the country in the late 1960s and 1970s, and have heightened in the 1990s and 2000s in many places, including Milltown and Fairview. Demographically, the populations have become more racially and ethnically diverse, and are more likely to be struggling in poverty. The economy has shifted, too. Once a robust manufacturing economy, the United States is now part of a technology- and financial-services-dominated global economy that supports fewer middle-class jobs and contributes to greater economic inequality. Finally, major political changes have unfolded, including the delegitimization and weakening of the social safety net, labor unions, and public institutions. Each development has been linked to the others and each has been fundamentally entwined with inequities tied to race, class, and age. These shifts have provoked concern, fear, and a substantial sense of dislocation among educators (Boyd 2003). Perhaps this is unsurprising, given the complex and evolving challenges with which public employees, schools, and a democratic society must contend.

This chapter provides an overview of these social, economic, and political shifts in the heartland cities of Milltown and Fairview and in the United States, and how they are intertwined with race and class inequities. It details how they have contributed to the current contexts of public schools and heightened the contradictions that confront school district leaders at nearly every step. In particular, I locate Milltown and Fairview and their schools in these broader developments and show how these broader shifts materialized and contributed to heightened contradictions in the two sites. In painting this broader macro-picture, I am arguing that the circumstances that prompted district leaders to adopt color-blind managerialism were deeply rooted in social, political, and economic shifts that were not of district leaders' or families' making, and that these conditions were not at all unique to these two places. Fairview and Milltown represent a microcosm of shifts in the "heartland" region of the United States, and color-blind managerialism was a response in Milltown and Fairview to these shifts and the heightened contradictions that they wrought. But these shifts—detailed below—also reflect a broader transnational movement of people, jobs, capital, and policy ideas. This, then, is a truly significant national and global story.

The Demographic Shifts: Migration, Immigration, and Increasing Racial and Ethnic Diversity

The first of these shifts, the rapid growth of racial "minority" groups in the country, was ignited in the mid-1960s and 1970s when a number of factors, including a series of immigration policies with unintended consequences, converged to lead to a dramatic increase in US immigration and migrant settlement by people from the Global South, predominantly Asia and Latin America. In 1965 Congress passed the Immigration and Nationality Act, also known as the Hart-Cellar Act. The Immigration and Nationality Act of 1965 abolished quotas that favored immigrants from Northern European countries, and set off unprecedented immigration from Asia—and, to a lesser extent, Africa and the Middle East—to the United States.[1] The act also established preferences for professionals and those with special skills, and prioritized immigration of family members.

For Asian immigrants, the Immigration and Nationality Act of 1965 overturned the Chinese Exclusion Act of 1882 and the National Origins Act of 1924, both of which had prohibited immigration to the United States from Asian countries. Subsequent immigration from those countries has intersected with global developments and home-country characteristics to contribute to distinct backgrounds, arrival patterns, reception into the United States, and a bifurcated class pattern. After passage of the 1965 law, Asian immigration ballooned, buffeted by preferences for family reunification and professionals in US law, as well as by US demand for workers in science, technology, and health care fields—but also by immigrant professionals escaping political instability and limited opportunities for advancement, and by some Asian countries exporting medical professionals as an economic development strategy (Ngai 2004). As a result, since the passage of the 1965 law, immigrants arriving from East and South Asian countries have had higher levels of education and economic resources than those they left behind, and higher than those of many other immigrant groups arriving in the United States. These factors have likely contributed to their children's relative economic and educational success in US schools.

US involvement in Southeast Asia and the end of the Vietnam War also brought Asian refugees and asylum seekers to the United States. In the 1980s, for instance, this included Hmong people who had allied with the United States during the Vietnam War and fled political persecution in Laos, or who had otherwise been displaced by war and had arrived as refugees, primarily in California, Minnesota, and Wisconsin (Zaniewski and Rosen 1998). Additional Hmong came in the 1990s when refugee camps in Thailand were closed, and between 2004 and 2006 when a last group of refugees who had been displaced from the 1990s camp closing arrived in the United States (Ngo and Lee 2007). Early waves of these refugees were often sponsored by churches; once the families were resettled, however, they were able to sponsor other family members to come. The most recent Hmong arrivals have resettled in the United States after much political advocacy and activism from within Hmong American communities. Those who came were often from modest rural backgrounds and were relatively uneducated, factors that seem to have contributed to more limited school and economic success in the United States.

While the Immigration and Nationality Act of 1965 expanded Asian immigration to the United States, it placed limits on legal immigration from within the Western Hemisphere where no limits had previously existed. Just a year earlier, in 1964, the US Congress ended the bracero program, which for twenty-two years had provided Mexicans with temporary visas to fill US farmers' demand for flexible, low-paid agricultural workers.[2] Despite these dramatic limitations, the demand for inexpensive, unskilled labor did not wane, and immigration from Latin America, predominantly by Mexicans, continued and even accelerated. The decline in legal migration options simply meant that migrants now entered the United States without legal authorization.

While traditional immigrant-receiving cities like Los Angeles, Chicago, and New York still have large numbers of new arrivals, many Latinx immigrants began in the late 1980s to settle in new destinations. These new destinations were located in metropolitan outskirts, smaller cities, and in parts of the South, Mountain West, and Midwest that had little recent experience with immigration, particularly with these "new immigrants" (Marrow 2005; Massey 2008; Wortham et al. 2002). The rising cost of living in coastal gateway cities, the shifting job market conditions in those places, and anti-immigrant sentiment in traditional immigrant gateway regions all contributed to migrants' decisions to leave these locales for new US destinations like Milltown and Fairview (Light 2006). Meanwhile, changes to immigration law in 1986 legalized some 2.3 million undocumented immigrants, making it easier for these individuals to move to other parts of the US for new opportunities (Massey, Durand, and Malone 2002). Other changes to this law led to the militarization of the Mexican-US border in the Southwest, causing migrants to cross the US-Mexico border at points further east, where border enforcement was weaker, or to establish their families in the United States rather than risk continued border crossings (Massey et al. 2002; Massey and Pren 2012). In their new destinations, migrants and immigrants found job opportunities and a lower cost of living. Agriculture, food processing, and other industries have also played a role in this movement through their strategies of recruiting among minoritized groups from across the country, especially in Latinx communities, to fill their low-wage jobs (Fink 1998). With resettlement, migration, or immigration underway, people have followed ethnic networks that provide links to jobs, community, and life among friends and family (Frey 2014).

In a process that began in the 1970s and accelerated in the 1990s, African Americans have also been leaving large cities such as Detroit, Chicago, Los Angeles, and New York, mostly for the cities and suburbs of the metropolitan "New South" (Frey 2014; Lacy 2016) and rural South (Stack 1996). They have migrated in search of better jobs, more affordable living in growing metropolitan areas, greater racial acceptance or tolerance, and the "call of home" and family (Stack 1996). These moves, then, have reflected shifting economic processes, including a fall in manufacturing jobs in the Northeast and Midwest, racial oppression and disillusionment in Northern cities, personal and cultural ties to the South, growth in the Black middle class, and the desire for a better quality of life that has characterized the movement of Americans across time (Frey 2014; Lacy 2016). This research does not directly indicate why African Americans might have been moving to Midwestern cities like Milltown and Fairview, but it does suggest some of the reasons why they were leaving major cities in the North and West more generally.

In Wisconsin, as in other Midwestern states, these demographic shifts have mostly converged in the 1990s and 2000s to create a new demographic picture, a local version of what demographer William Frey (2014) has called the nation's "diversity explosion." The first nations of Wisconsin—Menominee, Winneabego, Oneida, Potawatomi, Stockbridge-Munsee, and Brothertown, as well as the Lac Courte Orielles Band, Red Cliff Band, Fond du Lac Band, Bad River Band, Mole Lake Band, and Lac du Flambeau Band of Lake Superior Chippewa—are most concentrated in a few rural counties and a few of the state's cities. This is in part the effect of the massive history of colonization and violence that forced them to establish their communities on reservations. While some Native Americans moved to cities for greater opportunities, there is now a migration back to reservations as gaming brings greater economic opportunities to some Native communities. Up until recently, this predominantly white state has been home to relatively small populations of African Americans and Latinx people, most of whom lived in the Milwaukee area (Clark-Pujara 2017; Zaniewski and Rosen 1998). However, Asian, Latinx, and Black populations have been growing (Applied Population Lab 2007). The Hmong have been the largest group of the state's Asian population. Their numbers have grown through refugee resettlement, births, and migration from other states. Latinx families have been in Wisconsin since the 1960s, but the population of Latinx residents, both native-born and immigrant, increased rapidly in the late 1980s and early 1990s as predominantly Mexican immigrants arrived to fill farm labor positions, mainly in the dairy industry, and wage-labor positions in the service and manufacturing industries (Applied Population Lab 2007; Harrison and Lloyd 2013). Between 1990 and 2000, that population doubled (Zaniewski 2004).

Milltown

Milltown, home to a longtime Native American population, is a predominantly white city, but that has been changing along with the rest of the country. Milltown has been a refugee resettlement site. Hmong arrived there from the 1980s onward, through resettlement, family reunification, and migration from other states. Hmong are by far the largest and most visible refugee population in Milltown, though the city has also been home to refugee communities from Somalia, Sudan, Iraq, Laos, and Ukraine, among other countries (Refugee Processing Center 2018; Wisconsin Department of Children and Families 2016). The city's Latinx population, mostly Mexican immigrants, began growing in the late 1980s as meatpacking companies began to recruit workers from Mexico (Fink 1998), as previously noted. In the early 1980s, the Latinx population was virtually nonexistent, but it climbed to more than seven thousand people in 2000 and almost double that in 2010. In Milltown the Black population has been much smaller; African Americans began migrating there around 2000 and the population was just under four thousand in 2010. These individuals, many of whom were described as lower-income by Milltown district staff, joined a small number of African American engineers and other highly skilled African Americans who had been recruited to well-paying Milltown jobs.

Fairview

Although Fairview remains predominantly white, it has also become substantially more racially and ethnically diverse through the migration patterns just described. In contrast to Milltown, it has a longer history of African American, Latinx, and Asian residents, but a relatively small and heterogeneous Native American population. African Americans, in particular, have had a well-established community in the city since at least 1902, when the city's first Black church was founded, though African Americans had been counted amongst the city's population since 1839. The African American population in Fairview county began a period of rapid growth in the 1970s and again in the 1990s, by which time it had tripled. In 1990, more than 70 percent of African Americans reported having lived in a different Wisconsin county five years earlier, according to a 1995 community study. Local lore, rife with racist undertones about Black dependency and Black families being outsiders not from Wisconsin, held that this increase was due to African American families coming from the south side of Chicago for welfare benefits. But research evidence does not support the claim that Wisconsin was a "welfare magnet" (Corbett 1991), or that low-income African Americans migrated to Wisconsin (or anywhere else) as a result of the closing of public housing there in 2000 (Livingston and Porter 2014).[3] Furthermore, US Census data collected between 2006 and 2011 suggests that most African Americans migrating to Fairview County were coming from states other than Wisconsin or Illinois (a combined 65 percent; US Census Bureau 2011). As a whole, Fairview's African American population includes an established and economically comfortable group as well as a sizeable, economically struggling population, and shows evidence of economic strain across classes.

Fairview has also been the landing place for a large number of refugees, including Central Americans fleeing political instability in the 1980s and, since the 2000s, refugees from Sudan, Iraq, Liberia, and Bhutan (Refugee Processing Center 2018; Wisconsin Department of Children and Families 2016). Hmong, who were resettled in Milltown in the 1980s and again in 2006 from Laos via long-standing refugee camps in Thailand, are by far the largest refugee population in Fairview. They are also the largest Asian population in Fairview. East Asian families, immigrant or not, were not common in Milltown, but their arrival in Fairview has been particularly connected to local science and technology-related fields, as well as to the city's university.

In the 1990s, young low-income Mexican families from the Southwestern United States and from Mexico began arriving in Fairview, and they are now the largest Latinx population in the city, according to a 2006 community study. This group has joined Central American refugees, an earlier group of families who settled in the city, and a smaller group of Latinx residents who have arrived in Fairview for professional or educational opportunities. Taken together, the city is now home to a rapidly growing Latinx community of more than fifteen thousand people that includes longer-term residents with advanced education, stable careers, strong English proficiency, and no immigration status problem, as well as a more recent group of predominantly Mexican immigrants who tend to be younger, who have lower levels of education and English language proficiency, and are more likely to lack immigration papers.

Inevitably, as Milltown school board member Susan Leahy noted in the bagel shop, public schools have been first to reflect the growing diversity in Milltown and Fairview. Each school district saw dramatic increases in the number of students whose primary language was not English, the majority of whom were Hmong or Spanish speakers. In 1998, fewer than 10 percent of Milltown and Fairview students were designated as English learners (ELLs). Ten years later, ELLs were 20 percent of Milltown students and 17 percent of Fairview students. In that same time period, students identifying as Native American, Asian, Black, or Latinx grew to almost 40 percent of students in Milltown and almost half of Fairview students. In both districts, these changes primarily reflected an increase in Latinx students, though the percentage of Black students was also growing, and Blacks were the largest minoritized group in Fairview. In each city there also was an increase from 2000 to 2009 in the percentage of students living in poverty—from an already high one-third of Milltown students in 2000 to more than half of Milltown students in 2009, and from about a quarter of Fairview students in 2000 to almost half of Fairview students in 2009.

While student racial diversity was growing in Milltown and Fairview, teachers in both schools have remained overwhelmingly white. This discrepancy between teacher and student demographics mirrors national trends: about 50 percent of students in the nation are students of color, while 83 percent of teachers are white, a number that has changed little since 1999 (Kober 2012; Maxwell 2014; US Department of Education 2013). In Milltown, almost 97 percent of teachers identified as white, and just 3 percent were teachers of color. In Fairview almost 90 percent of teachers identified as white, and just 10 percent identified as people of color.

In the cities of Milltown and Fairview, more than 75 percent of city residents were also identified as white—much larger percentages than in the schools. This difference between school-aged populations and the residents as a whole reflects migration and immigration, but also an aging white population, a declining birthrate among whites, and an increasing birthrate among groups of color (Curtis and Lessem 2014). This data mirrors broader patterns across the country and nationally, where the child-aged population is more racially and ethnically diverse than the elderly population, even as the older, predominantly white population is living longer (Frey 2014).

Taken together, these demographic shifts have been reshaping the Milltown and Fairview communities and their schools. An increasingly racially and ethnically diverse population of students' and young families' educational opportunities and experiences will be linked to the decisions of the aging white middle-class population that makes up the majority of voters, leads local organizations and government, and teaches in the schools. These are not just demographic shifts but also societal ones. As they tried to serve a poorer and more racially diverse student population, Milltown and Fairview leaders were witnessing the inequalities that schools would be expected to address, and the concerns and demands of teachers and residents who were predominantly white and middle-class. They have ultimately tried to solve these issues with color-blind managerialism.

To be sure, racial and ethnic diversity was growing, and many families arriving to Milltown and Fairview since the 1990s were poorer than many existing residents. But with a changing economy, growth in poverty has not been limited to people of color who have arrived at "new" destinations in the United States. As will be discussed next, poverty was growing across all racialized groups, including white families, during this same time period.

The Economic Shifts: Transitioning Economies and Rising Inequality

The dilemmas and inequities in Fairview and Milltown school districts— and, ultimately, the adoption of color-blind managerialism strategies— were also deeply grounded in a second major shift, an economic shift. Since the mid-1970s the United States has seen a series of macroeconomic pressures including globalization of goods, capital, and labor (through documented and undocumented migration and immigration); growing capital markets and stockholder focus on short-term profit; and expansion of the service sector (Kalleberg 2011). Across the country, a product-driven manufacturing economy has become a technology- and finance-driven global economy. Similar economic shifts are evident in other countries, but in the United States these shifts have been accompanied by weakened worker protections and labor unions' declining strength.

Many US corporations have adapted to these macroeconomic pressures with profit maximization strategies, such as layoffs and organizational restructuring, that treat workers as costs rather than assets, and which elicit work from them through coercion and fear. The automation of routine manufacturing work and the passage in 1993 of the North American Free Trade Agreement (NAFTA) under President Bill Clinton further facilitated downsizing and the movement of jobs to low-wage countries.

The restructuring of meatpacking is one key example of the change to industry in the Midwest. The shifts in this industry's economic fortunes are tied broadly to processes of deindustrialization, labor rights, and racialized industry recruitment techniques (Fink 1998). Meatpacking companies and union organizing clashed bitterly during the early days of the industry, but the period from the 1950s to the 1970s marked a time of relatively peaceful compromise, reflecting a broader societal "bargain" between labor, capital, and the state. Wages were good, benefits were stable, and working conditions improved. Then, in the 1980s, the meatpacking industry went through a powerful period of mergers and consolidation. Local plants were folded into a national industry structure dominated by what were known as "new-breed" packing companies. In an era of declining state support for unions, these new-breed packers took a strong antiunion stance and relocated many of their operations to rural places, where they took advantage of low wages and a less militant workforce. These companies simultaneously drove down wages even further and sped up production, which meant they used up workers very quickly. What had once been decent jobs were no longer so attractive to workers. With high turnover and location in more sparsely populated areas, new-breed packers began to recruit pockets of workers from all over the country: Mexicans from the border areas, Asian Americans from California, Native Americans from reservations in South Dakota, African Americans from New Orleans. The results had a powerful effect on meatpacking communities, creating greater diversity and racial tension, as in Milltown, as well as divisions among new arrivals who were fighting similar problems of exploitation and discrimination in the workplace and animosity in the communities, but did so as separate racial and ethnic groups.

Strategies such as those used in the meatpacking industry, as well as others, have contributed to the growth in "polarized and precarious employment systems"—that is, the development of "good" jobs, particularly high-paid "knowledge-intensive" service-sector and manufacturing jobs, and "bad" jobs that are typically low-paid "labor-intensive" service-sector jobs (Kalleberg 2011). Formerly well-paying manufacturing jobs in the US Midwest and Northeast have been eliminated, automated, sent overseas, or relocated to so-called right-to-work states. In the Midwest and Northeast, remaining jobs now pay substantially less (Pew Research Center 2016). Wisconsin has the fourth-highest percentage of middle-income adults in the nation (Pew Research Center 2016). However, with globalization and the loss of well-paying blue-collar manufacturing jobs, financial security in middle-class households has deteriorated very rapidly in the state. Only eight other states have seen such a rapid decline in the real median income of their middle-tier households between 2000 and 2014 (Pew Research Center 2016).

As manufacturing jobs have declined, the service sector has grown nationally, albeit in bifurcated ways. Professional and technology sectors that involve "knowledge work" were growing and adding jobs in Fairview. In Milltown there was also some growth in technologically advanced manufacturing jobs, but more education is required for these better-paying manufacturing positions and "knowledge jobs." Labor-intensive, low-wage service work (e.g., retail, food service, or home health care work) is also growing nationally, and it represents a larger segment of the overall service sector, but the work is often part-time and unstable, without benefits or an upward career path. People working in the low-wage service sector—typically those with low levels of education—experience substantial difficulty in making ends meet (Boris and Klein 2012; Collins and Mayer 2010; Hacker 2006; Kalleberg 2011). Together, these economic developments, driven by global capitalism and without significant counterbalance from government regulation or labor union power, have contributed to a decline of the middle class and its feeling of security (Hacker 2006; Pew Research Center 2016). These shifts have contributed to a shrinking middle class and rising economic inequality in many parts of the United States and internationally; the outcomes have been widespread, but they disproportionately affect people of color and those with lower levels of education.

There are significant divisions in how groups experience the changing structures of employment and their economic prospects more generally. At the end of the twentieth century, "educational attainment increasingly divided Americans economically, socially, geographically, and politically" (Fischer and Hout, 2006, p. 241). Whether because such education is needed, or because employers simply believe that is the case, education is an increasingly important determinant of access to "good" jobs (Kalleberg 2011). It has been key to good jobs, or to having jobs at all, but minoritized groups are more likely to face disadvantages in acquiring the skills and credentials needed. This contributes to inequalities in the quality of jobs held by some minoritized and immigrant groups, and it increases racial wage gaps. For example, immigrants or refugees who arrive with little formal education may work hard, but will have few options besides low-wage labor, a problem likely to be compounded by racism, undocumented legal status, and limited English proficiency (Kalleberg 2011).

Racism plays an enduring role in unemployment. Black and Latinx communities tend to face greater disadvantages in educational access, and greater likelihood of employment discrimination, among other forms of racism. Social networks and segregated housing also contribute to disadvantages for Black and Latinx communities in accessing and securing higher quality jobs (Kalleberg 2011). For instance, African Americans have higher rates of unemployment than other racialized groups with similar levels of education (Fischer and Hout 2006); they are more likely to work in service jobs, and likely to be paid less for similar work. As macroeconomic shifts and employment strategies in the United States go unchecked by government policy or labor unions, people of color and immigrants are among the most economically vulnerable. These racialized disparities were exacerbated by the Great Recession of 2007–9 which was the United States' largest economic recession since the Great Depression.

These economic shifts, intertwined with racial inequity, were also bearing down on Milltown and Fairview.

Milltown

Milltown, an industrial city, faced the consolidation, "downsizing," and closing of several traditional manufacturing operations, including meat processing factories, as national conglomerates bought up local companies and subsidiary industries spread out in the 1990s. While advanced manufacturing, such as machine manufacturing, has developed and sectors like services, finance, insurance, transportation, and health are growing, fewer of the once plentiful low-skill, well-paying manufacturing jobs are available to the city's working- and middle-class populations, particularly those without a college education. Milltown residents described the local meat processing industry's new profit-raising corporate strategies of cutting wages and weakening the union. A tight local labor market, combined with the undesirability of this newly deunionized, low-paying, and dangerous work led to a worker shortage in the 1990s, and eventually to the recruitment of immigrants directly from Mexico to fill jobs.

As the meatpacking example suggests, Milltown's economic story is not just one of jobs moving out of town or going overseas. Even the jobs that remained or were created paid less than in an earlier era. While other kinds of industry in Milltown have adapted and done well, making it one of the more successful manufacturing cities in the Midwest, not all residents have benefited. The poverty rate has grown more quickly than unemployment, further suggesting that as Milltown's economy has changed, new jobs no longer pay as well (Engel and Longworth 2012). The median annual household income in Milltown County was an estimated $46,319 in 1997, approximately $6,500 more than in the state as a whole, and approximately $9,300 more than the national figure. Yet by 2009, Milltown's median household income had not grown as quickly as the state and national average; in less than a decade Milltown's middle class had fallen, and at $50,926, Milltown median household income now merely reflected the median state and national income (US Census Bureau 2017b).[4]

Growing inequality and poverty were evident in the increasing levels of poverty among Milltown families and students in its schools. Unemployment rose to new highs in 2009, the time of this study. At 12 percent, it was substantially higher than the national rate. Child poverty was a substantial problem. Ninety-seven percent of families in poverty included at least one child under eighteen. Almost half of Milltown's children were eligible for subsidized school meals and about seven hundred children were identified as homeless that same year (Wisconsin Department of Public Instruction 2017).

US Census Bureau data illustrates the enormous racial disparities in poverty and unemployment among Milltown families; almost 40 percent of Black families were poor, approximately four times the percentage of white families (10 percent), although far more white families (more than twenty thousand) than Black families (fewer than five hundred) lived in poverty (US Census Bureau 2009a). Almost 37 percent of Native Americans, 21 percent of Asians, 34 percent identified as "other," 19 percent who marked "two or more" racial-ethnic groups, and 28 percent of Latinx families were also estimated to be living in poverty. Unemployment patterns were quite similar. The unemployment rate for Native Americans (16.9 percent), Asians (12.3 percent), and Latinx (8.9 percent) were all substantially higher than for the white population (6.1 percent), with Black unemployment (25.8 percent) almost four times higher than white unemployment (US Census Bureau 2009a).

Milltown schools confronted challenges of student "transiency," as children without stable housing moved in and out of schools and the school district. Furthermore, falling income, wages, and job losses had fiscal implications for Milltown schools, which depended on local property values and wealth for their funding. These were some of the very conditions that Susan Leahy described as shaping the outlook of white Milltown constituents who questioned school spending for ELLs. With budget gaps, district leaders needed the support of the majority of the city's predominantly white voters, who were more likely to have lost well-paying jobs, given the disproportionate poverty of people of color in the city. In Milltown, both of the school funding referenda proposed between 2005 and 2009, in the period just before this study, had failed, though two different referenda were passed in the spring of 2010 (Wisconsin Department of Public Instruction n.d.).

Fairview

In contrast, Fairview had a relatively strong, even accelerating economy. In 1997 the median annual household income in Fairview County had been an estimated $47,607, only slightly more than in Milltown County. In the ensuing years, however, median household income in Fairview County had grown to an estimated $58,002 in 2009, and has continued to rise since then (US Census Bureau 2017a). The local economy was grounded in the education and government sectors, predominantly white-collar work that was not particularly susceptible to economic downturn. In addition, though manufacturing was waning, consumer services, health, and high tech have been robust and growing sectors in Fairview; the city's well educated workforce has started new businesses in these growing fields and attracted other companies to the Fairview area. Approximately 30 percent of city residents worked in the relatively stable or growing health, education, government, and social services sectors, with another approximate 12 percent employed in the professional, scientific, management, and administrative fields (US Census Bureau, 2009b), which fit more neatly into the global, finance-driven economy and often pay more. The city had 6-percent unemployment, a relatively low rate during the Great Recession. Overall, Fairview was experiencing steady economic growth in an already relatively prosperous and stable local economy, even in the midst of economic recession.

Nevertheless, there was also growing inequality in Fairview. This was particularly evident in the schools and among families. As noted earlier, almost half of the city's students were living in poverty, and more than eight hundred were identified as homeless (Wisconsin Department of Public Instruction 2017). There were also enormous racial disparities in poverty among Fairview families, 97 percent of which included at least one child under eighteen. An estimated 35 percent of Black families were living in poverty and only an estimated 5 percent of white families were, making Black families seven times more likely to be living in poverty. One local analysis suggested that the Black/white disparities in child poverty in the Fairview area were likely among the highest in the nation. In addition, an estimated 14 to 20 percent of Latinx families of any race, Asian families, and families identifying as "two or more" races were living in poverty (US Census Bureau, 2009a).[5] Unemployment rates in Fairview also reflected a racialized class structure, with a white unemployment rate of 4.4 percent compared to rates of 5.1 percent (Latinx), 6.4 percent (Asian), 10.7 percent (American Indian), and 14.5 percent (Black) for other racialized groups. As in Milltown, poverty contributed to many concerns about homelessness, students' basic needs for food and clothing, and student mobility in schools. While there was growing poverty in Fairview, the stronger economy put Fairview citizens, as a whole, in a better financial position to support the schools than in Milltown. Between 2005 and 2009, Fairview citizens approved three of five school referenda (Wisconsin Department of Public Instruction n.d.); this rate of success was historically low for that city, but it suggests that there was still fiscal support for schools among the voters.

The Political Shifts: Declining Support for Public Institutions

The third major trend that has sharpened the contradictions in school district leaders' work and deeply affected the Milltown and Fairview school districts is the shift in policy and ideology from a focus on government protection of citizens from the disruptions and instability of markets to a focus on reducing government and promoting free markets.

The quintessential example of government social protection in the United States is the New Deal, a spate of programs—like Social Security, Medicare, and the minimum wage—that the federal government initiated in the 1930s and 1940s in response to the Great Depression. These programs were intended to compensate for the poverty and inequality of a capitalist economic system and for other uncertainties by providing regulations and a social safety net for citizens, particularly for those who were least well off or were unable to work, such as the unemployed, disabled, elderly, poor, and widowed (Katznelson 2006). By both design and implementation, however, many people of color were excluded from these benefits, contributing to upward mobility for white people and the few people of color who had access to the programs, and a lack of such opportunities for the large numbers of people of color who did not (Katznelson 2006).

Beginning in the mid-1960s, with the initiation of the Great Society programs, public education became the key public institution of the US social welfare state (Kantor and Lowe 2006, 2013). Widespread free mass public education has always been an important part of the US social welfare state for white citizens (Howard 2008; Katznelson and Weir 1985), but the expectation that education solve a litany of social problems, like poverty, was a major shift from the New Deal focus on addressing poverty and material inequality through direct transfer of funds or provision of food, housing, and health care (Kantor and Lowe 2006, 2013). Many direct and robust poverty alleviation programs were abandoned or withered.

In the 1970s and 1980s, the idea of government as a countervailing force against inequality and poverty came increasingly under attack. Economic crises and inflation in the 1970s, the election of President Ronald Reagan in 1980, and the successful advocacy work of conservative think tanks contributed to a rise in views, based in neoconservatism and free-market orthodoxy, that questioned government spending and the social welfare state (Apple 2006; Pierson 1995). Instead, advocates called for smaller government, tax and spending cuts, and market models of social programs. This political ideology and approach, sometimes called neoliberalism, was vividly expressed in 1981 when in his inaugural speech Reagan declared, "Government is not the solution to our problem; government is the problem."

Under Reagan and subsequent US presidents, social welfare programs have been rolled back even further. The "Personal Responsibility and Work Opportunity Reconciliation Act," signed into law in 1996 by President Bill Clinton, forced single mothers into cycles of welfare and low-wage service work (Collins and Mayer 2010; Shaefer and Edin 2018). Children living in extreme poverty (on less than two dollars a day) rose sharply, nearly doubling between 1997 and 2007 before the onset of the

Great Recession (Shaefer and Edin 2018). Notable exceptions to the roll-back are the Earned Income Tax Credit, passed in 1975 and expanded in 1986 and 1993, which gives a refundable tax credit to low- and moderate-income families and is now the largest antipoverty program in the country, and the 2010 Patient Protection and Affordable Care Act (ACA), also known as Obamacare, which has contributed to a considerable extension of health insurance for US citizens.[6] Neither of these measures, however, will help those in the most extreme levels of poverty.

Between the exclusionary elements of earlier welfare policies and the rollback of welfare benefits in subsequent years, coupled with discrimination and economic trends that have hit people of color especially hard, there are significant racial disparities in poverty. In Wisconsin, for example, racial disparities exist across the board, but are especially stark for African Americans. In one ranking of child well-being, Wisconsin was the worst state in the country for African American children across a number of indicators, including education and employment outcomes, while it was also ranked among the top ten in the country for white children (Taylor 2014). The state ranked in the bottom quartile of states for the well-being of Asian children, and in the second quartile for Latinx and Native American children (Taylor 2014).

The attack on government that began in the 1970s and 1980s also extended to public education. With many social programs already cut back, and others being cut further, the public schools, one of the remaining legitimate institutions aimed at providing for the public welfare, became a disproportionate target for opponents of the state's social welfare role (Kantor and Lowe 2006, 2013). In 1983 a federally commissioned report, *A Nation at Risk*, famously argued that "the educational foundations of our society are presently being eroded by a rising tide of mediocrity" (National Commission on Excellence in Education 1983, p. 5). In the ensuing years, nearly every major school reform proposal has argued that the public schools are failing (Mehta 2015). Such attacks on public schools have contributed to their delegitimation (Boyd 2003).[7] Teachers have been increasingly characterized as self-interested, incompetent, or lazy, and have been targeted for attack (D. Goldstein 2014). More recently, the discourse of failure associated with high-stakes standardized testing and fomented by the efforts of conservative movement actors has further marked public schools as illegitimate (Apple 2006; Berliner and Biddle 1995). These problems of legitimacy have taken different forms.

In urban schools, which are often discussed as being synonymous with failure, the critique has taken a particular racialized character (Wheeler-Bell 2016).

Indeed, racism has played a complicated role in the delegitimation of public institutions and social welfare, especially as the country has become more racially diverse. Social movements of the 1970s brought greater attention to racial exclusion in public institutions, and as racial ideologies in the post–civil rights era made explicit legal racism less acceptable, public institutions were increasingly called out for their racism (J. Clarke and Newman 1997; Omi and Winant, 2015). The critique of public schools is grounded, in part, in the critiques by people of color that they have not fulfilled their obligation to serve communities of color well (J. Clarke and Newman 1997; Pedroni 2007). Racial disparity in student outcomes and school resources has contributed to these concerns. Wisconsin provides another example; at almost 93 percent, it has the third-highest white graduation rate in the nation, while its African American graduation rate is 64 percent (COWS 2017).

Opposition to or suspicion of government has also emerged through ideologies and identities that weave together antigovernment sentiment with resentment, at least some of which is racialized (Cramer 2016; López 2014; Omi and Winant 2015). This was evident in Wisconsin, for example, where state and local politicians, as well as media personalities, stoked and harnessed this sentiment through policy and campaign rhetoric that used dog-whistle racial politics (I. H. López 2014) to secure support from predominantly white constituents (Cramer 2016; Mac-Gillis 2014). Governor Scott Walker, in particular, leveraged issues such as a proposed high-speed train between the cities of Madison and Milwaukee as a dog whistle to appeal to white suburban and rural residents' belief that "urban" residents were the undeserving beneficiaries of "their" tax dollars.

Disinvestment, Competition, and Accountability Systems in Wisconsin

Over time, the broad challenges to the legitimacy of public schooling have created an opening for arguments that public schools are too broken to be fixed, and that radical alternatives such as privatization are necessary (Apple 2006; Berliner and Biddle 1995). Among the dramatic changes to public schools has been the advance of neoliberal state and federal policy tools that are inspired by market models of governance, and which have deepened inequality. These policies include state-imposed revenue limits, high-stakes accountability policies, and market-based competition reforms. These policies have eclipsed proposals to expand the social welfare state to better address poverty and inequality (Anyon 2005).

These policies also reflect a marked shift from earlier state and federal education policies like desegregation and the original federal Title 1 legislation, which focused on ensuring equity through additional resources and affirmative remedies for racial inequity. Market-based policies have often been promoted on the grounds that they will improve school effectiveness or "excellence" and have focused on increasing educational outputs, primarily measured in individualized student test scores, rather than remedying race and class disparities in the resources and opportunities available to whole populations of students. Policies that had been meant to ensure racial equity in schools were being eroded. A particularly notable example in K–12 education was the 2007 US Supreme Court decision *Parents Involved in Community Schools vs. Seattle School District No. 1* (2007). In this ruling, the court found that, unless required to do so under court-ordered desegregation plans, school systems could not use race as a primary or "tiebreaker" criterion for assigning students to schools. While they acknowledged a compelling interest in diverse schools, the justices found in a 4-1-4 vote that the use of race had to be more narrowly tailored to achieve that goal. This ruling was important to the story unfolding in Fairview, and to communities across the country that had tried some voluntary measure of racial desegregation in their schools.

Here, I focus on the way market-based policy tools have played out in Wisconsin as the particularities of the state's policies had direct bearing on the Milltown and Fairview districts. The national story of these policies is examined in greater detail elsewhere (e.g., DeBray 2006; Henig 1995). Wisconsin in the mid- to late 1990s and into the early 2000s was a hotbed of policy making that reflected the neoliberal impulse. These efforts reflected trends occurring in many states and at the federal level, including the 2001 No Child Left Behind Act (NCLB). The attendant pressures, discussed below, fall into three general types: disinvestment in education funding, increase in school competition, and a high-stakes accountability system.

Disinvestment in Education

State regulations designed to limit state and local public investment in schools have contributed to the transformation and decline of public funding for these school systems. State law limiting property tax increases has been part of the broader nationwide push for cuts to social spending by white conservative property holders (both individual homeowners and corporate interests; Edsall and Edsall 1991). These groups have advocated against rising taxes and redistributive government policies to protect their own fortunes and, in part, in reaction to racial unrest and the perception that redistributive policies were aiding African Americans.

In 1993 the Wisconsin legislature enacted a state-level strategy to limit local spending on education (Hall 2007; Lund and Maranto 1996; Mulcahy and Mulcahy 1995; Spicuzza 2010). Foreshadowing Act 10, the Qualified Economic Offer (QEO) allowed school districts to limit the scope of teachers' collective bargaining.[8] Along with the QEO, the legislature curbed the rise in property taxes by imposing new limits on school districts' yearly revenues from general state aid and local property tax levies.[9] Under the law, a district can increase its budget (by raising property taxes or offering bonds) only by putting it to a public referendum (Kava and Olin 2005; Spicuzza and Barbour 2010). However, revenue caps generally grew more slowly than costs, creating structural budget shortfalls and forcing school districts to inflict ever deeper cuts in order to balance budgets (Hall 2007; Lund and Maranto 1996; Spicuzza and Barbour 2010). High-poverty districts have suffered more than low-poverty districts under this finance system (Wittkopf and Robinson 2014).

With local community wealth deeply destabilized by declines in well-paying, unionized manufacturing jobs, and after many years of state budget cuts and state-imposed limits on school district funding, the Milltown and Fairview school districts had seen their budgets slashed by millions of dollars each year. The 2007–9 Great Recession only heightened the problem. In Fairview, state aid decreased by $5.7 million (12 percent) from 2007–8 to 2009–10 (Wisconsin Department of Public Instruction 2011). In Milltown, state aid decreased by $1.5 million between 2007–8 and 2009–10 despite increased enrollment (Wisconsin Department of Public Instruction 2010). During the 2009–10 school year, the Milltown district cut $6 million from an annual budget of approximately $240 million. That same year, Fairview leaders cut an estimated $3.9 million from its annual budget of approximately $330 million, even after receiving an additional $5 million from a 2008 local referendum (Wisconsin Department of Public Instruction 2018).

Since Milltown and Fairview school budgets had not kept pace with rising costs, and since state funding had declined, the districts had become increasingly dependent upon local revenue generation. Although the school population had rapidly become more diverse, the city's demographics had not changed as quickly. Thus, district leaders were more dependent than ever on the support of their cities' still predominantly white voters and taxpayers, and their willingness to pass school bond measures and increase property taxes. But, in the five years before the study, up until a 2008 referendum in Fairview, voters both in that more affluent city and in Milltown had indicated a reluctance to support referenda to raise those funds.

Growing School Competition

Growing competition between schools and districts has added to fiscal woes and exacerbated the challenges facing the public schools. Concurrent with a policy push to cut back government and limit taxes has been one to model the public sector more like the private sector by introducing market mechanisms and competition through charter schools, voucher schemes, open-enrollment policies, and virtual schooling. In 1990 Wisconsin instituted the Milwaukee Parental Choice Program (MPCP), the country's largest public experiment in school vouchers, which provides public funds for students in Milwaukee to attend private and religious schools. The MPCP was pressed by local conservative activists, but supported in part by African Americans frustrated with the inequitable education available to their children in Milwaukee public schools. The support of some African Americans for the MPCP is a potent example of how racial inequity in schools has contributed to the push toward market-based alternatives to public schools (Pedroni 2007).

Another policy which is part of the broader political shift toward market models of public education, but has received less attention, is Wisconsin's "open enrollment" law. Passed in 1997, the law allows parents to choose to send their children to any school district in the state, provided that the district is accepting additional enrollments. Interdistrict open enrollment has been adopted in forty-two states (Education Commission of the States 2017). In Wisconsin, the open enrollment law was "designed to encourage competition among districts . . . and to provide families with increased flexibility in their educational choices" (Bezruki et al. 2002, p. 3). Families no longer need to live within a school district's boundaries in order to enroll their children in that district's schools. Sending school districts must transfer state aid money to receiving school districts for each student who transfers out of their district, and must also pay for special education services for such students when applicable, thus contributing to net revenue gains or losses in different districts. The Wisconsin state school administrators association, state teachers union, and state school board association all originally supported the open enrollment law, under the condition that the costs would be covered for receiving districts, and limited so as not to threaten a district's viability (Witte, Schlomer, and Shober 2007). But as conditions changed—including the lifting of a cap on transfers in 2006–7—many districts have been threatened. Statewide, the numbers of students using the intradistrict transfer option (i.e., open enrollment) has increased dramatically (Kava 2011).

In Fairview, open enrollment was also expanded when in 2007, in response to the *Parents Involved* ruling, Fairview district leaders determined that they could no longer be certain that the district's implementation of the policy was legal, and ended it. The district had previously denied families' interdistrict open enrollment requests if granting such requests would upset the racial balance in the sending schools. Ending that aspect of district policy eliminated one of the main barriers to using the system to transfer white children out of Fairview schools.

Besides private schools, the main competition in both Milltown and Fairview came from neighboring suburban districts through Wisconsin's open enrollment policy. Net transfers from Milltown and Fairview were growing rapidly, with more than six hundred students (approximately 3 percent of the student body) transferring out of Milltown and more than four hundred students (approximately 2 percent of the student body) transferring out of Fairview in the year before I began this study (Kava 2011). Students mostly transferred to surrounding suburban districts, which were typically wealthier and whiter.

In schools and districts like Milltown and Fairview that have experienced a net loss of students, this competition exacerbates budget shortfalls as schools lose state dollars for each child who transfers out of their system. The political support and economic resources of the white middle class are therefore increasingly important to sustain the success of Milltown and Fairview public schools, even as the white middle class—not just families, but teachers and citizens too—has resisted change and shows signs of weakened support of the schools.

Heightened Expectations and Testing Pressures

Finally, the expectations that Milltown and Fairview public schools serve all students and bring them to higher levels of academic achievement and democratic citizenship are greater than ever. Within schools there is increased pressure to operate schools more like businesses, both due to a desire by educators to mimic legitimized school practices like "data-based decision making" (Booher-Jennings 2005; Clarke and Newman 1997), and due to educational professionals, or the "new managerial class," who find the need for their expertise in data analysis and management, and who find these mechanisms advantage their own middle-class children (Apple 2006; Clarke and Newman 1997). However, state and federal high-stakes accountability systems have added considerable pressures and sanctions from outside the school districts, whose leaders are now held responsible for raising test scores and other measurable outcomes. Simply giving their best effort is no longer enough.

Under the assumption that schools are solely to blame for poor educational performance, policy makers have designed state and federal accountability policies like NCLB. Through these policies, schools and districts face punitive consequences if they fail to achieve pre-established goals for improving test scores. For example, under NCLB, schools that did not raise test scores to meet externally established targets were labeled as failing, and faced punitive consequences. The tests upon which schools are evaluated are based are deeply disputed and often incorrectly used, and they best reflect a white middle-class background (Au 2016; Koretz 2008). Thus, they systematically reproduce inequalities, and mark Black and Brown students, low-income students, and the schools enrolling those students as failing academically. Nonetheless, the tests are often taken as a fair and neutral measure of achievement; and under high-stakes accountability systems, they are highly consequential.

Since 2003, when the first such ratings were reported, the state has added schools in both Milltown and Fairview to a list of "schools identified for improvement" (also called SIFI), a measure of school failure associated with the Wisconsin state accountability system and NCLB. In 2008–9, Fairview had seven of its forty-five schools identified as needing improvement, and Milltown had three of its thirty-six placed on the SIFI list. Standardized test scores indicated that there were racial disparities in student achievement. In Milltown, only about 20 percent of Black, 30 percent of American Indian and Latinx, and fewer than 40 percent of Asian (predominantly Hmong) students were deemed proficient on state standardized tests of mathematics in 2009–10, while approximately 60 percent of white students were (Wisconsin Department of Public Instruction 2011). Fewer than 30 percent of students identified as ELLs or as economically disadvantaged students were scored proficient. In Fairview, the disparities were wider between Black, Native American and Latinx students, and their white and Asian counterparts. About 15 percent of Black, 20 percent of Latinx, and 35 percent of Native American students were deemed proficient in mathematics in Fairview, although a majority of Asian (55 percent) and white (65 percent) students were marked proficient (Wisconsin Department of Public Instruction 2011). Furthermore, only 20 percent of Fairview's ELLs and economically disadvantaged students were deemed proficient in mathematics. Under NCLB, Milltown and Fairview were both targeted for improvement.

The story above describes the shifts in state and federal policy up until 2009, when I began collecting data for this study. But many of the political and policy shifts described here have continued or been heightened. While the QEO was repealed in 2009, revenue caps were maintained (Spicuzza 2010) and rising costs continued to outstrip those caps, leading to continued structural budget strains in both districts. The fiscal austerity measures seen leading up to this study were only more severely enacted in subsequent years. Following the lead of earlier policy makers, both Republican and Democrat, Governor Walker proposed Act 10, setting off one of the largest political conflicts and mass protests in the state's history.[10] Eventually passed by the state legislature, Act 10 called for severe budget cuts to K–12 public schools and the state university system, and a rollback of the rights of public employees to collectively bargain. In the following year, the Milwaukee voucher program was expanded, then adopted statewide in 2013. In 2015, the Every Student Succeeds Act (ESSA) replaced NCLB as the most recent reauthorization of the 1965 Elementary and Secondary Education Act. ESSA modified many aspects of NCLB, but retained provisions for regular standardized testing.

Change, Pressure, and Inequality in Fairview and Milltown

Demographic changes, shifting economic conditions, and political shifts have been deeply intertwined with race and class inequalities across the United States. Schools have been central to the economic and political shifts, and are among the first public institutions affected by the demographic changes. While it is well recognized that these changes have contributed to neoliberal school reforms in big city school systems (Cucchiara 2013; Lipman 2011; Rury and Mirel 1997; J. Scott and Holme 2016), related shifts also have sharpened the challenges facing smaller school districts across the country. The changes described in this chapter have heightened the challenges and contradictions of public schools as places that both help ensure social equity and democracy and also maintain status quo structures and inequities of race and class.

In the Milltown and Fairview school districts, a new policy context has not only weakened other parts of the social welfare state and challenged the legitimacy of public schooling, but has also put greater pressure on schools to alleviate growing poverty, raise academic achievement, and address increases in racial diversity. Top-down policy tools have contributed to severe district budget cuts, increased competition, and new pressure to raise test scores, deeply challenging Milltown and Fairview leaders' abilities to meet the rising expectations, and shaping their decision making in consequential ways.

Though both were changing demographically, the districts and their leaders represented contrasting political and economic contexts and trajectories, and thus were differently positioned within the changing political and economic contexts: in Fairview as a liberal, relatively prosperous, but increasingly unequal city, and in Milltown as a more conservative city with some advanced manufacturing and growth industries amid a more broadly stagnant or struggling industrial economy. The heightened inequality, made more evident and salient by racial-ethnic change as numbers of children of color grew and racial ideologies were activated, further challenged the legitimacy of the public schools in the eyes of still powerful white majorities and elites. These demographic, economic and political transformations created a profound need for school district leaders to act, and substantial challenges to their doing so.

An examination of the broader political, economic, and social shifts across much of the United States and in Milltown and Fairview high-

lights the web of racial and economic inequities that were tighten-
ing around school district leaders and their communities, and it brings
into stark relief the contradictions that trouble public schools across the
United States. While data indicate that political, economic, and social
shifts were transforming the Milltown and Fairview school district contexts, this was not how district leaders largely understood their situation.
Chapter 2 examines how they understood the changes.

Becoming "Urban" School Districts

In late October I headed just south of the highway that circles Fairview. I turned right off a heavily trafficked road, past a gas station and several plain but neatly maintained two-story brick apartment buildings. Elmwood, a Fairview neighborhood, was developed from farmland and forest into single family homes in the late 1950s and 1960s. In subsequent years an elementary school was built, spurring additional growth there. Construction of an outer ring of two-unit apartment buildings and multifamily residences in Elmwood and adjacent neighborhoods soon followed.

Janice Steiner and her husband moved into one of those single-family homes in the center of Elmwood. It sat amid low-slung modern houses that were set back on neatly trimmed emerald lawns along meandering streets. More than thirty years later, the trees had grown in, and the original homeowners had grown older. Their children have graduated from high school and college and moved on, as have Janice's. This "core" of middle-class white families remained for now, but the apartments and duplexes that surrounded them mostly housed low-income families, many of whom had school-aged children. More than 70 percent of children at the elementary school qualified for federally subsidized school lunches, and about 13 percent of the housing units were subsidized through government assistance programs. Families of color, primarily African American and Latinx, now called these outer rings of the neighborhood "home."

In a low chair in her den, Janice talked about the changes in the Fairview schools. A school board member and former teacher, Janice advocated and praised the school district's public school teachers. She recalled the changes in her neighborhood, in Fairview, and in the schools where she taught for twenty-five years before she retired. "When I came to Fairview, there were low-income students, first-wave Vietnamese and Hmong, and not many Hispanics. Then gradually, people from Chicago came and came for better life." Low-income families had settled across the city, except in the very wealthy areas where there was no low-income housing.

In her decades in Fairview schools, Janice had gone from teaching "teeny, tiny" first-graders in her first year, to teaching computer programming on Commodore computers in one of the city's first computer labs, to her last year co-teaching students identified for special education. Janice remembered her teaching days as being filled with innovative programs and difficult work, challenges that she and other teachers had resources and flexibility to address. She recalled her last classroom fondly. It had a music area, a living room area, a dining room area, and a workout area with an exercise bicycle. "When someone came in a little hyper, we said, 'Get on the exercise bicycle.'" Teachers adapted and problem-solved when students were a little out of hand. Janice's many years as a teacher shaped her thoughts as a school board member about the school district and about the changes occurring in the schools, especially the demographic changes.

Gradually this school became a high-poverty school, Janice recalled. In her last year of teaching, she had eighteen "high-risk" students and six "college-bound" students. She described that classroom as foreshadowing the changes occurring in the district. "That's what we are seeing now," she explained. "It was hard. A challenge." But, she added, "it was a very integrated classroom in terms of culture, and we had a bulletin board filled with all the aunts and uncles that went through Union Elementary before them. It was wonderful and safe, and teachers wanted to be there."

Yet those warm memories of teaching in a racially or culturally diverse classroom contrasted with the views of some parents and community members, and even with Janice's own view of the district at that moment. Janice had thought a lot about these issues. As I sat there, writing as quickly as I could, she explained her understanding of the changing demographics in the city and the schools. She described white families questioning educational quality in schools with low-income people and people of color, and exiting the district or transferring their children to predominantly white schools within Fairview. To Janice it appeared that there was a pattern of "white flight."

Janice explained this exit to suburban districts as the result of an ethos, under the previous superintendent, to "integrate and everyone will succeed, and the top [students] will take care of themselves." The result of this effort to ensure heterogeneous and inclusive classrooms, she believed, was "some very angry parents. It was a whole fiasco." Janice allowed that these parents had some valid complaints. But she noted that their children were not suffering. "These were the parents of children who were going to Harvard, Princeton, Yale. They would say it was despite the schools; I would say it was because of the schools."

Those parents were not the only ones complaining. As Fairview leaders tried to establish a pathway for lower-achieving students to take higher-level classes, a new set of parents had begun to complain that their students were not being properly served. "Now we are hearing it from the children of middle students."

Parents no longer seemed to defer to educators or respect their judgment. "It used to be that parents left the schools alone. Now a child named Dexter tells his mother he was bored in school and she says, 'How can you be bored in school?' and blames the teacher," Janice told me, her voice rising with disbelief. "And his teacher was one of the best teachers in the district! Everyone wants to participate, and everyone thinks they know."

For at least thirty years, the legitimacy of large urban public schools for middle- or upper-middle-class white families has been challenged around just such issues: poverty and minoritized populations, "white flight", and the efficacy of educational professionals. Now it seemed, the Fairview schools faced such questions as well.

To Janice, the contrast between these white or wealthier parents and the families of students arriving to Fairview was sharp. "Immigrant" parents she said, were struggling in life, but trying to do what's right. "They only want what's best for their child. I never met a family that didn't. I've seen them go off drugs to have a conference with me. Some of the lowest of the low. They care." Janice did not hear complaints from these families about school district efforts to add cultural relevancy for Black children to school programs, or plans to bus children to alleviate overcrowding and achieve greater racial and ethnic diversity in schools. Only the "white and well-to-do parents" complained about these things. But Janice added, "White folks care, too, but it's about their kid." In a sense, she acknowledged that parents, regardless of their racial position, desire what's best for their child. But she also made a distinction. To her it often seemed that what white parents wanted for their kids interfered with, or came at the expense of, what might be good for children of color.

Janice lamented the loss of interest in the democratic or civic goals of public schooling. She believed the schools were not only about individual advancement; they also taught democracy and contributed to society. "Schools train you as citizens, for a job," she said. "We train the lawyers, doctors, teachers, social workers. That's what we do in the schools." Parents who appeared to act solely with concern for the individual advancement of their own relatively privileged children, while the district tried to address the inequities of the "achievement gap," offended Janice's sense of educational mission and purpose. "I believe you define yourselves by how you treat people less fortunate than you. Some believe it is how you take care of yourself." Indeed, the conflict between schooling for individualized social mobility purposes and schooling for equity-minded democratic purposes strikes at the heart of the contradictions and inequities the school district seemed to face (Hochschild and Scovronick 2003; Labaree 1997).

This focus on only taking care of one's own was another instance, Janice concluded, of broader political shifts under way in Wisconsin. "You can see it in this election," she said, referring to the 2010 gubernatorial race between Scott Walker and Milwaukee's Mayor Tom Barrett, a Democrat. A Republican and a former executive of Milwaukee County, Walker won by running on a Tea Party platform of tax cuts, job creation, and rejection of federal funding to build a high-speed train between Milwaukee and Madison. This was a platform that successfully appealed to the racism of the highly segregated white votes in wealthy suburban and exurban Milwaukee enclaves (MacGillis 2014) and the racially tinged, antigovernment, antiurban resentment of rural Wisconsin voters (Cramer 2016). The political moment made particularly clear the reluctance of working-class, middle-class, and wealthier white residents to support and include communities of color, especially lower-income ones, as Janice pointed out. But the tenuous support or outright hostility toward communities of color was not new in the state (Clark-Pujara 2017; Collins and Mayer 2010), as is suggested in chapter 1 of this book.

Sitting in the comfort of her family home, amid her concerns about demographic change, budgets, "white flight," and the seeming erosion of a commitment to democratic and equitable ideals, Janice raised an urgent question. "The key question is: Can we do it? Can we educate a diverse population without being an inner-city school system?" The question hung in the air. Janice released a small sigh. "The answer is, we are not there yet. I don't know if we can. I do believe if a city can do it, Fairview can."

* * *

With well over a hundred thousand residents, the city of Fairview was no small town. Yet, to school board member and thirty-plus-year resident Janice Steiner, and many others, the idea of Fairview becoming an urban school system seemed like a troubling possibility rather than a geographic fact. Intrigued by the way she questioned the district's urban or "inner-city" status, I asked Janice what she meant by an "inner-city school system."[1] She replied, "Meaning poor schools with only low-achieving students, with no mix—a segregated city. Inner-city Chicago, New York, or Milwaukee, which is even closer." Like Janice, school district leaders and community members readily acknowledged that their districts were located in cities, yet the label "urban" suggested much more than a geographic location (Beauregard 2002; Leonardo and Hunter 2007; Macek 2006).

While cities are real physical places, "the urban" can also be thought of as a set of meanings, imagined in raced and classed ways. For example, the word "urban" frequently brings to mind people of color (Leonardo and Hunter 2007; Noguera 2003). It is not uncommon to find suburban school districts with growing poverty or large numbers of students of color referred to as "urban." This language has commonly been used to label places with concentrations of low-income people of color as dysfunctional. The implication is often that the people in these places are somehow the cause of their own circumstances, without recognition of the histories and politics of race and class exploitation that are so frequently at the root of those conditions. However, urban space and urban schooling have been perceived and represented in multiple, highly contradictory ways. Urban can be understood as poor or wealthy, as in decline or futuristic, as uncivilized or cosmopolitan, and as dysfunctional or innovative.

But urban imagery is not purely fantasy. Representations of urban space are grounded in policies as well as in social, political, and economic relations that have shaped urban development, and urban schooling, in very particular ways. Deindustrialization, suburbanization, racial housing segregation, and federal and state policy left many urban schools underresourced, physically deteriorating, and serving a minoritized student population that is struggling in concentrated poverty (e.g., Anyon 1997, 2005b; Kozol 1991). More recently, as described in chapter 1, globalization of finance, labor market changes, new policies, and demographic shifts have further contributed to "dual cities" where deepening poverty and skyrocketing wealth accumulation, and thus increasingly high levels of diversity and inequality, coexist and are intertwined (Mollenkopf and Castells 1991). Schools have been shaped by these raced and classed developments, and urban education policy has played a part in furthering these inequities (Lipman 2011). Taken together, invocations of "the urban" can signal real race and class inequities, but can—and often do—obscure the social, political and economic relations that have contributed to unequal conditions in many cities.

In this chapter I show that district leaders made sense of growing poverty and students of color, fiscal budget crises, declining achievement on standardized tests, and attacks on public education in terms of their districts "becoming urban," a narrative that tapped into highly racialized discourses about post–World War II urban transformation. In particular, school district leaders fixed their anxieties about these changes on the arrival of people of color, and on racist "white flight." This formulation of their circumstances masked the policy shifts and broader political and economic structures (described in chapter 1) that were impacting district leaders' work. Issues of power, inequality, and race were largely interpreted as issues of demographic change, culture, and individualized pathology or virtue. The notion of Milltown and Fairview districts as becoming "urban" forestalled a more radical critique of the situation. Nonetheless, the urban imaginary shaped Milltown and Fairview leaders' hopes and fears, their views of the challenges and contradictions they faced as they did their work, and the futures they charted for their more racially diverse and unequal school systems. Thus, these ideas contributed to the eventual adoption of color-blind managerialism.

How Fairview and Milltown Became "Urban"

"Fairview School District now describes itself as an urban school system. It never used to," former central office staff member Annalise Mayer declared. The idea that Fairview and Milltown districts were becoming "urban" expressed, in shorthand, the growing presence of communities of color, people living in poverty, and immigrant families. In the stories Fairview and Milltown district leaders frequently told about demographic change, for example, they recounted a narrative of predominantly white and middle-class "towns" or districts that had experienced the arrival of a succession of groups of people of color, many of whom were living in poverty. This was the case with Sharon Visser, a senior Milltown district administrator who identified as white. Sharon, who had herself once been a student in the Milltown schools, could speak to the history of Milltown, its school district, and the demographic changes that have taken place there.

She got right to the point. "We've had a lot of demographic changes," she told me. "We had basically an all-white district. We had a few American Indians. First, we had changes in our demographics of poverty." After poverty "came in," Sharon recalled the arrival of the Hmong as Milltown became a central area for the relocation of Hmong refugees. She described the "next big wave" as "our Hispanic population." Rewinding her story a bit, she remembered that throughout this time period there had been a small relatively affluent Black population. "All along, we've had a few African American students. Their parents were employed, usually as managers or above, CEOs, of some of our companies in the area." She continued: "Then we had our Hispanic group of people. We've had a lot. The first ones that came were really migrants, because of the farms around, and then we had the ones that were involved with [meat processing]." The last group was "African American families that are living in the lowest-income areas." In the previous year or two, many African American students had been moving to Milltown. "They are moving from Milwaukee and Chicago," Sharon said, adding an assumption that could also be heard in Fairview: that "a number of our families come because they are homeless and we've good services here." Whether it was entirely accurate or not, this narrative of demographic change, sometimes also including references to "white flight" or "middle-class flight," was broadly told among district leaders of both cities.

Reflecting the ways in which race and class are intertwined in everyday life in the United States (Omi and Winant 2015), district leaders' stories of demographic change emphasized both race and class change. Like other Milltown and Fairview leaders, Sharon described newly arriving minoritized groups as poorer than previous arrivals of the same race or ethnicity, emphasizing that demographic change also reflected a change in levels of poverty as new arrivals were perceived to be poorer than earlier coethnics (Turner 2015).[2] As another Milltown district administrator explained, "It's traditionally a white middle-class community, who's shifting to a much more diverse community culturally, ethnically, racially, and economically."

Both of these cities *were* experiencing notable shifts in the racial-ethnic identifications of their students. However, in telling the story of demographic change this way, district leaders located growing poverty in Fairview and Milltown as almost exclusively coming from or heightened by the arrival of people of color. They did not acknowledge the structural processes and shifts in the political economy that explain these changes.

Kevin Cole was an exception. A white Milltown administrator who worked closely with communities of color, Kevin was one of two district leaders who explicitly acknowledged demographic changes as being linked to broader social, economic, and political shifts occurring within and beyond the city. Kevin had also attended Milltown schools, and his own school experiences as a working-class kid, as well as his history teaching immigrant students, informed his understanding of the schools. When I first asked Kevin about demographic change, he mentioned the "waves" of Hmong, African American, and Latinx arrivals from the late 1970s on, but he also described a larger working-class population. Some poorer populations were moving to Milltown to work in the newly low-wage meatpacking jobs, he said, noting that in recent years Milltown's industries had been bought up and consolidated by out-of-state or foreign conglomerates, causing some secondary industries to be relocated elsewhere. "We have been hit by the economic shift," Kevin concluded. With 90 percent of students in some schools living in poverty, "we have almost an inner-city environment like we did in the 60s," he said, noting the "obvious parallel" between "low economic status and race" in school demographics. Kevin's framing of demographic change was uncommon among Milltown and Fairview district leaders for the degree to which he acknowledged underlying changes in the Milltown political economy— the global consolidation of industry, union busting, the loss of manufacturing jobs, and corporate recruitment of immigrant laborers—and the racialized dynamics of these changes as responsible for the growing poverty and its racialized nature in Milltown.

The notion of "becoming urban" also captured the deepening inequality that Milltown and Fairview district leaders observed in schools and in their cities. The monikers of "urban" and "suburban" conveyed the growing differences (in student populations, resources, opportunities, and physical conditions of schools) within each school system. They served as a shorthand for the deep contradictions within the school district and community, but they covered over the sources of those contradictions. One Milltown administrator called the east and west parts of the school district, nearest the downtown, the "inner city," and called the other parts of the district the "suburban" ones (see also Buendía et al. 2004). Kevin explained: "There is a dramatic contrast between some buildings that are very suburbanlike, and some that are very urbanlike and have urban students and problems. So there is a lot of contrast in terms of different needs."

In Fairview, several school district leaders talked about "a tale of two Fairviews," language that underscored the reality of Fairview as a kind of dual city. Katie Carlson, a young, white district administrator who worked in the district central office, explained: "You've got [an] affluent, smart, wealthy . . . real savvy, brainiac city. But then you also have a city with a lot of poverty. That it's a growing urban community where half our school students are living in poverty—that, people don't see." She wondered at "families who want organic lunch" but who did not even know about a whole group of Fairview students who "can't even afford forty cents for lunch, and are afraid of getting deported every day." The "really wealthy and really poor" in one school—"that is kind of the story of Fairview," she said.

Even as poverty and inequity have deepened considerably, more affluent families often remained oblivious to families struggling with poverty, as Katie recognized. Yet, for school district leaders who did take note of these inequities, the idea of two cities (or of "urban" and "suburban" parts of the city) illuminated the contradictory and inequitable circumstances and educational experiences of student populations.

In Milltown and Fairview, then, the term "urban"—and its association with immigrants, people living in poverty, and especially people of color—captured the demographic changes occurring, but also the student and school inequalities in the Milltown and Fairview schools. The poverty and inequality were concerning and disorienting. Gary Bradley, an executive administrator in Milltown and former physical education teacher who often spoke in sports analogies, called the fact that a majority of Milltown students were living in poverty a "really devastating trend. . . . It is difficult for me to reconcile that our children and families are in that position." Fairview school board member Janice Steiner, described at the start of this chapter, had been struggling with the seeming contradictions in her district for quite some time, and she felt uncertain about the district's future. Two representations of the urban, as a place of pathology and as a site of decline, further challenged district legitimacy and contributed to Milltown and Fairview leaders' fears that their schools were in peril.

Needy Students: The Imagery of Urban Pathology

With the arrival of greater numbers of students of color to the Milltown and Fairview schools, district leaders and other predominantly white and middle-class or wealthier residents were increasingly viewing these "good" school systems as "ghetto" or "inner city"—a common, pejorative, and deeply racialized construction of urban space that draws on cultural racism by explaining of racial inequality as a result of individual or cultural attributes of people of color (Bonilla-Silva 2003). Urban schools and students—invariably envisioned as low-income and of color—are imagined to be dysfunctional, disorderly, or unsafe, and urban students and families are seen as lacking the beliefs, values, and characteristics necessary for educational success (Leonardo and Hunter 2007; also Macek 2006).

The narrative of urban pathology and school failure helped district leaders account for two preoccupations in their work. One was falling indicators of student achievement. Fairview now had seven schools designated under the state and federal accountability system as "schools identified for improvement" (SIFI), and Milltown had three—additional evidence of shifts in academic achievement and a declining reputation. School district leaders described low achievement as arriving with families of color and low-income families who were in pursuit of a better life, but whose children were unprepared for school in Milltown and Fairview. Charlie Wills, a white former Fairview school board member, explained achievement as a mismatch where "the demands of the district educationally for the student and for the parent were far more rigorous than the community from which they came." A Milltown assistant superintendent described the district as having a "changing demographic from [a] primarily highly majority-white student population—high-achieving—to a district that now has much diversity and lower achievement, and a significant achievement gap from racial groups compared to white." In the less wealthy and less welcoming Milltown, one district administrator cited demographic change as "our biggest issue right now." He added, "The demographics are kids from very challenging backgrounds."

At the same time, and in a contradictory fashion, many district leaders also critiqued the rising anxious discourse among predominantly white middle- and upper-middle-class families: that Milltown and Fairview schools were no longer good schools, as they served a more diverse and unequal student population. Although these leaders also characterized low-income students of color as bringing problems to the district, these leaders denounced what they saw as these families' apparent fears of people of color and their perceptions of declining safety in the schools, concerns that closely mirrored the imagery of urban schools as pathological. For example, Jon Betz, a passionate Milltown teacher and union leader, explained: "It's 2009, and unfortunately we have schools that have reputations that are undeserved." Some people in the community, he said, have the perception that the schools are drug-infested, crime-ridden, and gang-ridden. A Milltown central office administrator explained that although parents might deny it, "white flight from the district" was based on parents' "perception of certain other children. Because they're feeling their children might not be safe at, quote, inner-city schools." Though this administrator did not use race words herself, she clearly signaled that she saw white flight as a result of white families' racist assumptions.

These perceptions were also evident in the more liberal Fairview. A Fairview school board member said: "People who aren't familiar with our schools, who kind of just draw their conclusions from reading the newspaper, think, number-one, that the schools aren't safe; and two, that they are not academically challenging enough. Both of those are kind of manifestations of a fear of the other." Charlie, the school board member, stressed the changes that had to be made to the schools in response to students who needed remedial education or bilingual services; but he saw a barrier in that "many people in the Fairview community—Black, Brown, white, made no difference—they perceived the immigrants as being folks who brought with them an awful lot of problems, and that they became a significant burden on the city's infrastructure, whether it be having to subsidize housing or . . . change the approach to educating students." To Milltown and Fairview leaders, white residents' "fear of the other," concerns about safety, or views of people of color as burdens as the schools became more diverse and unequal were triggering unfounded doubts about the schools by people who had little knowledge of them.

Indeed, local media and community members of different political persuasions also used imagery of urban pathology to express fears of increasing numbers of children of color. For example, a 1995 Fairview news article titled "School Colors" began by noting that Fairview and its suburbs were both seeing increases in public school enrollment. However, the newspaper reported, "the difference between the growth in the city and suburbs is stark. According to figures from the Fairview school district, all the growth in city schools is accounted for by minority students, many of them coming from poor families." Despite the presumptive inclusiveness of Fairview, the tone of this news coverage was more foreboding than welcoming. Milltown's local newspaper also ran stories on demographic change. A 2003 article contrasted the growing numbers of "minority" students in the Milltown schools with the city's predominantly white suburban school districts. The newspaper reported that "such differences can isolate minority students in an urban area's lowest performing schools," and noted that Milltown schools were the only ones in the area to be cited as failing in 2009 and 2010 under NCLB.

The discourse of urban pathology, reflecting cultural racism, implies that urban residents were to blame for the inequality of urban conditions because of their maladaptive cultures and individual choices. Specific policies and social, economic, and political relations that create such conditions, which are always part of the story, were ignored. Nevertheless, leaders in both districts understood the challenges of school achievement in terms of the arrival of more needy students, and negative perceptions of the schools in terms of white middle-class parents' and community members' beliefs that they were unsafe or of poor quality. Yet district leaders' own fears were less about gangs than about school budgets and white flight.

White Flight and Bankrupt Schools: Imagining School District Decline

District leaders' understandings of the changes in their districts mostly focused on their significant financial challenges, a concern captured in the imagery of urban decline. The discourse of urban decline highlights the postwar abandonment of cities by the white middle classes, a lack of resources, and a blighted or deteriorating infrastructure. Rather than emphasizing the culture or behavior of minoritized urban residents, as the urban pathology discourse does, the urban decline discourse centers on the fiscal and material deterioration of urban space, including schools, and the role of exit or "white flight" in hastening this decline (Beauregard 2002). "White flight," which became a central concern for district leaders, suggested a challenge to the sustainability of their districts.

Fairview district leaders and community members viewed student arrivals as requiring additional school district resources, from staff to structures to curriculum. These entailed increased costs that their school systems could not fully fund. Milltown and Fairview newspapers reported on the increased costs associated with the arrival of immigrant children and children living in poverty. As early as 1996, a news article in Fairview titled "Poverty, Diversity Boost School Costs" described the rising cost of hiring more reading specialists, special-education teachers, family-community liaisons, English as a second language and bilingual teachers, and assistant principals responsible for in-school discipline, as well as the costs associated with security and busing—all of which were implied to be associated with increasing poverty and growing "minority" populations. Janice described the students arriving at Fairview schools as "increasingly more intensely needy kids." She elaborated: "I'm talking about brain damage. From research I have done, this comes from poverty, kids coming from Chicago. They have witnessed crime, and this trauma has affected these children dramatically." Janice explained that these "kids coming from Chicago" and autistic children required costly one-on-one aides to meet their needs. "We are woefully underfunded for this by the state," she said. "This is draining us."

Janice's metaphor of being drained emphasized a loss of money related to rising costs associated with more "needy" kids *and* underfunding by the state of Wisconsin. Though Janice also used deficit notions of African American children, she also framed the problem as the state's underfunding of the schools. Staffing expenses have increased rapidly in both Milltown and Fairview in recent decades, in good part in relation to rising special education staffing costs. However, it is not clear that this rise in expenses was due in any large measure to the provision of aides to children from Chicago who were suffering from trauma, rather than to other special-education-related costs associated with services for white children or the district's previous focus on classroom inclusion as federal funding for special education was being cut. Increased expenditures were particularly challenging, perhaps unsustainable, in a context of budget shortfalls and the decline in state funding. As the district made policies to pay for low-income students' bus passes, lunches, and other basic needs, a different Fairview school board member explained the new reality as "more needs, fewer resources."

District leaders' anxieties about their districts' status and decline were crystallized in their concerns with white flight and its financial repercussions. Janice Steiner connected "white flight" or "middle-class flight" to what it meant to be a large urban school district. Consistent with a story of urban decline, Milltown and Fairview administrators and school board members frequently discussed the exit, or potential exit, of white or middle-class families to neighboring districts. For example, Janice explained that as Fairview had lost students to neighboring school districts through the open enrollment program, state funding for those students followed them out the door. She acknowledged that Fairview's talented and gifted programs weren't as good as they had been, but she rejected the claim that it was the reason why those children were using the interdistrict open enrollment policy to transfer their children from Fairview schools. "To me it was white flight," she said, noting, "Some have transferred within the city to 70 percent white schools, which shows it." This reminded Janice of large US cities. Indicating the ways in which she understood the exit of families from the district as a matter of both race and class, she explained: "When the district gets to 70 percent or 80 percent" of students eligible for a free or reduced price lunch, "you begin to see white flight."

There were many factors contributing to fiscal austerity in both cities but, like Janice, Milltown and Fairview district leaders fixed on white flight—or sometimes "middle-class flight" or "bright flight"—as a central factor in fiscal decline in their districts, and the almost inevitable consequence of a growing enrollment of students of color. This view focused on white families' individualized classed or racist choices as the explanation of fiscal decline, and it highlighted race and class prejudices as being of central concern. A central office administrator in Fairview described "the challenge for an urban public education district like ours" as that of not becoming like other communities "where non-low-income families disregard the value of the education there, and pursue education in the suburbs." Whether advantaged families were described as "white-flight" or "non-low-income," district leaders feared that more of them would exit their districts as the populations of low-income students and students of color grew. As the leaders considered how to address racial inequity, this framing contraposed racial equity against fiscal stability, and narrowed the kind of solutions that seemed practical to ones that would not scare those advantaged families, but rather cater to them. The underlying assumption that they could not lose advantaged families fueled color-blind managerialism.

Former Fairview district administrator Robert Dow, a white man known for being a straight-talking professional, described an "underlying fear of white flight" when diversity increases in a school district. Robert had been deeply involved in school integration efforts earlier in his career. Those struggles continued to inform his perspective on schooling, and as a senior district administrator he had been committed to ideals and practices of inclusion. Robert explained district concerns about exit as a powerful influence on school districts, and emphasized white flight as an issue more of class than of race. "It really plays out as middle-class flight," he said. "African-Americans, Hispanics that are middle-class, don't stay around either." Whatever the race, there was a fear that middle-class parents would leave for the suburbs, which were very accessible to Fairview. "That fear underlies everything. 'Cause one of the conflicts you have policywise in a district like Fairview that's changing is: How do you balance that? If you make the decision to always come down on the side of social justice and you lose all this tax base," then there is no money to address social justice issues that need attention, Robert explained. He described school boards and administrators as engaged in a "constant balancing act." Once white flight becomes a concern in a school board's mind, he said, it's a major concern. "It's a real factor. It's not a perceived thing. It's real in the sense that if your tax base drops off—" Robert let the rest of the sentence hang in the air. "So you'll always have this underlying fear as you balance policy: Am I cutting off my nose to spite my face? Or am I better off compromising on this issue and retaining the ability to affect the lives of these kids? That's kind of the fundamental issue." Robert's explanation captured the contradictions, or the "constant balancing act," that Milltown and Fairview leaders felt as they toggled between concerns about exit by some of their most advantaged families and their need to secure resources to serve some of their most disadvantaged families. As later chapters of this book will illustrate, this tension (or the perception of it) resurfaced repeatedly, particularly in Fairview, thus contributing to school district leaders' embrace of color-blind managerialism as they tried to adopt new policies to address racial inequity without alienating white middle-class families.

With trepidation, school district leaders' thoughts turned to postwar white flight in US cities like New York, Chicago, and Milwaukee when considering the future of their own school districts. The idea of white flight seemed to resonate strongly because, in Fairview at least, some of them had witnessed something similar in other cities they had lived in. Yet those cities provided few inspiring alternatives.

District leaders largely viewed exit as a product of families' individualized racism or a desire to send their children to schools with more advantaged children. This is the common way of thinking about white flight. However, this view often overlooks structural factors—such as older, underinvested, and physically deteriorating city neighborhoods; rising costs of public services for an increasingly low-income population; and federal mortgage incentives to buy homes in white neighborhoods— that were responsible for post–World War II white movement to the suburbs (Boustan 2017b; Massey and Denton 1993; Seligman 2005). White families' intentions may or may not have been racist, but those families benefited from racialized policies and practices, and the consequences of their moves were decidedly inequitable. Despite evidence of the *confluence* of individual attitudes with racist policies, structures, and economic motivations (Boustan 2017a; Rothstein 2017), the idea of white flight as mainly a consequence of individualized white prejudice persists, as it did in Fairview and Milltown.

Community members also discussed Fairview and Milltown as being on a slippery slope toward becoming white-flight school systems. For example, a former school board member of color who was an outspoken advocate for Latinx children described Fairview as "moving in the direction of a Milwaukee or other cities like that." He predicted that white parents would move out, and that parents of color would follow when they had the financial means to move their children to private schools or suburban districts. Similarly, Jerry Wilson, an older white man who frequently advocated for fiscal conservatism at school board meetings, said of Fairview, "We kind of know what Milwaukee is like, and we're on that slippery slope, unfortunately." Fairview district leaders seemed unprepared for these changes. Furthermore, they appeared to have lost control of conditions which threatened to overtake them.

The total numbers of students transferring from each district may have been growing, but they were not large, as will be shown in greater detail in chapter 4; and total enrollments were steady or growing. Nevertheless, the imagery of urban decline, in its attention to resources, captured the fiscal pressures that Milltown and Fairview district administrators and school board members were feeling. Through the urban-decline narratives, district leaders and the general public fixed the explanation for tighter school budgets on "needy" low-income families of color (particularly African Americans) who were arriving to their cities and driving up educational expenses at a time when resources were becoming increasingly scarce, and also on white upper-middle-class families perceived as being motivated by racism or individual self-interest to flee the schools and take their money with them. This focus ignored structures that precede and interact with families' mobility and school choices, including substantial declines in state funding for public education, state-imposed spending limits for schools, and ultimately the broader dislocations taking place in each city and beyond. Rather than highlighting and addressing issues of power and exploitation, it directed district leaders' understanding to concerns of culture, racist attitudes, and families, and to the kinds of policies that would address "white flight." Thus, as they sought new policies and programs, they were concerned by what they perceived to be a need to either staunch families' exit from the school district or risk their districts' ability to maintain functioning schools and address racial inequities.

Urban decline elicited deep fears and concerns among Milltown and Fairview district leaders and among many citizens, shaping their understanding of the challenges their school districts faced and the kinds of policies they embraced. But these were not the only ways in which they could have imagined the changes in their cities.

The Strengths of Minoritized Communities: A Counterstory of Urban Space

For a few school district administrators in each city, particularly school district administrators of color, the urban was a place of support and community for people of color. Indeed, urban spaces have also been recognized as places of authentic community that foster a sense of belonging, strong community-based organizations, and social solidarity for people of color (Leonardo and Hunter 2007; Lipman 2011). A few Milltown and Fairview leaders told a counterstory about urban space. They identified leadership, organizational resources, and community support as important benefits of urban communities. Seen in this light, "urban" spaces—that is, spaces with large minoritized populations—were positive places on their own terms, and Fairview and Milltown were not "urban" enough.

Pakou Xiong, a warm thirty-something Hmong American woman, worked with Hmong students and other Asian Americans in Fairview schools, and described her work as being guided by students' needs. For Pakou, Fairview lacked the vibrancy and activism of larger Hmong communities in Milwaukee and in the Twin Cities of Minneapolis and St. Paul. She considered these larger cities to be sites of political activism and community-based resources for Hmong families. From Pakou's perspective, Fairview compared unfavorably to those cities. She viewed Hmong people in Fairview as not very vocal or engaged in activism. However, people in Milwaukee she told me, "have a more active group. It could be because they have more grassroots community-based organizations that focus on Hmong. They also have community agencies there to service the community as well." Pakou described these agencies as beyond mainstream organizations like Catholic Charities and Lutheran Social Services. She emphasized that Hmong-run and -staffed agencies like those in Milwaukee provide "jobs that are created that can employ staff that are bilingual and bicultural."

Pakou also described the larger cities, which were seen as sites of dysfunction or decline by many white middle-class people in Fairview and Milltown, as places with deep community-embedded resources by and for Hmong people. Her comments highlight these cities as sites of Hmong cultural belonging, something she did not feel existed in Fairview. Pakou and I met at what had been described to me as a kind of Hmong community meeting place; but as soon as I arrived, she emphasized that the building was a health clinic and not a community center. This underscored her point. The Hmong community infrastructure was just not as robust as it could have been. From Pakou's vantage point— one not common among Fairview's predominantly white school district leadership—Milwaukee was enviable and Fairview was lacking.

In Milltown, several district administrators who self-identified as white also articulated a view of large urban areas as a place of family, support, and cultural belonging for communities of color. Having struggled to recruit teachers of color to their districts, they found that Milltown lacked a community and social network for them. As one white executive administrator explained, there was not much of a support system for Black teachers in Milltown: "We are not a Fairview, and we are not a Milwaukee. We are a Milltown, which has been, primarily been, very white. So once they [Black teachers] get up here, really there is not much to hold them here . . . in terms of how they grew up and what they value for their community."

Race and class mattered. Milltown lacked a middle-class Black community that would sustain Black teachers in the school system. Emphasizing the ways in which larger cities typically had bigger populations of color and a Black middle class, Sharon Visser, the Milltown administrator reported, "We have gone all over the United States trying to hire, and they don't wanna come here. When they do come here, they have been staying for a couple of years and leaving, because there hasn't been a population in Milltown that has been similar to them." Even though the district had a growing population of African American students, the majority of families were living in poverty. "They're our free and reduced group," Sharon explained. In speaking with African American teachers who had come to Milltown for a few years and then left, Sharon had learned that they had not felt they had a community. "We've asked them, 'Why don't you stay?' And that's what they've been telling us. There isn't a group of people that they can socialize with, that they wanna go out with, that they wanna date."

Of course there were strengths and resources within the communities of color in both cities. The office where I sat talking with Pakou was one example of this in Fairview. And, while not necessarily attractive to middle-class Black educators, the growing low-income African American community in Milltown certainly had collective and individual resources that were valuable in addressing educational inequities. One African American mother I met there, Sedona Richards, worked tirelessly and without pay to help Black parents advocate productively for their children in the school district. Yet the voices of people of color who were embedded in communities of color, like Pakou and Sedona, were few and far between in these school districts, and were mainly peripheral to the executive leadership teams or school board meetings where many decisions were debated and made.

For school district leaders, the urban imaginary helped explain the difficulty of attracting African American teachers or Spanish-bilingual teachers who could potentially help address the needs of growing African American and Spanish-speaking Latinx student populations whom the school systems were not adequately educating. Still, this explanation highlighted the people who were *not* there, while largely overlooking resources that were in the communities and leaving unexamined the structures that precluded the development of a larger or strong Black middle class. For example, not only were the schools having difficulty attracting and retaining Black professionals; the Milltown police department had hired its first Black police officer only in the past year.

The view of urban space as offering authentic community, cultural recognition, and a place of strength and resourcefulness was a promising point from which to consider and envision urban schooling. It rightfully challenged assumptions of Fairview and Milltown as having been idyllic, warm, small-town communities for everyone, and it suggested the support, relationships, and decentering of whiteness necessary to better serve students of color and their families. However, as Milltown and Fairview district leaders developed their visions for the kinds of districts they wanted to become, and pursued policies like auditing and marketing, even Pakou and Sharon never seriously considered the development of strong, authentic, political communities of color to be a promising model for their own cities. To be sure, urban space imagined as a place of authentic community is not without its problems. It still focuses on individualized actors or specific groups, rather than on policies and structures that provide the meaning, context, and possibilities (or lack thereof) for their actions. Furthermore, it is susceptible to the dangers of essentializing racial-ethnic groups and their preferences and values (Leonardo and Hunter 2007). Nevertheless, a vision of urban spaces as positive, authentic spaces of community, power, and resources for people of color offered an alternative vision for the school districts. It could have catalyzed ways forward, such as stimulating existing or burgeoning minoritized-community leadership and political action, and it might have provided an alternative to the depoliticized inclusion and community implied in the color-blind managerialism the school districts did adopt. But this was a path not taken.

Imagining a "Diverse" Cosmopolitan Future

In contrast to the imagery of pathology and decline that portended a bleak future arising from the increasing numbers of low-income students of color and white or middle-class flight, central office administrators in both Fairfield and Milltown school districts simultaneously and paradoxically embraced cultural diversity as a welcome and hopeful change for their school districts, and as a solution to these perceived problems. The imagery of cosmopolitan urban space—modern and technologically advanced, and thus innovative, but also a contemporary crossroads for different cultures, lifestyles, and people from around the world (Leonardo and Hunter 2007)—offered Milltown and Fairview district leaders a vision of growing racial diversity as part of a promising new future.

District leaders sometimes expressed a belief that growing populations of students of color offered an exciting cultural addition to their cities, one that portended a positive, future-oriented turn for their districts. Fairview district administrator Katie Carlson captured this sentiment when she said of her colleagues: "I think as our population grows, people are more in tune and accepting that Fairview is changing and that this is our new reality: global, twenty-first [century], multicultural, multilingual world. And we'd better embrace it, because it is not changing." Milltown administrators such as Elaine Belvedere and Tara Randall enthusiastically expressed their appreciation for ethnic diversity and their enjoyment of working in an "urban" district. Both administrators sent their own children to racially diverse schools in the city, and described those experiences positively. As Elaine said of the demographic changes in Milltown: "It's been a challenge, but I think it's been a wonderful change for our district. I mean, I'm glad to be part of the urban district. I think I'd have a hard time going to a smaller, primarily middle-class Caucasian school district. I just don't think that's where the world's gonna be." Like others in both Milltown and Fairview, Elaine viewed the increasing racial diversity as part of what defined Milltown as an urban district. Consistent with an imagined cosmopolitan space, Elaine described racial diversity as where the global future lay.

Tara also talked about the positives of "diversity." She noted the "small businesses that have started up in the inner city because of the diversity," and the revival that had brought to those areas. She was enthusiastic about the interesting things that were coming with growing racial and ethnic diversity in Milltown. Tara had tried to raise her kids to appreciate people and things for their differences. "I think when a lot of people move in from big cities they're looking for that," she said. "They're looking for the sushi bars and the Indian restaurants and, you know, it just kind of makes Milltown a more interesting place to live."

Tara's description of increased "diversity" as bringing economic revitalization to the "inner city" and cultural experiences for her own children (through friends made at school and experiences eating at sushi or Indian restaurants) hewed very closely to urban cosmopolitan imagery.

Yet such a view was not without its problems. Undergirding this shimmering view of the positives of diversity was a material inequality highlighted by the dual cities concept. Unspoken and maybe unrecognized were the inequalities that allowed for such a scene to take place: the low-wage work characteristic of the restaurant industry, the likelihood that such work was performed by immigrants of color, and the relative privilege that allowed white residents like Tara and her family to be able to eat out. Furthermore, Japanese people (or, more likely, the Chinese or Malaysian immigrants running sushi restaurants) were not significant populations in Milltown, and neither were Indian or Indian American families. This hints at the fairly abstract way in which this view of urban space allows racial and ethnic diversity to be celebrated, commodified, and consumed, all while inequality is ignored.

While positive, the cosmopolitan urban imagination does not tell the full story any more than the other ways in which urban space is typically imagined. In the focus on diversity and celebrating culture, the imagery of cosmopolitan urban space can still comfortably coexist with and gloss over the social, economic, and political inequalities that make the imagined cosmopolitan urban space possible. The segregated neighborhoods, evictions from gentrification, and low-wage service workers, often people of color, are typically absent from this imagery. The imagery of cosmopolitan urban space is the dual city, but only from one side: it highlights culture, diversity, and prosperity over power and exploitation.

Nonetheless, in emphasizing the idea of racial diversity as a vibrant, valuable attribute, the imagery of cosmopolitan urban space provided district leaders with a positive, hopeful vision for the Milltown and Fairview schools. Rather than a pathologically broken city in decline, the image of urban space as cosmopolitan suggested opportunity: a wealthy, racially, and ethnically diverse city full of promise for the future. Such narratives and visions provided a template for color-blind managerial solutions. As I will describe in chapter 4, this imagery of cosmopolitan diversity influenced the ways in which school district leaders marketed their schools. But, while this representation of the city was attractive and useful for presenting a positive view of diversity for Milltown and Fairview leaders, it rendered economic inequality and other struc-

tural aspects of city life invisible, ultimately making it a problematic tool
as district leaders attempted to address the inequities and contradictions
in their work.

Contradictions and Ambivalence in Becoming Urban

The changing political, economic and demographic contexts of school
districts—seen through the lenses of an urban imaginary—suggested
many uncertainties, even fears, amid the other contradictions, dislocations, and unknowns of public education in Milltown and Fairview. District policy makers' conflicting ways of making sense of growing poverty
and racial-ethnic diversity, falling academic achievement, ongoing budgetary crises, tenuous public legitimacy, and families' exit out of their
districts, as well as the contradictions these entailed, was a key factor
in the development of their perspectives. From pathology, to decline, to
spaces of authentic community, to cosmopolitan future, the urban imagination primed a specific set of narratives for understanding changes in
Fairview and Milltown, and especially for understanding educational inequality and race in their school systems.

While providing a comprehensible narrative for the changes occurring in Milltown and Fairview schools, becoming urban explained poverty and school district circumstances as the result of mobility, where
the poor families of color were moving in and the wealthier, predominantly white families were leaving. The urban imaginary—particularly
imagery of pathology and decline, and the respective focus on poor people and white flight as problems—offered a channel for broader anxieties in these cities. This view tended to locate the issues in individuals—
particularly the families of color who were increasingly coming to
Fairview and Milltown, and the white families who were exiting the district. Absent in many of these descriptions was explicit recognition of
the underlying changes in the US economy and politics, and the racialized dynamics of these changes (described in chapter 1) that explained
the growing poverty, the racial and ethnic diversity, and the budget cuts
and achievement patterns that district leaders perceived.

The urban imaginary was also the established framework from which
Milltown and Fairview imagined their futures, as Janice Steiner did. The
narrative of urban decline, the metaphor of slippery slopes, and the discussion of white flight tell a story of declension and suggest a sense of

inevitability as to what the future would hold. The story captured district leaders' broader anxieties about the changes that were occurring (Beauregard 2002; Leonardo and Hunter 2007; Mollenkopf and Castells 1991). Indeed, from concerns about school safety, to sanctions under accountability policy, to the lack of success in educating for racial and ethnic diversity, teachers, administrators, and school board members harbor a general fear that public education in America is no longer politically viable (Ginsberg and Cooper 2008).

Yet, like Janice, Fairview and Milltown district administrators and school board members did not accept that their districts were or would inevitably be sites of urban decline or urban pathology. While they expressed a sense that this shifting identity marked a turning point, and expressed a fear of white flight and of their districts becoming like some in the "inner city," they also maintained that the future of their districts was still being written. As they struggled to define and chart futures for their more racially and ethnically diverse school systems, the urban imaginary also shaped how they considered which policies and programs were appropriate and necessary. Though the authentic community was largely dismissed, cosmopolitan imagery, in particular, was a source of hope and suggested a potential opportunity in growing racial diversity. It also suggested hopeful, albeit limited, paths for Milltown and Fairview school districts. The ways in which they tried to respond to demographic changes, white flight, and inequality are the subjects of the rest of this book.

Together with chapter 1, this chapter provides a deeper examination of discourses and racial meanings that shaped and were the foundation for policy making, leadership, and color-blind managerialism. The particular directions that Fairview and Milltown school district leaders took were not preordained. But, as these chapters have shown, that they furthered inequalities is also not surprising, given the structural and ideological terrains upon which they worked. The ways that these played out in particular color-blind managerial approaches in each city are the topics of chapters 3 and 4.

Managing Accountability by Monitoring Achievement Gaps

A t the start of every school year, the Milltown superintendent held a back-to-school meeting for teachers and staff across the school district. Traditionally, the meeting had been mostly a social event. "Four or five years ago," said Assistant Superintendent Elaine Belvedere, "it used to be, 'Rah-rah. You're back. And let's have a good social.'" That was in 2004 or 2005, but things had changed. Several Milltown district leaders recalled one particular back-to-school meeting as marking a turning point for the school district. NCLB had been signed into law in 2002. With pressure from the law's new focus on raising test scores across groups of students, district leaders began to examine standardized test data from Milltown's schools, specifically data disaggregated by categories of student socioeconomic status, English language proficiency, disability, and race. The results of this review set off a new sense of urgency among district administrators, something that was palpable during the back-to-school meeting.

With approximately 1,700 teachers, principals, custodians, paraprofessionals, central office administrators, and school board members in attendance, Milltown's superintendent presented data on the levels of proficiency for different groups of students and on the district's "achievement gap," the disparities in test scores between different racial groups. Other disparities, such as in graduation rates or the overrepresentation of certain groups identified for special education, were also sometimes referred to as "gaps." It was the first time the data had been shared publicly in this way. Harriet Fields, a longtime school board member, using language that echoed NCLB, remembered the moment when the data was presented.

> I can recall hearing a gasp in the audience when the data was put up there, because I think teachers realized that we weren't doing as good a job as we thought we were, and that we were indeed leaving some children behind. And those kinds of things are really powerful, because I think people come to school day after day thinking, "Well, you know, we're doing a good job."

But the standardized test score data collected to meet the provisions of NCLB seemed to suggest otherwise. As the superintendent explained at the meeting, there was an urgent problem.

The message that Elaine Belvedere remembered from that meeting was: "We need to pay attention to learning data." "It wasn't a popular message to give," she recalled. "But it needed to be said." As she explained further: "If you're a teacher in your own classroom not connected with the data and all that's going on with the changes in our district, you're not gonna know [about the achievement gap]." Teachers who were busy with their classroom concerns didn't have the districtwide data or the districtwide perspective, she explained, but what they saw was startling. "We noticed a huge trend," she recalled. "Our achievement gap is pathetic." To judge from the standardized test data, the school system did not seem to be doing well. Students of color were not being deemed proficient in mathematics and literacy, and there were major gaps between aggregate test scores for students of color and for white-identified students. While 83 percent of white fourth-graders in the district had been scored proficient or advanced on the state tests, fewer than 50 percent of Latinx and African American students had been (Wisconsin Department of Public Instruction 2013). As a result of this data, the superintendent and school board members agreed that it was time to confront the issues in their midst.

The district administrators' decision to introduce this data (and the serious inequities it seemed to reveal) at that back-to-school meeting was thought to be an important step toward addressing the issue. Milltown Assistant Superintendent Sharon Visser explained the contradiction she felt they faced: "We'd been hiding behind it before. Basically afraid to let the community know, because we've had an awful lot of white flight. But by not confronting it, we were not doing a service to our kids, either." Addressing the inequities that they saw in test score data seemed to imperil the support of the white middle-class families and residents whom Sharon called "the community." Nevertheless, the district leaders said that confronting "achievement gaps" was the right thing to do, and like school districts across the country, they had to respond to state and federal test-based accountability pressures. "I don't remember a debate about it," Elaine said. "I think we were all wanting to say, 'We can do better.'" They thought they were doing the right thing, but they worried about "community" and district teachers' support.

No longer a feel-good social event, this first districtwide staff meeting and teacher professional development training of the school year was, Elaine said, especially intended to communicate to district staff: "Glad you're back. Hope you rested up. Cause we gotta get goin'. There's a lot of work to do."

While data highlighted the problem of "achievement gaps," it also created other problems. These included the challenge to legitimacy that data could cause by suggesting that these school systems were not accomplishing their expected civic functions, and needed to spur teachers to cooperate to change what happened in their classrooms. Though the district leaders were not entirely sure how to address these concerns, the use of data as a key decision-making rationale seemed to provide them with a role and some ideas for moving their district forward.

* * *

Milltown district leaders were not alone in their concerns. In fact, as NCLB was kicking into gear, the numbers also troubled district leaders in Fairview. Although Fairview was a wealthier "liberal" city, the data there suggested an even more unequal system. In 2004 only about 60 percent of Black and 55 percent of Latinx fourth-graders there were deemed proficient or advanced on state tests, compared to 88 percent of white fourth-graders (Wisconsin Department of Public Instruction 2013). Taken at face value, as they usually were, these numbers were troublesome for a school system expected to ensure a quality education, student success, and educational opportunity for all.

Though high-stakes tests and the accountability systems in which they are embedded are frequently presented as measures that can disrupt inequality, substantial research now shows that they are rife with raced and classed inequities (Au 2009b, 2016; Berliner 2013). Standardized test scores reflect the racial biases of the tests, and are better predicted by a person's socioeconomic status or zip code than by any other factor (Berliner 2013; Valencia and Suzuki 2000). Often connoting precision and fact, and thus seen as beyond question, numbers involve numerous social judgments that reflect the people who have made them, and they are only one way of describing reality (D. A. Stone 2002). However, even as the failure of students of color and students living in poverty is designed into the tests, these tests are framed as "objective" and "neutral" measures of ability. The monitoring systems of which those tests are a part are also widely treated as fair, efficient, and rational, even as persistent achievement gaps between low-income children and wealthier students and between students of color and white students (Ladson-Billings 2006; National Research Council 2011) mean that low income children of color and the schools that serve them are consistently labeled as failures. This veneer of neutrality amid inequity, in the true fashion of abstract equality, leaves the suggestion that low average test scores for low-income children and children of color are simply a reflection of their individualized deficiencies, or perhaps those of their teachers (Leonardo 2007). These tests, and the monitoring systems of which they are a part, operate through color blindness to obscure the historical and contemporary contexts of structural racism, poverty, and inequitable political power within which data, merit, and "rational" decision-making processes are embedded (Au 2016; Ladson-Billings 2006). Reviewing the history of standardized testing and the research on the outcomes of high-stakes accountability, Wayne Au (2016) argues that high-stakes testing is a racial project of neoliberalism. Similar to the arguments I make here, Au argues that through notions of meritocracy, the neoliberal policy of high-stakes accountability is proposed to be a mechanism of equity when it is actually an instrument of racism.

Despite the ways in which high-stakes testing and accountability systems serve as mechanisms of inequality, Fairview and Milltown school district leaders and many residents in both cities used standardized test scores, and responded to pressures from high-stakes accountability systems in a number of consequential ways. In this chapter I examine Milltown and Fairview's homegrown data monitoring efforts to understand how and why district leaders came to adopt this approach, which can be understood as an example of color-blind managerialism. I argue that as student populations grew more racially diverse and unequal, the low test scores and heightened accountability pressures were a predictable and visible result of the social inequity and the inequitable standardized testing and accountability policies that produced them. This presented Milltown and Fairview district leaders with "achievement gaps" and related challenges to district legitimacy. Addressing these issues in a moment of fiscal austerity, however, presented them with considerable challenges as they tried to remedy inequities without blaming students, and without imperiling support from the predominantly white teachers and white middle-class residents upon whom they depended for school district support and operation.

I show that, after efforts to train teachers to be more sensitive to the complications of teaching across lines of race and culture drew resistance, the district leaders embraced data-monitoring strategies as an equity-oriented intervention that would remedy "achievement gaps." They viewed monitoring as a way to act more efficiently or effectively to change the schools at a moment when fiscal pressures and accountability pressures were strong. In Milltown they adopted data-monitoring systems focused on "the basics," and in Fairview they embraced strategic planning processes to achieve "excellence for all." Despite the differences in their data-monitoring approaches, both Fairview and Milltown turned to (and recreated) the color-blind managerialism of high-stakes testing. Data monitoring and the official antiracisms associated with it obscured the racism and inequality of standardized testing and high-stakes accountability policies, and legitimized data-wielding district leaders over teachers and families of color. In both cases district leaders' efforts undermined rather than advanced racial equity.

Heightened Testing and Accountability in a Raced and Classed Monitoring System

Even if district leaders had not always recognized "the achievement gap" in the years following the passage of NCLB, as they peered at the computer screens, test score reports, and school-level data, the numbers sparked what to them seemed undeniable evidence of racialized inequity and demographic change in their school districts. Harriet Fields, a Milltown school board leader and a white woman, described herself as very concerned about the racial disparity in achievement among Milltown students, something that she became aware of when first dealing with NCLB. Harriet had first gotten involved in the schools when she advocated for one of her own children. That experience reinforced her belief that the school board needed more parent representatives. "I just got interested in making sure that parents who couldn't always advocate for their children like I could, had someone who understood that," she explained. "And, you know, I really believe that what you want for your child, you should want for all children."

"When I first got on the board, there wasn't a real attention to the changing demographics" Harriet said. That had changed with NCLB, which had not existed when Harriet first started as a school trustee in the late 1990s. "We realized that student achievement had to be our focus. And then when we saw how children of color were not achieving at the same levels as their white peers, we realized that we needed to serve all children equally well, and we weren't doing that." Harriet had not recognized existing inequities or considered demographic change much at all before seeing this data. Now it was her number-one concern.

In Fairview, mid-level administrator Annalise Mayer made similar observations about the role that NCLB had played in spurring attention to racialized inequities and to the education of ELLs in that city. Annalise recalled that NCLB had triggered Fairview leaders' awareness of demographic changes and racialized disparities in achievement. "It made a previously invisible group of students visible," she explained. While she was not a fan of NCLB, she noted that it got the district's attention "in terms of race and awareness of the fact that not all students were white anymore . . . and just the rising level of poverty." Fairview school board member Jen Kemp recalled, during an interview one day in a Fairview coffee shop, that the growing numbers of students who were living in poverty and not well-prepared in their previous schools had hit the district "like a storm." According to Jen, a white woman in her forties, things had changed dramatically. "I mean we were doing okay, and then all of a sudden it was, 'Oh my gosh, 40 percent of our kids are failing algebra in ninth grade.'" The achievement data announced a problem with great force, and drew attention and concern to what school board members like herself might otherwise not have noticed.

While academic achievement data produced through NCLB were garnering a lot of attention, district leaders also confronted data indicating racialized disparities in the identification of students for special education and "gifted" education, gaps in graduation rates, and more, as offices in Wisconsin's Department of Public Instruction and the US Department of Education initiated programs—some of them voluntary—to inventory racial disparities in schools. In addition to state and federal data sources, Fairview had a number of homegrown reports—often pre-pared in response to demands or concerns by constituents of color—that surfaced additional points of concern. Most notably, the state had identified both districts for racial disproportionality of students identi-fied for special education, and they were required to develop a plan and show improvement. "Clearly, something's not right here," Mike Easton, a retired Fairview administrator, recalled thinking when he first exam-ined special education data that showed that almost one-third of African American students in Fairview were in special education. For Milltown and Fairview district leaders like Jen, Harriet, Annalise, and Mike, stan-dardized test data and analyses of disparities between groups seemed to transparently and self-evidently demonstrate grave problems of ineq-uity: "achievement gaps" or other unmet expectations for the most mar-ginalized children in the school district.

When I spoke with district leaders in 2009 and 2010, it was increas-ingly clear to them that existing practices were not leading to markedly improved test scores in Milltown and Fairview. The achievement data in Milltown, for example, was not much different from when district leaders had launched the transformative back-to-school meeting mentioned ear-lier. In 2009 the numbers of students of color, students living in poverty, and ELLs had increased, and yet only about 20 percent of Black, 30 per-cent of Native American and Latinx, fewer than 40 percent of Asian, and approximately 60 percent of white students were deemed proficient on state standardized tests of mathematics (Wisconsin Department of Pub-lic Instruction 2011). Fewer than 30 percent of ELLs and economically disadvantaged students scored as proficient. Despite the racism and in-equality of these tests, when district leaders looked at the data they did not question it. Furthermore, district leaders took the meaning of this data as self-evident: there was a problem with the schools.

While data illuminated "achievement gaps," and district leaders de-scribed it as spurring their recognition of inequity, it mostly arrived with accountability pressures linked to NCLB which put schools and dis-tricts on the hook for meeting targets for achievement that were mostly based on standardized test scores. If schools did not meet these targets across each of their student subgroups (determined by poverty, racial-ized groups, English proficiency, and identification for special educa-tion), they faced sanctions which increased over time. Repeated failure to make targets would result in schools being placed on lists of schools identified for improvement (SIFI) and assigned statuses, like "corrective action," that required different levels of sanction. Schools identified for "school improvement status" were required to develop and implement improvement plans, to offer all students in the school the option to transfer to another school and provide transportation to that school, and to make privately provided "supplemental educational services" available. By law, the "corrective action"-level schools had to make changes like replacing relevant school staff, instituting new curricular programs, or restructuring their internal organization. Schools in "restructuring" status were required to reopen as charter schools, replace their staff, contract with private management companies, or make other major changes. Districts could be determined as being "identified for improvement," as well.

Under this accountability system, schools with larger numbers of subgroups that traditionally did not do well on these tests—such as students of color, students living in poverty, ELLs, and students identified for special education—were more likely to be labeled as failing by the standards of test-based accountability systems. Besides known biases of standardized tests for students of color and low-income children, more diverse schools and districts like Milltown and Fairview are likely to be identified as failing under NCLB, due to being evaluated on a larger number of subgroups (Novak and Fuller 2003; Kane and Staiger 2002). For example, schools with a sizable number of children from immigrant families might have the same students counted within racial-ethnic, low-income, and ELL subgroups. Fairview leaders had discussed a similar situation in their district.

In a system where targets were raised every year until a goal of 100 percent proficiency for each subgroup was reached in 2014, it seemed likely that the numbers of SIFI schools would continue to rise, providing a sense that things were only going to get worse. Carl Bertram, a district administrator who closely tracked school district achievement measures in Milltown, explained accountability pressures that Milltown expected to confront by saying, "We are gonna be under the gun, dramatically." Seven years after NCLB was signed into law, and with the districts' embrace of data analysis and professional development efforts, student test scores had not budged enough to keep up with rising expectations. As table 3.1 shows, a small number of Milltown schools were identified as needing improvement under NCLB, and these schools were facing increasingly severe sanctions. Reflecting on the situation, Carl, who was very knowledgeable about the intricacies of the assessment sys-

TABLE 3.1. **Milltown schools identified for improvement (SIFI) status and sanctions, 2002–11**

	Level 1	Level 2	Level 3	Level 4	Level 5		
	School improvement, year 1	School improvement, year 2	Corrective action	Restructuring planning	Restructuring implementation	% SIFI	Number SIFI
	--------> Increasingly severe sanctions -------->						
2002–3		1				3%	1
2003–4							
2004–5							
2005–6							
2006–7	3					8%	3
2007–8	2	1				8%	3
2008–9	1	1	1			8%	3
2009–10	1	1	1			8%	3
2010–11	1			1		6%	2

Source: Wisconsin Department of Public Instruction, Office of Educational Accountability, schools identified for improvement (SIFI) in Wisconsin districts (data files: 2002–11). Data calculated by the author.

tem, was stressed but hopeful. He said that the pressure to increase test scores would "eventually turn out to be a good thing," but explained, "We have an unsustainable financial situation here, with nonproductive [test score] results." According to him, the district had only "maintained the status quo."

In Fairview, too, accountability pressures were on. School board member Jen Kemp explained the situation, saying that under NCLB, "if our kids don't achieve at a certain level, and we have [a] big achievement gap between the haves and have-nots, then we're punished." Jen noted, "We already have two schools that are on the SIFI list." As table 3.2 shows, a small but increasing number of schools in Fairview were being identified as failing. In 2007 and 2008, two Fairview schools had been identified at level 2, the second year of school improvement status. Another year of failing to meet AYP targets, and they would be in placed into "corrective action." The district could expect greater pressures and financial costs down the line. Sanctions involved a loss of federal Title I funding for "failing" schools, and at each level NCLB required districts to incur additional costs, including added costs for transportation of students to other schools, and payments to private entities for "supplemental educational services" (Burch 2009). These costs further contributed

TABLE 3.2. **Fairview schools identified for improvement (SIFI) status and sanctions, 2002–11**

	Level 1 School improvement, year 1	Level 2 School improvement, year 2	Level 3 Corrective action	Level 4 Restructuring planning	Level 5 Restructuring implementation	% SIFI	Number SIFI
	--------> Increasingly severe sanctions -------->						
2002–3		1				2%	1
2003–4	2					4%	2
2004–5	1	1				4%	2
2005–6			1			2%	1
2006–7			1			6%	3
2007–8	2	2				8%	4
2008–9	5	1	1			13%	7
2009–10	3	1	1	1		11%	6
2010–11	1	2	2		1	11%	6

Source: Wisconsin Department of Public Instruction, Office of Educational Accountability, schools identified for improvement (SIFI) in Wisconsin districts (data files, 2002–11). Data calculated by the author.

to district leaders' fiscal worries. In 2009 and 2010, after the end of data collection for this study, Fairview was named a "district identified for improvement," one of four Wisconsin school districts cited as repeatedly failing to make district targets.

It was not only that problems of inequity and accountability pressures required a response. Data also challenged the legitimacy of the Milltown and Fairview districts, calling into question district leaders' expertise and effectiveness at their jobs. Standardized test data, labels from accountability systems, "achievement gaps," and disparity analyses all suggested that students, schools, and districts were failing. The visibility of such data without an alternative analysis of its causes implies that there is a level playing field for the tests, and thus locates the achievement gap as a problem of the low-income students, ELLs, and students of color who are most disadvantaged by the tests and do not do well on them. It can also suggest that the teachers, schools, and districts are to blame.

Many district leaders admitted to me, in private, that they were not solving the "achievement gap" problem in their districts. Milltown administrator Carl Bertram explained, "[We] don't know how to address the achievement needs of minority students. And [we] have in the past performed very well, and now we have all these different kids and, you know, life is different; it's a struggle. So we're trying to figure out what to do with that." In Fairview, a former board member of color expressed a mixture of concern about achievement and uncertainty about how to improve it, saying, "We don't have the grasp or a good handle on the achievement gap between kids of color and nonkids of color. If you're white, if you're middle-class in Fairview, you will do well. If you don't, then you will struggle." Methods that had been successful in educating white middle-class students did not appear to be generating high levels of achievement for students of color, low-income students, or the growing numbers of ELLs. A Fairview assistant superintendent acknowledged, "We haven't found the right practice to change what they are learning."

As Carl noted, people outside the system were also not happy with achievement in the school district. Pointing to what he viewed as complacency among some district teachers and principals and the way standardized test data undermined district legitimacy, Carl explained: "People inside the system are happy with that, but more and more people outside the system aren't." It wasn't entirely clear whom Carl was referring to, but he was clearly identifying a sense from "outside" that the schools were not doing well. Milltown assistant superintendent Sharon Visser put a finer tip on the matter, as described in the introduction to this chapter: Milltown leaders feared that publicizing falling achievement scores would undermine white middle-class and upper-middle class support and contribute to families leaving the school district for other schools.

In Fairview there was a similar sense that white community members were questioning district legitimacy. Fairview had always touted the academic success of its students and schools on websites and in school board meetings. They highlighted the awards that teachers and students won, the colleges that district graduates attended, and the number of high school students recognized nationally for academic achievements. But, as Fairview school board member Jen Kemp explained, district leaders had been worried about the parents who had been "in the past very supportive of our schools," but were beginning to raise objections to the district's focus on low-income students and achievement gaps.

Blaming Teachers, Not Students

As they thought about the achievement gap problem and how to remedy it, district leaders resisted the idea that students were to blame for the racial disparities in standardized test score data. Instead, they focused on the roles of schools and teachers in these inequities. Describing teachers as using cultural deficit thinking (Valencia 1997) or a cultural racism frame (Bonilla-Silva 2003), district leaders explained racial inequality as the result of teachers' values, attitudes, and beliefs. Much as Castagno (2014) found in her study of a Utah school district, the district offices claimed that the onus of inequities lay in schools, an explanation that abrogated responsibility for equity within district offices and positioned them to take roles as good and responsible actors.

Milltown school board member Harriet Fields emphasized the importance of understanding *why* achievement gaps had come about, and not just blaming kids. Sitting at a dusty table before a four-hour Milltown school board meeting where the board would consider a report on a new reading program, progress reports from three high-poverty elementary schools, and a strategy for a projected $7 million budget deficit, Harriet explained: "Being able to be honest about race, being able to face the fact that your school isn't doing as well as it should and could for children—that's a big step." A quiet woman even in school board meetings, Harriet nonetheless declared with force and conviction: "Espouse platitudes all you want, but what's happening between that child and the classroom is really the most important. And teachers who in their mind say, 'Well, you know, I'm gonna focus on these kids because this child's parents don't wanna help them'—you just can't have that kind of attitude." However, Harriet worried "that there are a number of teachers who don't necessarily believe that all children can learn. And to the extent that they really believe that, I am concerned that they may not work as hard to understand children and give them what they need. You know, 'cause I really believe that if they didn't learn it, you didn't teach it." Harriet laughed, but she was serious: teachers needed to change.

Fairview and Milltown school district leaders understood teachers and their teaching as responsible for the "achievement gap" and accountability pressures in the district. District leaders, particularly in Milltown, identified the problem as a predominantly white teaching staff's cultural mismatch, biases, and lack of expertise in working with students of color, especially African American students. This wasn't entirely far-fetched. In 2010 approximately 97 percent of Milltown staff and almost 90 percent of Fairview staff were identified as white, far greater than the populations of white-identified students in these districts; and there were very few teachers of color in either school district.

Like Harriet, Milltown administrator John Resnik, a white man who had been a leader in Milltown's district equity efforts for years, regarded many teachers as having low expectations for students of color and therefore failing to recognize or take responsibility for those students' academic outcomes. This concern had prompted the earlier cultural competency training that John had helped to organize. John drew in his breath as he explained to me that it had taken years to get teachers to adopt the mindset of: "Me, I as a teacher, have to do something different here." There had been growth, John said, but there was still a long way to go. All staff, including teachers and principals, had to change their belief systems to believe "that all kids can learn," he said. Pacing around his office in a tweedy sport coat, he searched for a report on the results of a 2007 survey of the beliefs of Milltown teachers, administrators, and school board members. He flipped through the report and began reading me the results that showed that teachers were blaming students and their families for student achievement, rather than believing all children could learn and identifying their own ability as teachers to make a difference.

That evening, I browsed a copy of the report. As John promised, the survey results were quite interesting. Conducted to help the school board focus on improving student learning, the survey—which allowed respondents to choose more than one answer to each question—indicated that 60 percent of teachers who participated in the study believed that *parents* had the "biggest impact on student learning." The next most common response was *students* (59 percent) followed by *teachers* (51 percent). The same survey showed that the opposite was true of school and district administrators. Most administrators identified teachers (77 percent) as having the biggest impact on student learning, followed by students (42 percent) and parents (28 percent). Although research has repeatedly shown the strong influence of poverty and inequality on student achievement (Berliner 2013; Sirin 2005), very few respondents (fewer than 7 percent across groups) chose "family income" as having biggest impact on achievement. Notably, the survey implicitly framed achievement as the result of individual effort: there was no option on the survey to identify lack of health care, inequity of resources, or similar factors, although some Milltown teachers noted those in the write-in section of the survey.

Earlier in the decade, Milltown and Fairview leaders had tried to use professional development to identify and address teachers' presumed racial biases, cultural incompetence, and lack of urgency to address "achievement gaps." John Resnik remembered back to 2003, when district leaders had tried to convince teachers that "all kids can learn." One way they tried to do this was with a one-day cultural competency workshop that focused on getting teachers to recognize and understand cultural differences, see how existing school approaches might disadvantage students of color, and learn culturally competent practices. School board members and administrators also participated in the training.

Similarly, in Fairview in 2003 and for several years thereafter, district leaders introduced the Difficult Discussions program, which brought in a facilitator to lead staff in conversations and reflection on their own beliefs about race. They also focused on addressing teachers' presumed prejudices and differential treatments. Fairview district leaders hoped that staff members "would examine their own prejudices and thinking about their beliefs around race and how their beliefs might be affecting the students that they were teaching," Annalise Mayer explained. Former school board member Charlie Willis recalled that the Difficult Discussions program was "targeted to try and get at that issue of, even if the same two kids are approaching at you in terms of academic ability, how can you treat that kid a little different than this kid? And so try and get at, What are your experiences about race, where did you grow up, what do you think about these things? It was trying to be introspective." In bringing in this kind of professional development, Milltown and Fairview district leaders described their intention as being to establish open and explicit discussions with teachers about their racial biases or cultural competencies, and their role in racialized inequalities.

However, district leaders mostly viewed the previous race discussion program and cultural competence professional development training as a failure. District leaders in both Milltown and Fairview reported that these programs had provoked opposition from their predominantly white teachers, and concluded that the teachers were offended by the trainings, rejected the call to confront their biases, or simply were not going to change what they did. "It got crazy, we got people upset; it was 'one more thing that the district's making us do,'" John Resnik recalled. "You know, it was all that attitude around 'If you would only let me teach, I will be able to do this work.'" Former Fairview school board member Charlie Wills recalled that "a lot of folks felt threatened" by the Difficult Discussions work, "and felt that by that person's [the discussion facilitator's] presence, you were calling me a racist kind of thing." The effort garnered "response that was negative; some positive too," Charlie said. But whatever the balance, as Monica Collins recalled dryly, the overall conclusion among district leaders was, "That did not go over too well."

One of Fairview's few administrators of color, Monica Collins, agreed that Difficult Discussions had been contentious, but she didn't think of the program as a failure. She remembered it as making a strong and much-needed statement to teachers that "we focus on race and equity." She thought the professional development had been good. Milltown administrator Kevin Cole also described the Milltown training as being of "excellent" quality, and noted that the workshop was valuable because "it was showing our concern" with racial inequity. He and Monica recognized the negative response this professional development had caused, but thought it was important to be explicit about the need to address racial inequality; they were not particularly worried about teachers' discomfort in addressing cultural biases and race. Monica explained white teachers' responses as part of what happens when one tries to explicitly discuss race and raise racial consciousness. She said that "part of raising consciousness is, people feel uncomfortable because most European Americans, most of the majority, don't talk about [race]. . . . I mean, that's what the research shows." Reflecting back on Difficult Discussions, she acknowledged that there were some things they could have done better, but she also thought that the discomfort was "unavoidable for white people."

That teachers objected is not surprising, as Monica noted; district leaders' decisions to introduce race-conscious or cultural competency professional development implied teachers were racist and not teaching well or that they needed to change what they were doing in their classrooms. Due to the prevalence of color-blind ideology, people across the political spectrum from far right Tea Party adherents to liberal left activists claim to "transcend racism" (Burke 2017). Under such conditions, raising issues of race may be upsetting (DiAngelo 2011) or seem impolite to people who are "educated in whiteness" (Castagno 2014). Furthermore, though district leaders interpreted teachers' opposition to the professional development as racism, there may have been other reasons for teacher resistance, such as stress at being asked to do more under intense accountability regimes and with limited resources, or being held responsible for problems of poverty and generational structural racism.

Milltown and Fairview leaders grappled with what they viewed as teachers' denial and indifference to changing their practices to meet the needs of a more diverse student body. But in the end, district leaders did not feel they could ignore teachers' responses. In Milltown, the cultural competency training lasted only one day before district leaders concluded that it had failed. The Fairview program persisted for three or four years, but it was ended too, over concerns about teacher opposition. School district leaders' commitments to these explicit examinations of race or pedagogical change appeared fragile when confronted with school district teachers' opposition. Remnants of that work may have continued on in different corners of the school district, as Monica Collins mentioned, but the professional development programs were eventually abandoned as districtwide initiatives.

Given the ways in which high stakes testing and the "achievement gap" construct low test scores as evidence that *schools* and people in them (like teachers and students) are failing, and the prevalence of discourses which link teachers to school failure under NCLB (Goldstein 2011), it was not particularly surprising that district leaders framed teachers as the problem. Indeed, the idea that teachers' beliefs and school practices were the cause of achievement and other disparity data went largely unquestioned among Milltown and Fairview leaders. District leaders were not necessarily wrong in thinking that teachers held racial biases that would affect, even if unconsciously, race and class inequity in classrooms. Research on implicit bias has demonstrated pervasive, unconscious racism, including among teachers and those who endorse egalitarian beliefs (for a review see Staats, Capatosto, Wright, and Contractor 2015).

Still, this way of making sense of the situation framed racial inequality as an issue of teachers' individualized shortcomings and located the problem at individual staff member or school levels. District leaders substituted an individualized student deficit explanation for a teacher deficit explanation (Turner 2015). This focused them on remedying teachers' knowledge, skills, attitudes, and cooperation and made it difficult to also recognize—or address—the broader race and class inequalities located in the test data itself, the accountability system, the school system, and the society more broadly, the very factors that made achievement disparities so predictable.

Under pressure to eliminate "achievement gaps" and avoid labels and sanctions under NCLB, Fairview and Milltown district leaders still needed a way to address these problems without blaming students or delegitimizing the schools. But, taking note of the negative response to the professional development trainings from predominantly white staff, they didn't think they could continue those kinds of programs and risk resistance from the teachers whom district leaders depended upon and felt they needed to keep happy. They still felt the teachers needed to change, but with cultural competency and racism-focused professional development derailed, pressures to raise test scores unabated, and with no new resources forthcoming due to declining state funding and the possibility of additional cuts, the district leaders knew they needed another plan.

Navigating Contradictions of Accountability by Monitoring Schools

As Milltown and Fairview school district administrators and elected school board members continued to focus on changing schools and teachers to eliminate racialized disparities, they turned to rationalizing decision making through the examination and analysis of data. A key component of this approach was the addition of performance monitoring and evaluation mechanisms. Performance monitoring, as a broader phenomenon, draws inspiration from the field of financial accounting, but proliferated outside of finance in the 1980s (Shore and Wright 2000; Strathern 2000). Beyond just providing a source of information about how the schools were doing, or serving as a way to pinpoint problems, practices of auditing can serve as mechanisms of control over schools, teachers, and students. Particularly in education, quantified data is used as a means of efficiently altering performance, enacting accountability, or achieving other outcomes demanded by political and economic relations (Coburn and Turner 2011; Espeland and Sauder 2007; Shore and Wright 2000), most notably in NCLB. In adopting these practices, in effect, the Milltown and Fairview districts enacted their own data-based accountability systems in their schools.

The choice to take on this kind of approach mirrors a growing body of research which documents many instances of educational leaders who, confronted by normative or political opposition from staff or elite parents, drop equity-oriented challenges to the status quo and adopt color-blind, techno-rational approaches as a relatively uncontroversial alternative to their earlier efforts (Evans 2007; Holme, Diem, and Welton 2014; Trujillo 2013; Wells and Serna 1996; Welton et al. 2015). However, the Fairview and Milltown leaders did not see the expansion of data-monitoring as an abrogation of their obligations to equity. They viewed it as a next logical step in those efforts. They described such approaches as a primary way to address achievement gaps and improve schooling for students who differed from the white, middle-class, monolingual English-speaking students the schools had been adapted to serve. Performance monitoring was appealing to these district leaders because it seemed to be a rational way to prioritize goals and increase efficiency while still addressing equity goals, as well as accountability and budget pressures. In both districts, as we will see, they expressed a view of data use and performance monitoring as a solution to "achievement gaps." Thus, in an example of color-blind managerialism, district leaders presented a color-blind examination of data as an antiracist act.

There was much overlap in these districts' managerial approaches, which emphasized using standardized data such as test scores, performance, continual monitoring, and planning in processes that were assumed to be rational, value-neutral, objective, and fair. The differential experiences of students of color in schools, concerns about teacher racism, or lack of preparation to teach students living in poverty or coming from marginalized racial backgrounds were largely ignored in favor of rational planning and seemingly objective measures. Yet, there were differences between the two districts. Milltown and Fairview embraced different logics about how better or more rationally to address achievement data, thus contributing to different kinds of performance monitoring systems and different official antiracisms in the two districts.

Milltown: Monitoring Schools and Back-to-Basics

Sitting in an empty conference room in 2009, school board member Harriet Fields explained that a year earlier, as state and federal government pressures bore down on them and a new superintendent joined the school district, "our board work shifted to a greater use of data and a greater use of breaking that data down by ethnicity, by school, gender, [and] socioeconomic status, so that we could really understand where the board needed to focus its energy." Harriet felt this had allowed them to really prioritize their time and attention. Budget cuts, too, created a need to prioritize their work. Assistant Superintendent Elaine Belvedere added, "With dwindling resources, it becomes more of a challenge, But I think that we've gotten so good at using data to prioritize and make decisions."

Two priorities stood out. By looking at the data, Harriet said, "we have identified that there has to be really two basic focuses: one is read-ing, and the other is math." Milltown district leaders articulated a "back-to-basics" focus to solving "achievement gaps." They emphasized read-ing and mathematics. One thing they had cut was their membership in National Student Achievement Association, a national network focused on equitable education. The focus on reading and mathematics is not sur-prising, given that NCLB made standardized reading and mathematics data readily available, and that district leaders were accountable for im-proving it. Across the country, high-stakes testing policies have contrib-uted to narrowing schooling to tested subjects and concepts in schools under pressure (e.g., Au 2007; Diamond 2007; Diamond and Spillane 2004; McNeil 2000) and squeezing out bilingual education, multicultural education, culturally relevant pedagogies and other approaches explic-itly intended to connect to the knowledge and learning of low-income children of color (e.g., Au 2009; McNeil 2000; Menken and Solorza 2014; Wright and Choi 2006).

In addition to a focus on mathematics and reading, Milltown leaders had also set a goal for "student engagement," variously described by dif-ferent district staff and school board members as an effort to improve attendance and dropout rates, student behavior, or student interest in school. John Resnik explained: "That engagement piece is in response to the changing demographics." Earlier cultural competency trainings and strategic goals to improve cultural responsiveness as a way to ad-dress growing racial diversity had morphed into an ill-defined, color-blind student engagement commitment, a goal stripped of explicit con-frontation of race.

In 2008 and 2009, Milltown leaders rolled out new school-level and district-level data retreats, professional learning communities, and pro-fessional learning plans to improve instruction and address achievement gaps. When the cultural competency training did not seem to change teacher practice earlier in the decade, "We felt we needed to change the whole mindset around the training model, and so we did," John Resnik explained. Data retreats and performance monitoring seemed like a promising tool to change teachers' practices in schools but also to ad-dress equity issues (e.g., the achievement gap). John emphasized, "It re-ally gets back to, at a district level, to really make our schools account-able." Kevin Cole explained that they were using professional learning communities "to affect teachers' strategies and make teachers more ac-countable," and he emphasized the equity focus: "It is concerned with equity and that is heard from the top. It's not just about being aware, but also about changing how things are done." These data initiatives—school reports to the school board, data retreats, teachers' examination of data in teams, and so on—were all officially antiracist ways of addressing inequality. Every school was now required to conduct data retreats at the beginning of the year, and to continue examining data in an ongoing manner. Elaine Belvedere explained of principals, "They're always looking at data." School-level teams were expected to identify concerns about student learning, and teacher leaders would train other teachers in the "strategies that you use to prepare kids for the test."

Data monitoring in Milltown took many different forms. Teachers were required to develop professional development plans based on data from their school's data retreats, and to participate in teams that met for an hour on seven mornings spread across the school year. District administrator Mary Wilson had helped develop the professional development plan, and she said she personally reviewed all the logs to make sure that teachers and principals were following the process correctly. She noted that when teachers wrote about things unrelated to their professional learning, such as blaming kids or their families, "those kinds of discussions do not advance their professional learning and growth." Beginning in the 2009–10 school year, principals were required to prepare reports on their schools' progress across different standardized measures, and to present the results at televised school board meetings. About three principals presented their reports at each meeting.

At about 8 p.m. just a few days before Thanksgiving, Rich Hanes was about to give the last principal's report of the evening. Rich had only been a principal at the school for a few months. The chair of the committee introduced him as a "veteran of one trimester at Edgar Elementary School." The school board members seemed eager to hear how things were going. Rich said, "I am proud to be a new member of Edgar Elementary, but I am not alone. One challenge is, we have eighteen new staff members at Edgar." Edgar Elementary School was the highest-poverty school in the district. "One challenge is the high socioeconomic status disadvantage, and we too have a transient population." Harriet asked him about transiency. "We probably average two to three students a week," Rich told her. "At the end of the year there is probably 20 to 30 percent turnover." "Transience" and "transiency" were the terms people in the district used to talk about midyear student transfer in and out of schools. Left unsaid, and perhaps not always fully realized, was the underlying poverty and insecurity that contributes to housing in-stability and thus student mobility or transience. The first principal who had presented, Devon Elementary School principal Christina Peterson, had reported increasing transience, but she estimated that 70 percent of students were stable, and noted that homeless families were choosing to stay at Devon even after finding housing in other parts of the city. She explained that she had made a real effort to connect with families. Cary Schroeder, the second principal to present to the board, had reported she was seeing increased poverty in her school, adding, "This year we are a targeted assistance school, though, and Title I school. . . . So we are seeing extra assistance." As the Title I designation indicated, they were also seeing greater poverty. These three principals faced evidence of stu-dent poverty. But Rich, at least, said that his goal for the year was "get-ting better at using data. We need to have clear learning targets. That is my own passion. As we are starting to analyze our goals, we are getting better at that. The special education rolls are still high, but we learned that the majority aren't identified until they are behind grade level." He called these "the brutal facts," but he saw some small hope in the data. Rich noted that reading test scores for Latinx students and ELLs had been improving each year. "They already start in a hole, but each year we are closing a gap. Hopefully we'll see longitudinal and growth pat-terns emerging. . . . Now we need to figure out what we were doing and how to bring this to the rest of our populations." Rich explained that he had applied for a supplemental grant to do this work. Despite the lim-ited resources and the student poverty and mobility which undermined achievement, Rich looked the data and saw improvement.

The board stayed another hour. There was a student council report to hear, a budget strategy to address an expected $7 to $8 million deficit, a legislative update on proposed new powers for the state superintendent to take over failing schools, a report that Wisconsin school finance was ninth worst in the country, a proposal for a mayoral control bill in Mil-waukee, and a bill that would require school districts to report all spend-ing over twenty-five dollars. Not only was poverty and student mobility distressingly high, but schools faced additional concerns about achieve-ment and efforts from above to control the schools. When the meeting adjourned, the board members cheerfully wished each other a happy Thanksgiving, and headed out into the night.

Everyone left pleased with the reports they had heard and the pleas-ant interactions. The transient students were still transient; they were still going to be evaluated, labeled, and sanctioned by tests and a monitoring system that were stacked against them. For example, with such large numbers of student moving so regularly, test scores didn't seem likely to reflect any school improvements that might exist. However, no plans to explicitly address all of those problems had been raised. At the next month's meeting, a new set of school principals would report. At a casual glance it seemed that enormous effort was being made to address inequities in the district. That, after all, was what district leaders said the reports were for. But as much as anything else, data use seemed to play a crucial underlying function of demonstrating the efforts and legitimacy of district leaders, rather than providing a real solution to inequity.

District leaders saw data retreats and professional learning plans as ways to improve school-level practices and classroom teaching—that is, to make schools more rationalized, accountable, and efficient, and thereby raise literacy and mathematics achievement. They plotted a path to improving test scores with neither specific attention to teachers' cultural competency with children of color, nor attention to power and race. Nothing precluded district or school site leaders from race-conscious work or from pursuing more structural solutions, and many schools were trying to strengthen relationships with families or carrying out mitten drives and backpack giveaways as well. But without a framework or specific goals that addressed school or social determinants of inequality, nothing in this approach required transformative work either. Even if the teachers wanted to work on raising the students' reading or math scores, the professional learning and data retreats they embarked upon more directly responded to NCLB policy pressures and the priorities embedded within the testing system, rather than explicitly confronting race and class inequality. Data monitoring was also adopted in Fairview, but it looked different than in Milltown.

Fairview: Strategic Planning, Evaluation, and Excellence for All

In 2008, with changing demographics, achievement gaps, and ongoing budget cuts, but also with middle-class white parents who were dissatisfied with the school district's curricular offerings, Fairview's superintendent, Ben Sedlak, initiated a community-involved strategic planning process for the school district. A committee of more than sixty individuals—representing diverse racial and ethnic groups, business and local city officials, religious leaders, heads of community-based organizations, an advocate for fiscal conservatism and school constituencies (e.g., "gifted" education families, the teachers union), and district staff— participated in crafting a new strategic plan.

The Fairview school board adopted the strategic plan in 2009. At eighty-five pages in length plus appendixes, the new document was hefty. It detailed five strategic objectives (in the areas of students, curriculum, staff, resource capacity, and organization), eighteen action plans with as many as thirteen "action steps," and between one and seven performance measures for each action plan. In several ways it departed from Fairview's previous strategic plan, passed in 2000 and revised in 2008, which had been two pages long and listed three objectives.

Fairview school board member Jen Kemp explained the decision to write a new strategic plan as a proactive effort to take control of the situation. There had been a time, she said, when the district had plenty of resources and parents were happy; but Fairview was no longer in those "golden years" with the money, time, and luxury to see things ahead of time. "We're gonna start planning," Jen declared, "because things are never gonna go back to the way they were. It's only gonna be getting more and more different as we move to the future. So we're looking at a five-year plan to try to handle what is happening now and what is to come. Every decision that we make is based on that document."

District leaders emphasized having a strategic plan, aligning district efforts with it, and measuring progress on it as an equity effort. In other words, the rational examination and evaluation or monitoring of performance was viewed as an act of antiracism. "I think that strategic plan was one attempt to name that [racial disparities in achievement], and to begin to put some activities or action steps underneath it," a Fairview assistant superintendent explained.

The strategic plan goals had changed as well. One assistant superintendent noted, "This district had a superintendent for fourteen years and had three goals for fourteen years: improvement in attendance, completion of algebra by the end of ninth grade, and reading at grade level in third grade." In contrast to the back-to-basics vision recently taken up in Milltown, or the old strategic plan in Fairview, the new Fairview strategic plan included a broader, more expansive set of objectives. These included accelerated learning, civic education, cultural relevancy, recruitment and retention of staff, rigorous evaluation, and prioritization and allocation of resources.

In the strategic planning process, Fairview came to adopt an ethos of "excellence for all" (Schneider 2011; Turner and Spain 2016). The super-intendent described the plan as calling for a "dual focus on ensuring im-proved achievement for all kids while we eliminate our achievement gap. So it's a both/and concept." The inclusion of advocates representing dif-ferent points of view brought a greater focus on achievement of Afri-can Americans through a plan to infuse in the curriculum greater cul-tural relevancy for African American students, the demands of Latinx communities for more bilingual education, and attention to hiring staff of color, for example. But the emphasis on serving "all students" also signaled the inclusion of predominantly white middle-class families who were advocating for greater identification of and attention to "talented and gifted" children, and a shift away from the previous superintendent's focus on addressing achievement gaps among of low-income children of color (Turner and Spain 2016). In this sense, the strategic plan may have moved forward some aspects of equity in response to the concerns of communities of color who were involved in the planning. But the super-intendent's quote also suggests that "excellence for all" served as an of-ficial antiracism that drew on notions of abstract equality in community participation. The strategic plan was positioned as addressing the con-cerns and needs of communities of color and making the schools more equitable in that way, but equity was also framed as equally making space for the participation of predominantly white middle-class parents and shifting attention to their "non-low-achieving" or "gifted" students (read: white) by potentially reinstating structures of sorting that have been shown to reproduce social inequities (Oakes 1985; Tyson 2011).

The new Fairview strategic plan reflected what district leaders viewed as an important new approach: an elaborate system of monitoring school district work and evaluating it through measurable performance indica-tors. Evaluation was not the only focus area; the plan also set multiple performance measures for each of the focus areas, and prescribed regu-lar evaluation and reporting to the school board and community on the district administration's progress toward meeting them. For example, as a result of the strategic plan, the superintendent initiated a yearly "State of the District" speech to the public. In the ensuing year, the plan was discussed in terms of having made "a commitment to evaluate." School board members spent considerable time discussing an evaluation of a reading program and hearing reports on the mathematics program, the Talented and Gifted program, and more. Fairview leaders viewed this planning and evaluation—especially the strategic planning process—as ensuring their attention to narrowing achievement gaps, but in ways that also brought in greater participation and support from predominantly white middle-class constituents. In this way, not unlike the data monitoring in Milltown, the Fairview strategic planning and evaluation process continued to be limited by what was acceptable to white middle-class families.

In sum, Milltown and Fairview district leaders adopted data-monitoring practices as official antiracisms in a racial project of color-blind managerialism. They seemed to address inequity while also maintaining support of white teachers or families. The ways in which they did this and the discourses they drew on differed. Each school district had its own particular official antiracisms and data monitoring systems. In Milltown, a plethora of back-to-basics data retreats and reports focused on mathematics and reading replaced a wider list of priorities, including cultural relevancy, that had been prioritized under a previous superintendent. In Fairview, district leaders downplayed more explicit efforts to raise achievement for children of color and low-income children, with a detailed strategic plan and evaluation of performance measures, and a focus on reaching high levels of achievement for "all students" and developing "twenty-first-century skills." This is not to say that there were not important differences between the two forms of data monitoring. The Fairview strategic plan approach had some advantages over the data monitoring in Milltown in that it was more inclusive. By including communities of color in the strategic planning discussions, the Fairview approach came to lift up issues of cultural relevancy and bilingual education that reflected the concerns of some in the African American and Latinx communities. Reflecting these groups' concerns, and those of white-middle class families who advocated for talented and gifted programming for their children, the strategic plan moved beyond a pure focus on improving standardized test scores to include additional areas of achievement and curriculum. In its focus on school district–level policy and practice, it also included attention to institutional change over individual-level blame. In this way, the Fairview process represented a more inclusive and broader form of data monitoring than in Milltown. However, in both sites the agendas of these initiatives were largely set by district leaders, white middle classes and elites, and federal policy. And in both cases use of data devolved into a focus on monitoring.

To district leaders, data- and performance-monitoring initiatives seemed to respond to problems of inequity. But the districtwide uptake of these approaches focused on standardized test measures, which are not objective. They disadvantage kids of color and kids living in poverty, and thus further inequity (Au 2016; Berliner 2013). These approaches also fail to confront structural racism in schools or the deeper structures of race and class inequity that led to the predictable "failure" on the standardized tests by students living in poverty or students of color (Khalifa et al. 2016).

Data monitoring was not simply a way to wield control of schools, or a sign of district leaders' weak resolve on equity, though it may also have been both of those things. Data monitoring conveniently helped district leaders to navigate the multiple pressures they faced in relation to achievement data and inequality, and it was grounded in the broader political pressures to raise test scores without more funds or social supports for families living in poverty, and without greatly upsetting the white middle-class families upon whom the schools depended. As programs to build cultural competency and race consciousness among teachers stalled, color-blind data monitoring became a strategy for navigating contradictory pressures on the schools. In Milltown, a focus on using data to narrow achievement gaps contributed to limiting notions of academic achievement for students of color. In Fairview, the strategic planning process reflected a move from focusing on the achievement of students of color to an abstract equality approach to the setting of educational goals in schools. As part of a larger pattern of color-blind managerialism, we can see a process where in the name of race equity in education, confrontation of racism and to a lesser extent attention to student culture become anathema to the officially sanctioned policies and practices of schools (see also Au 2016). And, as is discussed next, data monitoring also legitimized district leaders by pushing the problem and blame to the school level and presenting district leaders as acting rationally.

Legitimizing Districts and District Leaders While Perpetuating Inequity

While data use seems unlikely to solve the problems of inequity because it does not actually address the sources of inequity, data monitoring did seem to help solve some problems of illegitimacy for district leaders. Around the country and across the globe, policy makers exalt data use and data-based decision making as the way to improve schooling. Such approaches have become a marker of legitimacy in the field of education, and the "good" or responsible educator is someone who makes decisions based on data (e.g. Booher-Jennings 2005). For district administrators and school board members, data use and monitoring offered a seemingly legitimate role in school improvement and educational equity. District administrators, in particular, have the potential to represent what Apple (2006) has called an "upwardly mobile professional and managerial new middle class" that supports data use and benefits from it professionally and personally, thus ensuring its own success through expertise in data techniques.

In setting up data-based approaches, examining and planning with data, and using data to manage teachers and hold schools to account, Milltown and Fairview district leaders were positioned as having a role and authority in addressing racial inequities and improving schools. Central office administrators and school board members played crucial roles in designing and directing data-use activities in Milltown and Fairview, including deciding on the kinds of measurement tools the districts would buy, designing and reviewing school-level data reports, and processing district and school data in various ways. But school board members did those things too. They often oversaw the monitoring systems, whether it was Milltown principals' school reports at board meetings or the review of the strategic plan and the oversight of administrators' progress on that plan in Fairview. As Elaine Belvedere explained at the beginning of this chapter, "If you're a teacher in your own classroom, not connected with the data and all that's going on with the changes in our district, you're not gonna know [about the achievement gap]." But she recalled that district administrators had noticed gaps in the achievement data. Data use initiatives at the school level, in particular, gave central office administrators a role in supervising the production and reporting of data in schools. For instance, Milltown district administrator John Resnik described the district's role as being to respond to data generated by schools. He acknowledged that district administrators had not yet formulated a response to the schools, but data use nonetheless positioned them as having one.

The focus on data as a means to improve schooling also suggested that decisions could be confidently made even though district leaders were largely without a particular answer on how to improve educational success for students of color, English learners, and children living in poverty. Two district leaders specifically described themselves as not knowing a lot about curriculum or pedagogy, but as being able to use the data to make decisions. In Milltown, district administrator Carl Bertram explained his selection of a literacy intervention for secondary school students: "I don't claim any great expertise in reading, but no one else stepped up, so I did it." He viewed the quantified data from the program, and thus the ability to quantitatively evaluate the program, as a sufficient basis on which to make educational decisions. In Fairview, school board member Stephen Harris also professed a lack of expertise in curriculum, yet during a school board meeting he asserted the ability to make a decision about a literacy program on the basis of an evaluation report:

> We have to act on what the evaluation tells us. . . . We couldn't see any statistical effect two years ago. It is small this year. Given the cost, it doesn't seem like much of a great thing. Why don't we do as [Elementary School 6] does? . . . They are getting great results. . . . I'm not a curriculum expert. Are we just doubling down on what we have? I would like to hear about what is going on at [Elementary School 6].

While the quantitative data of the reading program was not the only information the school board reviewed in its evaluation of the reading program, this board member argued that the board needed to make the decision indicated by the statistical analysis. While not denying the utility of practitioner knowledge of implementation and program alternatives, this board member was nonetheless prepared to make decisions to end a literacy intervention on the basis of the statistical analysis alone. Again, the data and the will to "act on what the evaluation tells us" were viewed as sufficient.

By ostensibly demonstrating antiracist concern and a motivation to act on the data on behalf of communities of color, these monitoring systems also positioned district leaders as ethical and good people working to address inequalities in their school systems. District leaders described standardized test data, achievement gap analyses, and other measures linked to state and federal accountability policies as commanding their concern, awakening them to their ethical obligations, and providing the springboard for their action. For instance, school board member Harriet Fields told me that Milltown had not succeeded in raising the achievement levels for students of color. As she explained it:

There's an element where we are failing, and those are the students that we have to focus in on. And they're silent, and they don't advocate for themselves, and neither do their parents. So I think that one of the roles of the board is to make sure we keep our eye on that.

While the desire of Harriet and other district leaders to take responsibility for school system failure was admirable, it was not without its problems.

First, though Harriet may not have been entirely aware of them, parents and community members of color were regularly advocating for students of color. One example was Sedona Richards, a Black mother and parent advocate who worked without pay to help other Black parents advocate for their children. She saw her work as trying to foster understanding by helping Black parents navigate an unfamiliar school system and helping white district educators understand the diversity of Black culture. Sedona explained that Milltown had high numbers of Black students placed into special education, but added, "There are some kids that don't need special ed, but they need some support to acclimate to this area." Sedona had found the district "open to new strategies" and "open to change," but also "very protective." She told me, "I was here maybe five years before the district really understood that I'm here to help." Indeed, over time she had been recognized as a member of parent advisory committee, and two Milltown district officials referred me to her as a person with an important role and perspective on the districts' response to demographic changes. The perception that students and families from low-income and minoritized groups do not or cannot advocate for themselves may reflect more about district leaders' perceptions of families of color than about the actual advocacy landscape in the Milltown school district.

Additionally, data use and monitoring created identities for Harriet and her colleagues as antiracist, data-using leaders. District leaders painted teachers as racist or unwilling to change, and themselves as holding teachers accountable for racial equity and as not blaming students. Although overt white supremacy has never gone away, in the context of the increasing color blindness of the post–Civil Rights era, being an antiracist is generally a positive identity or position (Burke 2017; Castagno 2014; Cole 2012). Thus, district leaders, as the people attempting to intervene in educational inequity, are elevated to a kind of exceptional white-person status, or as "white saviors." When white people claim to be saving people of color they often garner recognition and validation, which can advantage them without advancing justice and the security of people of color. In fact, a white savior orientation can infantilize or position people of color as being incapable of speaking for or saving themselves (Cole 2012). Harriet's sincerity in addressing achievement gaps, like that of her colleagues in Milltown and Fairview, seemed genuine; she spoke against racial inequity and worked to change existing school district practices. However, such concern also helped district leaders cultivate positions as people who, in the midst of evidence of racial inequity, were part of the solution, not part of the problem.

Under the increasingly intense scrutiny of public schools, and accountability pressure to raise test scores and eliminate racialized disparities in student outcomes—and also with uncertainty about their schools' ability to address these things—the use of data positioned Milltown and Fairview district administrators and school board members as rational and antiracist leaders who were addressing racial inequity through planning, use of data, and their commitment and hard work.

Conclusion: Leaving Racial Equity Behind

In a moment of delegitimizing developments, data and performance-monitoring approaches helped Milltown and Fairview district leaders navigate those challenges by seeming to offer a way to address achievement gaps while maintaining their own legitimacy and that of the schools, as well as the support of white families and teachers. Data monitoring was presented as a way to address the achievement gap, raise test scores, and ensure that students were getting the basics, or that district efforts would achieve excellence for all. That seeming ability to navigate school district contradictions, the promise of being able to make everyone happy, is the appeal of data monitoring systems. Although addressing "achievement gaps" through examination and monitoring of standardized test data was an officially antiracist action that legitimized the district and its leaders as trying to solve a problem of inequality, it in fact contributed to inequality. The district leaders noticed inequality or "achievement gaps" but failed to address racism, and focused instead on the color-blind and techno-rational improvement of students and schools (Au 2016; Trujillo 2014). In this way they contributed to the racial project of color-blind managerialism.

Data monitoring of various sorts is found in school systems across the United States (Marsh 2012), so it is important to recall that while there is some evidence that data-based decision-making processes raise achievement test scores (Carlson, Borman, and Robinson 2011), and while high-stakes accountability style systems have in some circumstances led to school improvement, there is generally a lack of evidence that these kinds of approaches meaningfully boost achievement or decrease achievement gaps; they may instead contribute to dropout rates and suppress graduation rates (e.g., Au 2007; Darling-Hammond 2010; National Research Council 2011). Moreover, research has repeatedly found that schools under high accountability pressures, which disproportionately serve low-income children and children of color, can do harm. They tend to limit students' access to untested subject matter, they focus on a narrow subset of students, and they use or adopt didactic pedagogies that limit students' access to opportunities for critical thinking and other skills (e.g., Au 2007; Booher-Jennings 2005; McNeil 2000). These effects are concentrated in schools with large numbers of low-income students of color. Thus, high-stakes use of testing seems to exacerbate social inequity while being presented as against what President George W. Bush famously called, in his support for high-stakes testing, "the soft bigotry of low expectations."

Despite these equity concerns, a critical function for the test-heavy data approach in Milltown and Fairview was to counter the delegitimization narrative that the data had suggested. As district leaders turned to data—which places students, teachers, and schools in the sights of "reform" efforts—they used it for rhetorical prodding and monitoring to rationalize and alter what teachers did in schools to address inequality. Their interpretations of the roots of achievement gap data and other data centered individual teachers' psychological conditions and biases and the schools' organizational apparatus as being responsible for racial inequities. A view of teachers as the problem and schools as a solution allowed them to stake out an antiracist position against racial bias, cultural incompetency, and unresponsiveness to a changing student population. However, this position also connected to color-blind and individualized discourses associated with NCLB and data-based decision making that implied that teachers and school leaders were almost solely responsible for improving outcomes (R. A. Goldstein 2011; Kumashiro 2012; Leonardo 2007), even if these outcomes were not solely of their making. Regardless of how it helped or hindered students, the official antiracism of data use and performance monitoring placed district leaders in a positive and moral light, obscured their investment in data-use approaches, and legitimated the continued white middle-class professional control and authority over schools, now as antiracist data users.

While district administrators and school board members were elevated through the use of data, communities of color and teachers had a limited official role and tenuous legitimacy in this system. Teachers and communities of color are likely to hold knowledge of learning, children, and equity that is necessary to improve schooling, and they are likely to articulate the importance of race, for example, to school decisions and policy (Khalifa et al. 2014). Valorizing the work of the individual district leaders who act in antiracist ways, or who try to do so, may also undermine the collective efforts of those they are trying to save, or others who are doing important work, and it may offer a simple story of heroism that obscures the complex raced and classed "patterns of power" that have contributed to the problems they seek to address in the first place (Burke 2017; Cole 2012).

Race inequality continues through use of these tests and control of schools. While data use contributed to the legitimation of district leaders' authority to make decisions about schools, the district leaders largely abandoned race-conscious or culturally relevant professional development in the face of teacher opposition to those efforts. Catering to white teachers and families took precedence over racial equity. Furthermore, despite recognizing the "transiency" of low-income student populations and often trying to provide for students' basic needs at school, leaders rarely probed or addressed the pernicious roles of structural racism, poverty, and government policy in producing opportunity gaps and educational inequities in student learning and achievement (Anyon 2005; Berliner 2013; Carter and Welner 2013), nor did they seek to address them. They focused their attention "down," toward fixing and controlling teachers or fixing organizational systems, instead of looking "up" to address broken school funding mechanisms or the collapse of social protections (beyond public education) as inequality rose. To be sure, district leaders felt they had little choice but to end the race-conscious professional development that they believed had provoked such consternation in the teachers. District leaders are limited in the ways they can change classroom practices, and they cannot easily fix broken school funding systems or restore social protections on their own. Recognizing these limitations underscores the insufficiency of individual-level explanations of racial inequality, and also of good intentions, in understanding and challenging racial inequity.

Data and a sense of declining achievement were not the only factors that district leaders understood as posing challenges to district legitimacy. As the populations of low-income, African American, Asian, and Latinx students grew in Milltown and Fairview and the specter of "white flight" grew sharper, district leaders also saw a need to make "diversity" acceptable.

CHAPTER FOUR

Managing Competition by Marketing Diversity

It was 11:15 a.m. in late November 2009. The early morning bustle of elementary school children arriving to school was over, and the school day had settled into its routine. Thirteen elementary school principals and four central office administrators were sitting around tables in the middle of a windowless meeting room at the Milltown district central offices. The principals had left their campuses for a special meeting to discuss a plan to market the school district.

Tara Randall started the meeting with her characteristic enthusiasm. "This is a major issue. We have had amazing turnover. I'm thrilled you are here. This is an important issue, and thank you for coming." A transplant from the East Coast, Tara had worked in corporate and nonprofit public relations before coming to Milltown, and she brought both informality and a bit of color to her work at the school district where she was the one-woman communications team. She passed around handouts on the number of Milltown students enrolling in other school districts. "It was a real shocker when I saw it," she said.

The data in the handouts showed the district having lost more than five hundred students through open enrollment in the previous school year. For each student who had transferred out of Milltown schools, roughly $6,500 would go with them. "If you look at the data, Boulder Hills [a large neighboring suburb] is making a killing off of us," said Tara. "Ron, I think you said that 20 percent of their enrollment comes from open enrollment." Ron, an elementary school principal in the group, confirmed he had said this.

The situation in Milltown stood in contrast to that of its wealthier neighbor. The principals looked at the open enrollment data for each of the elementary schools. Tara continued, "We don't have a lot of choicing in. We have choicing out. And our people are putting our schools down. We are shooting ourselves in the foot." She said it was not just teachers who were speaking poorly of district schools; it was clerical staff, and "those grocery store conversations."

More than that, there were new school rating websites. Tara handed out pages printed from one of them, SchoolDigger.org. On the handout was a screenshot of one of the website's school pages, which awarded schools stars and publicized standardized test scores, among other information. Tara explained to those gathered before her: "When people move to an area, these are the websites they are looking at. And they don't make us look good."

The principals looked at the printouts. On one, a district elementary school, Cleveland, was compared to other schools in its vicinity by proficiency on state standardized tests. Cleveland served large numbers of Latinx students, many of whom were English learners. Like many other low-income schools around it, it had earned no stars in the SchoolDigger rankings. Reagan Elementary, which was predominantly white and geographically closer to the suburbs, had one star. While a few district schools had received three, four, or five stars, like the suburban schools, most had not.

The room was hushed. Principals quietly flipped through the handouts. Tara continued: "The other thing is that the first thing that you see when you open up a school page is the ethnic count." Below the comparisons of proficiency were a bar chart and tables that compared elementary school enrollments, disaggregated by race. "So, parents that see color—" Tara's voice trailed off, leaving unsaid the kind of negative effect that district leaders assumed that racial enrollment data—which showed that the Milltown schools were, on the whole, significantly more racially diverse than neighboring suburban schools—would have on prospective home buyers and district parents.

Tara noted that the district schools were being compared to wealthier suburban districts. "If that is their comparison, we look bad," she said. Indeed, the suburban middle schools had almost all been given four stars, and had more than 85 percent of their students rated as proficient. These schools, the website showed, were also overwhelmingly white.

After a few minutes, the principals started questioning how the websites determined their school ratings. They pointed to discrepancies between the number of stars assigned to a school and its students' levels of proficiency on state tests, or between what they knew of the schools and how those schools were rated on the website. Tara explained that the district's marketing efforts were needed because things like achievement data, enrollment numbers, or even stars on a school-ranking website were fueling inaccurate and negative perceptions of district schools, particularly among white parents. This was the reason why Tara had called the meeting. "That's what we are fighting: the perceptions versus what we know is really going on," she said.

Marketing was not entirely new in Milltown, but with the increase in students "choosing out" of district schools, Tara and other district leaders had decided to develop a marketing plan and ramp up their marketing efforts. They were ready to counter the achievement data, the changing enrollments, the supermarket conversations, and the news reports they believed were provoking negative perceptions of their schools and causing what they presumed were white middle-class families to leave the district. Not just reputation but money was at stake.

* * *

Fairview and Milltown had long employed staff responsible for public relations. However, as competition increased in those districts, and as media reports amplified the increasing populations of students of color and the poverty, low test scores, and occasional violence in and around the schools, the district leaders grew increasingly concerned, and renewed their focus on marketing in 2009. In Milltown they launched discussions and coordination with school principals, as in the meeting recounted at the beginning of this chapter. They also recruited an intern to work on marketing, and allocated funds toward advertising on billboards, television, and school flyers. In Fairview, where the project was eventually canceled due to budget crisis, the district began initial steps in a marketing campaign that included a forty-thousand-dollar allocation to hire public relations consultants, a community meeting to solicit feedback on marketing and district communications, and a request for marketing proposals from private consultants.

This chapter examines plans to market the racial diversity of the Milltown and Fairview school systems as another example of color-blind managerialism. The findings demonstrate that Milltown and Fairview leaders turned to marketing, and particularly to marketing diversity, as a

way to navigate contradictions of school district competition in the raced
and classed marketplace of schools. In particular, as their school populations became more racially diverse and unequal, they faced an obligation to make their schools more inclusive. They also felt a need to maintain the support and enrollment of the predominantly white middle- and
upper-middle-class constituents who were advantaged and empowered
in the inequitable system. District leaders believed that these families were developing negative perceptions of the schools as they came
to serve more students of color and students living in poverty, and they
explained the exit of families to suburban districts in terms of "white
flight" and individualized racism.

   I show that to remain competitive in a raced and classed "market"
that favored families with resources, and to thus retain support of district schools, Milltown and Fairview district leaders tried to market district "diversity," commodifying images of communities of color to con-
vey egalitarian cultural values, and using limited notions of diversity
and multiculturalism to attract or retain predominantly white middle-
class and upper-middle-class families. Their efforts sometimes benefited
communities of color, but diversity and cultural inclusion became official antiracisms that projected a veneer of equity while justifying and
obscuring the inequities of school district competition and simultaneously creating new inequities. Through their marketing decisions, district leaders largely positioned white middle-class families as "valued
customers," targeted their priorities in district policy, and sought to offer them educational advantages. The two districts' particular strategies
for selling diversity differed in ways that were more or less problematic.
However, this story underscores the similarities in their efforts and how
they contributed to reinforcing existing status inequities and whiteness
in the two school districts.

Heightened Competition in a Raced and Classed Marketplace

Both of these traditional public school districts were experiencing increased competitive pressures at the end of the decade. There were only
a small number of private or parochial schools in each district, and no
voucher schools. Instead, the main competition in both Milltown and
Fairview came from neighboring suburban districts, through Wisconsin's "open enrollment" law. The law, described in greater detail in chap-

ter 1, allows students to enroll in a school district even if they do not live within that district's boundaries (Bezruki et al. 2002). Because funding is often tied to enrollments and policies typically are designed to shift funds from the sending schools, these market mechanisms can also exacerbate declining fiscal resources in schools or districts that lose students to competitors as Milltown and Fairview did. This has created incentives for schools to vie with each other to attract students.

Locally, the competitive environment in which Milltown and Fairview schools operated greatly intensified after the cap on open enrollment transfers was lifted in the 2006–7 school year. In Milltown, district respondents described the breakdown of an area superintendent's "gentlemen's agreement" to refrain from advertising during the open enrollment period. Some neighboring districts began actively recruiting students to their schools. In particular, a new superintendent at Boulder Hills School District just outside Milltown had begun openly advertising and courting parents as a remedy to his large suburban district's falling enrollment.

Milltown school board member Rose Polaski explained the impact this was having on her school district. "We're losing a lot of kids to different districts" through the interdistrict transfer program, she said. This was especially the case along the Boulder Hills-Milltown border, where she lived. Rose noted that a different wealthy suburb had released a new promotional video and was holding meetings to recruit students to their district. "We're kinda behind the eight ball," she said. "We don't really sell our district the way we should."

At the end of the decade, competition was ramping up in Fairview too. In 2008, after the cap on transfers was lifted in 2006–7, the school district's leaders ended a policy of denying transfers out of the district if such transfers would upset the racial balance at a student's home school. This decision was prompted by the 2007 Supreme Court ruling *Parents Involved in Community Schools vs. Seattle School District No. 1* (2007), stating that school systems could not use race as a primary or "tiebreaker" criterion for assigning students to schools. School systems across the country have also interpreted the ruling with caution, and have opted to alter their student assignment systems to rely less upon a student's individual racial identification (McDermott, Frankenberg, and Diem 2011). In Fairview this change eliminated a main barrier to transfers by white children out of the Fairview district. At the same time, virtual schools, operated by private companies contracting with school districts in other parts of the state, were beginning to advertise in the Fairview area. Through a combination of open enrollment and virtual schooling, the district also faced competition from schools outside their immediate geographic vicinity.

Both Fairview and Milltown faced increasing competitive pressures and net loss of students through the open enrollment policy. Total student enrollment numbers changed little between 2004 and 2009 (just 1.4 percent in Milltown and 1.5 percent in Fairview), but transfers out of the districts were growing rapidly (see table 4.1). By the 2009–10 school year, just a few years after the cap on transfers had been phased out and the Supreme Court had issued the *Parents Involved* decision, the net numbers of students transferring out of the district rose to more than four hundred students in Fairview and more than six hundred in Milltown (Kava 2011). These were still small percentages of the overall Milltown and Fairview school enrollments, but the numbers were steadily increasing.[1] In Milltown there was a 141 percent growth in net transfers out of the district in the 2004–9 period. In Fairview there were fewer net transfers out of the district, but the number of transfers grew much more rapidly (711 percent) in that same time period. Looking at the open enrollment data and the rapid growth in transfers to wealthier and whiter neighboring suburban schools, Milltown and Fairview district leaders were worried.

District leaders perceived exit as a modern-day form of "white flight," where predominantly white middle-class or upper-middle class families were mainly using the open enrollment system to leave the city schools

TABLE 4.1. **Five-year total school district enrollment trends, 2004–9**

Year	Milltown total student enrollment	Milltown transfers (in less out)	Fairview total student enrollment	Fairview transfers (in less out)
2004–5	20,292	–179	24,863	–35
2005–6	20,314	–184	24,452	–47
2006–7	20,070	–207	24,755	–82
2007–8	19,534	–307	24,670	–156
2008–9	20,573	–432	24,496	–284
5 year % change, 2004–9	1.4%	141%	–1.5%	711%
2009–10	20,332	–639	24,628	–435

Sources: Wisconsin Information System for Education, data dashboard. Open enrollment pupil transfers and aid adjustments data, Wisconsin Department of Public Instruction (https://dpi.wi.gov/open-enrollment/data/aid-adjustments).

as Fairview and Milltown student populations became more racially diverse and more likely to be struggling in poverty. Fairview and Milltown district leaders believed that the families exiting their districts were predominantly white.[2] As was explained in earlier chapters, the white-identified families had much higher per capita income and much lower levels of unemployment and poverty in each city. The open enrollment law was designed, intentionally or not, to be most convenient and manageable for the wealthier, predominantly white families who lived in neighborhoods bordering the suburbs and could transport their children between districts.[3] Furthermore, Milltown district leaders described white parents voicing their belief that schools with students of color were not good schools, and threatening to exit the district—most notably during debates about redrawing high school boundaries just a few years earlier. In Fairview, district leaders knew that district policy had previously denied many white families permission to transfer out of the school district, on the basis that it would negatively affect racial balance in the sending schools. It is not clear whether the district leaders knew that most families exiting their districts were white and middle-class or upper-middle-class; but they believed that to be the case.

By 2009, the Milltown and Fairview school districts had between 30 and 35 percent more students of color than their respective neighboring suburban districts. The city districts also served far more students living in poverty, and more students labeled "limited English-proficient." Milltown and Fairview were growing more diverse than their suburbs—which were also diversifying, but to a far more limited extent.[4]

Fairview's superintendent, Ben Sedlak, explained that awareness of demographic change "can create in some people a kind of flight instinct where they think, 'This community has changed so much, maybe I need to think about not being a part of this community anymore.' You can create a worry in terms of, 'What is this all going to end up costing us because of this problem?'" This interpretation, that there was "white flight," resonated with common discourse about the histories of Milwaukee, Chicago, and other metropolitan areas as Black populations grew in those cities in the postwar era, as noted in chapter 2. This idea was also reinforced by the race and wealth distinctions between Milltown and Fairview cities and their suburbs. Both cities are surrounded by suburban districts that, on average, have considerably higher percentages of white students and considerably smaller percentages of students identified as economically disadvantaged and "limited English-proficient" (see table 4.2).

TABLE 4.2. **Milltown and Fairview student demographics compared to those of all school districts in their counties, 2009-10**

	Milltown district	Milltown suburban districts	Fairview district	Fairview suburban districts
White	60%	91%	50%	85%
American Indian	5%	3%	1%	0%
Asian	8%	2%	10%	3%
Black	7%	2%	24%	6%
Hispanic	20%	2%	15%	5%
Economically disadvantaged	52%	17%	47%	18%
Limited English-proficient	20%	2%	17%	5%

Source: Wisconsin Information System for Education, data dashboard.
Note: Figures have been altered slightly to maintain anonymity of the two city districts. Due to rounding, the student racial-ethnic percentages do not always add up to 100. Since there is no standard definition of a suburb, suburban districts are defined here as all school districts in the county in which each city is located. This data was combined to calculate suburban student populations for each district. Group labels are those used in the Wisconsin Information System for Education.

Milltown and Fairview district leaders were alarmed, particularly because they feared the net transfers would further undermine their already tenuous finances. A Milltown executive-level administrator explained:

> We have major financial problems, and with that number of students leaving, that's like six million dollars leaving the district, that we have to pay out to other districts. Last week, actually, we just had our first [marketing] meeting of principals who are now becoming concerned.

The figure this administrator used was not reflected in the data I collected from state records, but it does capture the feeling among school district leaders that this was a large financial loss for the school district, and that a response was needed. Fairview's administrator Todd Stone explained: "How the district is perceived, that's a very important topic that actually is part of our new strategic plan. The board is very concerned about families who open-enroll out of the district. . . . It's still well less than 1 percent of our potential students, but that's a concern because as students leave, that affects your funding and other factors [important] to perception in the community."

Open enrollment has resulted in economic costs to each district. Districts that lose students must pay receiving districts a per-pupil amount equal to a statewide average school district per pupil cost. The per-pupil transfer amount was $6,498 in 2009–10 (Kava 2011). Net open enrollments out of Milltown, the more working-class school district in this study, cost the district approximately $3.5 million in payments to other school districts in the 2009–10 school year alone (Wisconsin Department of Public Instruction 2010). Fairview, the wealthier district, paid approximately $2.6 million to other districts in that same period (Wisconsin Department of Public Instruction 2010). Furthermore, districts that, like Milltown and Fairview, had a net transfer-out of students were prohibited from increasing their property tax revenue limit to compensate for lost funds (Kava 2011). Table 4.3 illustrates the total budget figures over time, and the growing percentage of the budget change related to transfers.

The loss of funds from net open enrollment out of these districts compounded the fiscal pressures and looming budget cuts that Fairview and Milltown faced. While the money lost through open enrollment was only a small percentage of their budgets, it still amounted to millions of dollars, and the loss appeared to be growing at a time when both districts were contemplating cutting millions of dollars from their 2009–10 budgets.

In Milltown, district assistant superintendent Sharon Visser explained that the agreement not to advertise "just hurt Milltown. And our superintendent now says we've got to really let people know what we are doing, and advertise it." In her meeting with the elementary school principals, Tara Randall also argued that that advertising had become essen-

TABLE 4.3. **Net transfer aid as percentage of total budgets, 2004–10**

Year	Milltown total budget	Milltown net aid transfers	Percentage of budget	Fairview total budget	Fairview net aid transfers	Percentage of budget
2004–5	$219,565,654	($824,157)	0.4%	$319,472,601	($257,458)	0.1%
2005–6	$229,649,805	($901,496)	0.4%	$322,965,384	($329,812)	0.1%
2006–7	$232,641,964	($1,164,202)	0.5%	$330,759,620	($500,880)	0.2%
2007–8	$240,496,583	($1,691,469)	0.7%	$337,133,823	($908,757)	0.3%
2008–9	$239,019,136	($2,360,726)	1.0%	$347,186,032	($1,611,893)	0.5%
2009–10	$253,618,317	($3,499,343)	1.4%	$353,464,261	($2,567,504)	0.7%

Source: Wisconsin School Financial Services Data Warehouse, audited comparative total district cost data (costs of instruction, pupil and staff support, operation and administration, transportation, facility, food, and community services). Wisconsin open enrollment pupil transfers and aid adjustments.

Notes: I have indicated here the net transfer aid, the amount taken in from students open-enrolling into the district minus the amount paid out for students transferring to other districts. The net aid figures capture the total loss related to open enrollment; however, it is important to note that, in their discussions of open enrollment, district leaders often used figures representing only the cost of the transfers out of the districts.

tial, saying, "It's gotten to the point where the gloves are off, and now we're gonna try to counter that [recruitment by other districts]. . . . I'm looking at the numbers and the money [*laughs*]. . . . We can't avoid it anymore." She estimated that, with design work done pro bono, the cost of advertising would be less than that of losing one student to a neighboring school district.

Marketing, then, was a response to the increasing numbers of students who were transferring out of the school districts and the financial pressures district leaders felt, in part, as a result of net transfers out of the districts. And, as noted above, from the start it was primarily aimed at fending off the exit of white middle-class families, whom district leaders believed to be primary users of the transfer program. The concern expressed in both districts for retaining these families reveals a raced and classed school marketplace that itself reflected race and class inequities in these cities. Open enrollment policy facilitated the movement of families who lived in the mostly wealthy neighborhoods bordering the suburbs and had the economic means to transport their children to other school districts. Such families were most likely white, given the racialized wealth disparities in Fairview and Milltown, which reflected deep racial disparities in socioeconomic status and political participation in Wisconsin and across the United States (Elbow 2014; Taylor 2014), and which scholars argue are largely the result of historical patterns of racial exclusion of African American families, in particular, from property ownership, voting, and wealth generation (Conley 2010; Katznelson 2006; Massey and Denton 1993; Oliver and Shapiro 2005). But the state open enrollment law and increased competition with suburban schools were not the only concerns that spurred district leaders' interest in expanding their marketing.

Negative Perceptions in an Unequal Marketplace

A connected reason why Milltown and Fairview district leaders saw a need for marketing plans was that they believed their school districts were increasingly being perceived in negative, inaccurate, and racist ways by predominantly white residents, or in what district leaders—in a demonstration of how white residents were centered and normalized—often referred to as "the community." The district leaders worried that achievement data, news coverage of homeless students and safety issues, and

even their own staff conveyed a negative image of the schools. Enrollment data demonstrating racial composition and poverty levels at schools
also seemed to play into negative perceptions by "community" members. Mirroring the assumptions about white flight and urban decline described in chapter 2, many district leaders believed that transfer from district schools was based, at least in part, in white upper- and middle-class
parents' negative perceptions that schools with students of color, particularly Black students, were unsafe or not academically rigorous.

Karen Warner, a white Milltown school board member, was one of
these concerned district leaders. Karen worried about the undeserv-
edly negative reputation that she saw the schools were getting as a result
of demographic change. She felt that at Marshall High School her children had gotten a good education—indeed, one of them was headed to
an Ivy League university—and that they had made friends and played
on athletic teams with students from all different racial and ethnic backgrounds. But members of "the community" increasingly viewed the high
school as a bad one. She said:

> Marshall is a white-minority school. It's got a high poverty rate. . . . [People]
> look at those numbers and then jump to all sorts of conclusions because of
> that, and one of the biggest conclusions they jump to is that the academics is
> subpar; "It's a terrible environment to send your kids to school in." . . . I don't
> think our community is ready to embrace the diversity that's kind of pour-
> ing in. . . .

Karen had been an active parent at Marshall for many years, but as other
parents and community members looked at the demographic data on enrollments, they appeared to discount the school, assuming that it was
bad without knowing much more. Karen declared that this was one of
her biggest concerns with the rapidly changing demographics. For that
reason, she was involved in the Board Speakers' Bureau and planned
to join the Marshall public relations committee to "help the community
understand what a great place this is to send your kids to high school."
Karen was not optimistic, though. "People don't even want to hear it,"
she said.

Indeed, the view that "white-minority" schools are subpar is a deeply
engrained trope in US education (Leonardo and Hunter 2007; Posey-
Maddox and 2014; Roda and Wells 2013). Despite Fairview's more racially

inclusive climate, leaders in that district, like their Milltown counterparts, were concerned that test data, student demographics, and local news fueled negative perceptions and uninformed assumptions about their schools. Much like Milltown school board member Karen Warner, Stephen Harris was a white Fairview school board member whose children had attended Washington High, a racially diverse and economically unequal high school in the district. Stephen believed that his own children had benefited from their experience there when they had gone on to college and in the rest of their lives, and he suspected that other students had benefited as well. But, he explained:

> People who aren't familiar with our schools . . . who kind of just draw their conclusions from reading the newspaper, think, number one, that the schools aren't safe, and two, that they are not academically challenging enough. Both of those . . . are sort of [long pause], well, in different ways, are kind of manifestations of kind of a fear of "the other," you know, just thinking that "these kids aren't like my kid. They look different."

Though he was reluctant to do so directly, Stephen, in evoking "the other," was expressing suspicion that racism lurked behind white parents' and white community members' perceptions of the Fairview schools. It appeared to him and to other Fairview leaders that white parents had largely viewed the schools as good when the student populations were predominantly white, but were beginning to view them as low-quality as the student populations became more racially diverse.

The negative perceptions of district schools were not just about children of color, but also about deepening poverty. At the elementary principals' meeting in Milltown, one principal told her colleagues, "Whenever our newspapers are at my school, it's always about poverty, and I sometimes think I am the queen of poverty." Her comment was met with laughter, as she was frequently featured in the news, but she was serious. She noted that the newspapers rarely featured positive stories about other Milltown schools, either: "Wright [High School] had *Les Mis[érables]* and it was fabulous, and there was nothing in the newspaper about that."

In both Milltown and Fairview, local elites also voiced concerns about the ways the school systems were perceived. Business leaders in both cities, for example, expressed the importance of a positive view in "the community." In an interview, a prominent white business and

political leader whose children had attended Milltown's Marshall High
School said:

> Marshall High School was regarded as a underperforming school simply be-
> cause of its diversity. It had nothing to do with its faculty, its program offer-
> ings, its athletic teams. That offended me significantly, and it was an extraor-
> dinary insult to a very good school, and because of that impression, was doing
> it far more harm than anything else that was going on in the school. . . . I
> learned, unfortunately, that it wasn't just a general community view of those
> schools; there was also a great deal of subtle bigotry attached to it, and even
> some blatant racism.

Business groups viewed the public schools as important to the economic
vitality of the city, and sponsored training projects and workforce development linked to local manufacturing. In Fairview, in particular, a
group of community leaders involved in strategic planning had emphasized the need to focus on "positive branding of the FSD [Fairview
School District] school experience and publicize the benefits of graduat-
ing from FSD." They had identified a goal and a communications plan as
being district priorities.

As white residents without children made up a large percentage of
the local voters, their perceptions were essential for passing school bond
measures and raising local property taxes. White Milltown school board
member Susan Leahy explained:

> You try to get the media to focus on, you know—that's fine, focus on the nega-
> tive stuff, but also focus on the positive stuff. . . . Only 17 to 20 percent of the
> households in Milltown that register to vote—those that have a big impact on
> some of what we do—have school-age kids, so there are a [lot of] people who
> are pretty removed from the schools. . . .

The school district was significantly more racially diverse than the city
population at large, reflecting age-stratified racial differences resulting
from immigration and migration to Milltown by younger people and
families of color, a declining white birth rate, and the aging of white
baby boomers. District leaders hoped that having more positive media
coverage, getting information to these older, white residents who were
presumed to vote, and engaging those residents in school issues would
address the negative perceptions of district schools. In this sense, these

older white residents were sometimes the target of marketing, particularly in more fiscally challenged, politically conservative, and less inclusive Milltown. As Tara Randall had explained to the elementary school principals at the marketing meeting, however, the district leaders mainly described their marketing efforts as being focused on the school competition they faced, and the need to curb enrollment of families out of district schools.

District leaders emphasized the "negative perceptions" being circulated about their school districts. However, families' reasons for transferring were not clear-cut. In the marketing meeting described at the start of this chapter, Milltown principals recalled families turned off by Milltown's larger class sizes, old school buildings, and safety concerns at one middle school, and families attracted by new school facilities, winning sports teams, and the opportunity to place their children in gifted and talented classes in neighboring suburbs. In a district survey that returned only twenty-five responses, Milltown parents' explanations for exit likewise included access to gifted and talented classes. In Fairview, a district survey of exiting parents listed school environment (e.g., safety, drugs, "liberal philosophy," and "my children are becoming the minority") and proximity to home as major reasons for families' decisions to transfer out of the district. These responses suggest that "white flight" was not necessarily about racism, or not *only* about racism, but also influenced by a desire to take advantage of suburban schools' resources and by exiting families' wealth or residency in a border neighborhood.

To district leaders, marketing seemed like a necessary and logical next step, given the negative perceptions that were circulating in the media and in their communities more broadly. As Rose Polaski said, "If you aren't gonna market your school district, all the kids are gonna go, 'cause all they're gonna hear is the negativity in the paper." Tara, too, explained, "The perception is out there, you know, and if we can't sell ourselves, who's going to sell us? You know, that's kind of the stance that we have to take."

Navigating Contradictions by "Marketing That Diversity" and Making It Pay

As other traditional urban public school systems have done, Milltown and Fairview began to think more seriously about marketing in order to remake a negative image after low test scores, news coverage, and the presence of students of color in some schools left the school districts with a poor reputation among some of their residents (see Cucchiara, Gold, and Simon 2011). The marketing plans were intended to cast a more positive view of the school districts to city residents in general, but were primarily focused on attracting and retaining families who were transferring to neighboring districts through the state open enrollment system, and thus contributing to a loss of state enrollment funding in each school district. Milltown and Fairview district leaders positioned these families as "valued customers" (Cucchiara 2008; see also Ladson-Billings and Tate 1997), a particular segment of the population of school-aged families whom they sought to attract.

District leaders hoped to appeal to upper- and middle-class white families through a variety of measures and messages. "Diversity" was a main message, as I show below, but it was not the only one. The leaders continued previous practices of highlighting student and school achievements, and also attempted to appeal to status-anxious parents seeking upward mobility for their students. In Milltown, for example, they wanted to highlight student success and the choices available within a large school system, such as the option of early and late start school days. Tara posted student and teacher awards and celebrations on social media, the school district website, and district flyers. "We put a lot of good stuff out there that doesn't make the media . . . a lot of student achievements, and schools that might not be considered high-achieving schools, although their kids *are* there [doing well]." While Milltown sports teams frequently struggled, particularly in comparison to those in neighboring suburban districts, the Milltown superintendent promoted opportunities for sportsmanship and playing time when talking to parents who were eager to have their children participate on more competitive teams in the suburbs. In Fairview, a district where academic success was held in particularly high regard, an administrator involved in district communications identified the "progressive education" and students' academic success as two of the key messages the district wanted to communicate to the community. The district website and promotional materials prominently featured the numbers of students who had been recognized nationally for academic merit. Marketing was an opportunity to put out positive messages and accomplishments that were not otherwise visible, and to reassure parents of the value of the education in their districts.

In each district, however, "diversity" was a key message related to these other ones. Worried that parents did not like the "racial mix" and of Milltown and Fairview schools, and were pulling students out because of misperceptions or racist assumptions about their quality, policy makers felt compelled to address the "diversity," or presence of children of color, in their districts. In Fairview the superintendent described the district's communication efforts by saying:

> What we're really truly trying to do, while we are open and clear about our challenges, is to also be promoting diversity as a value-added concept . . . to the point where it may serve as a clear positive separator for us and the other districts in [the] county.

They hoped that they could reverse negative perceptions of the districts, and that the racial identities of students of color would give them a competitive advantage over less racially diverse neighboring school districts. Milltown school board member Rose Polaski said simply, "We need to market that diversity, and we need to market all the great things that we have in Milltown."

Despite ongoing inequities and a resurgence of explicit white supremacist ideology, in the post–civil rights era purported "color blindness" has ushered in greater, but limited, acceptance of racial diversity and cultural inclusion in US society (Berrey 2005; Leong 2013; Omi and Winant 2015). Integrated schools and multicultural education are often upheld as ideals in the field of education. However, the facts that schools are increasingly racially and socioeconomically segregated (Orfield, Kucsera, and Siegel-Hawley 2012) and that legislators attempt to ban ethnic studies classes (e.g., McGinnis and Palos 2011) make evident that the color-blind era is more an ideal than a reality. Indeed, Milltown and Fairview district leaders did not believe that reframing the presence of students of color into something that upper and middle-class white families would view as attractive would be a simple task. They doubted that simply articulating a value of racial diversity would be sufficient for addressing the racialized concerns and the potential for district transfer of "valued customers." Milltown assistant superintendent Sharon Visser explained about marketing: "We tried the little cliché, you know, about 'Diversity is good.' But we've got to go beyond just the little cliché. We've got to show what with diversity is good. And how it enhances student learning."

District leaders sought to sell or frame diversity as offering value to upper- and middle-class white families. Their marketing approaches highlighted the instrumental benefit for upper- and middle-class white children of attending school with children of color. They emphasized the need to appeal to white middle-class parents' self-interest in concrete ways. Fairview school board member Stephen Harris said, "No one's going to sacrifice their own kid to their notions of political correctness." He felt that it was a challenge "to promote an image of the community or our schools as providing—seeing diversity as a strength." He explained:

> It can seem like this "Kumbaya" stuff. But there's more to it than that, and you've got to be able to extract the value from that in a way you can convey in a reasonably persuasive way, and that's something we have been working on. . . .

In fact, Stephen had recently conducted a Facebook survey asking recent graduates of Washington High, where his children had graduated, about the benefits of having attended a racially diverse school. He felt that this kind of information helped to show how students benefited from diversity. As his reference to "Kumbaya" and the language of being "able to extract value" suggests, he did not believe it would be sufficient to argue that the presence of children of color was of inherent worth. Indeed, it seemed that white community members already denied that worth, and Steven hoped they could change that view.

Discourses of global cosmopolitanism were fundamental to the efforts of district administrators and school board members to market racial diversity to upper- and middle-class, white families. Global cosmopolitanism—a discourse that ties racial and cultural diversity to global change—presumes an increasingly interconnected, cosmopolitan world that requires learning about and from difference, and developing specific skills and knowledge. In part, the appeal of global cosmopolitanism is that it conveys innovation and futurity (Leonardo and Hunter 2007). And, as noted in chapter 2, this is a relatively positive image of racial diversity in urban spaces. This vision is appealing to a subset of white middle-class and elite parents in the United States and in other countries, who seek out "multicultural" schools—especially those that are not too diverse, have immigrant populations, and offer opportunities for multilingualism (Dorner 2015; Palmer 2010; Reay et al. 2007).

Parents in both cities had expressed some enthusiasm for educational programs that teach "foreign" languages and "world" cultures. Over the last half of the decade, parents in the more liberal Fairview had signed up on waiting lists for the dual-language immersion program where children learned English and Spanish together. They wrote letters in the local newspapers about the benefits of language education, and made phone calls to district leaders indicating their strong interest in such a program. In Milltown, where the county had enacted an English-only law, many school board members nevertheless touted the dual-language immersion program for the popularity it had among a subset of monolingual English-speaking parents. They noted the enthusiasm for a local private high school that had just started an International Baccalaureate (IB) program, an option that promises an internationally recognized high school diploma. Thus there was some evidence that such a vision of diversity, especially one linked to the discourse of global cosmopolitanism, was appealing to some parents in both Milltown and Fairview, as it has been more broadly (Dorner 2015; Flores 2016; Palmer 2010; Reay et al. 2007). Not surprisingly, the appeal of global cosmopolitanism appeared to be stronger in relatively racially inclusive, and more liberal Fairview than in the more conservative Milltown.

Fairview

Fairview district leaders sought to use their association with students of color, what Leong (2013) has called their *racial capital*, to market their districts as having value for white children. Racial capital is akin to social capital in that it emphasizes the value (e.g., status or reputation) that can be gained from *being associated with* people of color, even if the quality or depth of the relations are minimal.

Fairview leaders—operating in a political context that expressed inclusivity of immigrants and people of color—framed interracial friendships, social skills, and cultural knowledge as potential benefits of racial diversity for all district students. The Fairview superintendent explained the message he sought to promote:

> . . . It's that type of message . . . that our children are inheriting from us a world of vast differences. And, by the fact that this district has become more

diverse, there's great opportunity for our kids to learn how to deal with differences as they're young and as they're traveling through their educational experience with us, in part through their curriculum, but in part solely through the educational environment called school, you know—that they get to be with different kids.

As suggested by the language of "inheriting from us a world of vast differences," this administrator presented the district, through the racial diversity of its students, as preparing children for a global future. This framing melded an emphasis on skills for individual students' social mobility in a globalizing economy (getting ahead) with more democratic skills for living with others in multicultural society (getting along; Reay et al. 2007). Implied in the superintendent's language is the importance of actual interracial interactions or relationships, and of being in school with students of color. This thicker view of diversity acknowledged a gain that students of color might enjoy from this arrangement, and it assumed physical mixing between racialized groups. Nonetheless, leaders expressing these views appeared to position racial diversity—whether as getting along or as getting ahead—as something to gain "value from" (Reay et al. 2007). In using students' racial identities to bolster their school systems' reputations and competitiveness, district leaders attempted "deriving social or economic value from the racial identit[ies]" (Leong 2013, p. 2153) of students of color in their districts.

Furthermore, as competition tightened at the end of the decade, district leaders in both cities also enthusiastically developed or expanded, and promoted, instructional programs that developed bilingualism in Spanish and English (dual-language immersion programming in Fairview) and an internationally recognized education (IB in Milltown; Turner 2015). Through its diploma program, language requirements, and courses that count for college credit, the IB program offered credentials and cultural capital for success in competitive college admissions and a globalizing economy. The dual-language immersion bilingual programs, in which speakers of Spanish and English were taught both languages and learn academic content in both languages while sharing the same classroom, promised what Reay and colleagues (2007) have called *multicultural capital*, the cultural capital associated with the cultures of people of color. Reay and colleagues found that middle-class white parents in England enrolled their children in multiracial schools in part so that their children would acquire the multicultural capital for success in a competitive global economy. Milltown and Fairview district leaders sought to evoke this kind of language and imagery to frame their districts as preparing children for the future.

Milltown

Milltown's advertising campaign included several television advertisements. In one, uptempo music plays as school scenes flash across the screen. A young white boy holds colorful letters and shows them to his teacher as the words "ABCs today" flash across the screen, followed by "CEO tomorrow." An older Asian boy with glasses is painting alongside two classmates, a white redheaded girl and a white girl with brown braids, and the words read, "Art in the classroom today," followed by "Art in the museum tomorrow." Finally, a Latina teenager is shown staring at a spinning model of the human heart. Across the screen, the words read, "Anatomy class today," and then, "Heart surgery tomorrow." Interspersed is footage, played at a rapid speed, of racially diverse–looking students walking through school hallways. The video ends with the tag line, "What's your tomorrow?" Another advertisement, aired several months later, begins with the same music and diverse students moving through the hallways, and says, "6 foreign languages"; the Latinx girl looking at the model heart is followed by two white teenagers wearing chefs' whites and chopping food; on both pictures are superimposed the words "34 ways to earn college credit." Next to a white teenage girl playing the violin is displayed the words "2011 International Baccalaureate." The advertisement ends with several blond-haired white children walking down a hallway and the words, "More for your tomorrow." Both videos show a cautiously diverse array of students superimposed by language conjuring up an innovative, high-culture successful future consistent with the imagery of global cosmopolitanism. The ad emphasizes that the skills, knowledge, and cultural capital one can gain in diverse Milltown schools will set students on their way to aspirational high-status futures.

In Milltown, the value of diversity was heavily wrapped in appeals to academic rigor, and strongly invested in serving and developing the cultural capital of white families. In meetings, flyers, and advertisements promoting the IB program, Milltown district leaders' messages emphasized it was a rigorous course of study with an internationally-recognized diploma, responding to perceived cultural capital needs of upper- and middle-class white students. A flyer prepared for the opening of the program, for example, highlighted it as "the single, truly international, pre-university high school program," and noted the emphasis on "high academic standards" in subject areas. The flyer also advertised cost-saving advantages of the program, noting that it was "Tuition-Free IB!" (a contrast to the IB program recently offered by a local private school in the area) and that it provided "greater opportunities for transfer credits to post-secondary schools for students achieving sufficiently high results," noting the potential for "$15,000–$60,000" savings" in college costs. In contrast to the Fairview strategy of trying to appeal to an association with people of color, the effort to sell multicultural capital in both districts drew on a thinner notion of the value and conditions of diversity.

Rose Polaski had been involved in the marketing efforts discussed earlier in this chapter. Like most of her colleagues on the school board, she was a lifelong Milltown resident whose children had graduated from the city's schools. But, unlike many of her colleagues, she had a background in business. Regarding her decision to run for a school board seat, she explained: "There are many people with education backgrounds or volunteer backgrounds, and I just felt that the board needed a little bit more: people with more financial, business, marketing backgrounds . . . plus my love of the community, and my faith in the Milltown public school system." Rose's entrepreneurial instincts and belief in the schools pushed her to look for things in the district that could be framed to appeal to "consumers," and then to infuse those messages with enthusiasm.

"A lot of people don't know we have this great culinary program at Wright High School," she told me one day in mid-January 2010, just as the district was developing radio, TV, and print advertisements to highlight the unique programs not available in other school districts. "I always bring that up. And I try to make it more personal. . . . Coming from business, you know, it's an automatic sell for me. . . . I'll say, 'Do you know that you can take Chinese if you come to Milltown Public Schools?' No, they don't know that. 'Do you know you can take *Italian* if you come to Milltown Public Schools?' Nobody else has that. . . ."

Rose's ideas, whether or not they would impress their target "customers" in the "market," were heavily influenced by the discourse of global cosmopolitanism and its promise of multicultural capital and job skills. Perhaps unsurprisingly in a city like Milltown, which had passed antiimmigrant ordinances, and where there were no people of color in school district leadership positions, marketing of multicultural capital was abstracted from actual interaction with children of color. Chinese and Italian were not primary languages spoken by children in the district—an indication that these classes were likely intended not for communities of color, like the Latinx and Hmong English learners who were contributing to making Milltown school district more diverse, but for the monolingual English, middle- and upper-middle-class parents desiring high-status language skills for their children.

Though the Milltown and Fairview educational "markets" both adopted diversity and global cosmopolitanism as a vision for their districts, they understood and communicated its value differently, and to different effects. In Milltown, a city less welcoming of immigrants and people of color, district leaders promoted diversity as an abstract idea loosely associated with actual students of color in their school systems and more heavily focused on skills, credentials, and other (multi)cultural capital for a global future for white families. Notions of diversity captured by language courses like Italian and Chinese and IB, appealing though they may have been to the middle-class white families, were not explicitly designed to ensure any interracial or intercultural interaction between students, or to provide educational advantages for students of color. Furthermore, these programs were removed from the actual backgrounds of children of color in Milltown and did little to promote their status. Indeed, the notion that languages other than English are "foreign" reinforces status hierarchies about who is, or can be, a "real" American.

In part, this speaks to the nature of the diversity discourse itself, which can obscure the work and underlying dynamics of racial hierarchy and power (Castagno 2014; Leonardo and Hunter 2007; Moses and Chang 2006). Multiple education scholars have found that racial diversity is one of the first priorities that is discarded when it seems to clash with other goals held by upper and middle-class whites, such as raising test scores, creating neighborhood schools, or reducing costs (Diem et al. 2014; Frankenberg et al. 2015; Lee 2005; Lewis and Diamond 2015). In other words, those families' investment in maintaining their advantages typically overshadows a commitment to diversity. Indeed, diversity and global multiculturalism were largely imagined in the service of selling Fairview and Milltown schools to the predominantly white middle- and upper-middle class families who were believed to be exiting the school district—a point that reinforces the privileged status of these families as being able to make demands. That communities of color would gain from this multicultural capital, or have their concerns addressed, was not assured.

Interest Convergence and the Possibility
of Advantages for Students of Color

Julio Garcia, a respected professional and political actor in Fairview, was known as an advocate for Latinx communities. He was often seen rushing into political and community meetings after work, still wearing a sport coat and tie or a sweater vest. For years, Julio and a Fairview Latinx advocacy group he worked with had been involved—along with many other parents, nonprofit leaders, and local advocates—in getting area school districts to pay attention to the needs of the growing Latinx student population in Fairview County. Julio recalled that the dual-language immersion bilingual programs that had become part of the efforts to attract white, middle-class families in the Fairview school district had begun with the considerable hard work and political navigating of teachers, parents, and community members as ways to improve educational services for Spanish-speaking Latinx youth. Teachers and Latinx community members had worked for three years to get the first Fairview dual-language immersion bilingual program, a charter school, approved by the school district in 2004. Five years later, with increased demand for foreign language instruction from monolingual English-speaking white families and a desire to halt "white flight," the school board decision to expand dual-language immersion bilingual programs to additional Fairview schools came more easily.

"Unfortunately, and you have heard it before," Julio said, reflecting on the school district's decision, his voice turned to mock horror, "Oh, my gosh. Fifty percent of the students in the school district are students of color. We have to stop the white flight!" He chuckled at this constant school district focus on white middle-class families, but continued seriously. "There was always a tension there. 'Oh, we don't want to really scare the majority community.' And the other side is, 'But we need to recognize that . . . this new demographic of kids is as entitled to a good education as anybody else, and we need to have practices that help them.'" So, Julio concluded, "there was a give and take, or a balance."

Julio recognized that district leaders hoped to use dual-language immersion programs to attract or retain white middle-class families in Fairview. That wasn't his motivation, but he saw the strategic benefits for his cause. "We actually leverage the voice of those who traditionally had a voice into giving us the opportunity to have a voice," he explained. It was "unfortunate" that it had to happen that way, that the school board decision was made to expand dual-language immersion "not because we asked them, but because *they* asked them," Julio said, emphasizing the influence that white families who wanted more dual-language immersion programs had over school board members who didn't want to scare off the "majority community."

The dual appeal of dual-language immersion education—to serve Latinx ELLs while also serving the desire of white middle-class parents for their children to be bilingual—also made these programs attractive to school district leaders, as many of them told me. "Some may view [dual-language immersion programs] as an attractor for white families to stay in public schools, which I think is some element—there's a huge element of truth in that," a Fairview administrator explained with some disappointment. "It's not just about creating bilingual, bicultural kids. It's keeping Fairview from being a white-flight community."

Julio accepted pragmatically that unequal responsiveness was part of the racial politics involved in securing programs that he believed would provide cultural and academic opportunities for Latinx children in the district. But it was a perpetuation of inequity. The expansion of dual-language immersion reflected what legal theorist Derrick Bell (1980) has called interest convergence, the phenomenon whereby racial justice is advanced only when these efforts are seen as aligned with those of advantaged white groups and policy makers. Though dual-language immersion would not have occurred without the advocacy and organization of teachers, parents, and immigrant advocates, interest convergence underscores the point Julio Garcia grasped from his everyday experience: race and power are the terrain upon which marginalized and minoritized groups struggle for equity. If the past was any indication, they would not have otherwise achieved this expansion of dual-language immersion. But interest convergence offers a limited advancement against race and class injustice (Alemán and Alemán 2010; Bell 1980; Castagno 2014). Because the policies and practices advanced through it are dependent upon being acceptable to white people, it is people of color who have to change or sacrifice to fit the needs or concerns of white people. Any forward motion is typically on the terms of white supremacy, and is unlikely to fundamentally or deeply alter structural inequities. For example, two middle-level managers noted that even with the expansion of dual-language immersion, many ELLs would remain underserved, and resources were needed for those students even though they were not in classrooms with white students.

Like dual-language immersion, IB also resonated with a discourse of global cosmopolitanism, and became a part of Milltown marketing even before the program had been started. The IB program had originally been suggested by the superintendent as a way to attract students to two underenrolled high schools. Teachers at one of these schools, Whitman High School, ran with the idea, enthusiastic about the model of education, and hoping that it would benefit their racially diverse low-income students. Stephanie Wahl, a school administrator, explained the appeal of the program:

> Too often Whitman has had the reputation of being a school, an "inner-city school" . . . and has had negative connotations to it, in terms of the low socio-economic [status], which is our profile. We do have great diversity in terms of student backgrounds, religions, students of color; but that doesn't mean that Whitman should not and cannot have opportunities for the students that will help them excel.

Thus, while adding an IB program promised greater educational opportunities, as Stephanie and her colleagues at Whitman saw it, and was a way to "change perceptions" and address Milltown district leaders' concerns about open enrollment, the IB program neither originated from communities of color in Milltown nor appeared to respond to their desires for their children. It may have increased some educational opportunity, but it was largely seen as a means to attract white middle-class families, and it was used as a mechanism of marketing and competition for these families more generally. As in Fairview, color-blind managerialism contributed to some interest convergence in Milltown, but it did so in ways that limited attention to the concerns of communities of color (itself an indication of inequity) and to structural or institutional inequities.

Reinforcing Racial Hierarchy: Valued Customers vs. Communicating to Communities of Color

District policy makers' efforts to market to upper- and middle-class white families contrasted with their orientation toward "communicating" with families of color. This was made clear in the way they perceived the differing expectations of the two groups, and in how they related to them.

One evening in late February 2010, when the Fairview marketing and communications work was just getting under way, Fairview district leaders organized a community meeting. They were planning to hire a private firm to develop a school district marketing plan, but first they sought public input. Flanked by several school board members in a middle school cafeteria, before a mostly white audience of about forty people and crews from two local television stations, Fairview superintendent Ben Sedlak introduced the purpose of the meeting: improving communication with a diverse set of families.

"Every day," Ben began, "we send messages at the school and district level. . . . It is our responsibility . . . to do it in good ways and effective ways." He acknowledged the importance of connecting with all families, and the challenge of connecting with immigrant families speaking a variety of home languages. "As a public organization, we have a complexity of size and language [to address], so that all our families can connect," he said. After a brief pause, he went on to frame the meeting as being about the need to compete for families "in the marketplace." He said, "I think of us as living in a time characterized by choice. All families make choices about where they get their education from. There are a lot of people in the marketplace, and many high-quality opportunities in this community, and even virtual ones. We have excellence. How can we help people understand that, and how can we improve?"

While the superintendent was suggesting that families of color could also be consumers, his comments about families looking for excellence who had many opportunities and might choose non-district schools paralleled district leaders' talk in reference to predominantly upper- and middle-class white families—not families of color, or poor families of any race. Fairview policy makers spoke simultaneously of marketing and communications; yet, in this meeting and in other ways, it was quickly apparent that improving communications and marketing efforts were aimed at different groups of families. While the school districts worked very hard to woo white middle-class parents as valued customers, they treated low-income communities of color more as beneficiaries of district services, and handled outreach to them differently.

As one administrator, Tara Randall, busily prepared the marketing plan in Milltown, for example, she made no mention of targeting families of color. Instead, she discussed the district's efforts to ensure that communities of color received school notices and announcements that were already communicated to families, including information on school registration, school calendars and deadlines, and the availability of translation services. In particular, she described efforts to translate materials into Hmong and Spanish, improve accessibility to digital communications, and distribute flyers in laundromats and ethnic grocery stores. Of the demographic change influencing her office's work she said, "You know, we need a lot more translated. Particularly in Spanish, that's about 20 percent of our student population. It's huge. . . . The Hispanic families do access the Internet. So, you know, we want to make it easier for them to get information." She cited the importance of making sure that "ethnic media" got information from the district. Her concern, like that of her Fairview colleagues, was to provide information to families of color, especially those who did not speak English.

Fairview and Milltown leaders expressed little concern that families of color might leave their school districts, though middle- and upper-middle class families of color could and sometimes did so. Furthermore, the district leaders never mentioned the possibility of trying to attract or retain more families of color—of any class—to the district. Rather, they tended to worry that the presence of students of color, who were assumed to be low-income, incurred additional expenditures on services like bilingual education, special education, or subsidized free school activities. Advertisements and school promotional brochures were not translated into languages other than English, and there was no plan to distribute them in the targeted ways Tara described. The lack of marketing to those families underscores the raced and classed nature of the marketing in Milltown and Fairview. District leaders viewed it as a measure that would contribute to the financial survival of schools serving thousands of students—increasingly low-income students and students of color—and provide a positive view of them as racially diverse. But in the end, the marketing signaled the status of white middle- and upper-middle-class students as "valued customers," and sought to provide them with certain desired rewards.

Conclusion: Managing School Districts in a Racialized Marketplace

The marketing of diversity, as an example of color-blind managerialism, was a response to the contradictions and the challenges to legitimacy that these two racially diverse and unequal school districts faced when they operated in a raced and classed marketplace of school competition. In a context where student needs and outcomes reflected race-class oppression, and where families' disparate ability to make such choices is also overspecified by race and class, marketing diversity "solves" contradictions of serving an increasingly racially diverse and economically unequal student population under increasing conditions of marketlike "competition."

Fairview and Milltown were facing pressures of competiton, test-based accountability, and constrained resources as the school districts became more racially diverse and unequal. The leaders in both districts worried about the financial repercussions. They were not alone in this. Marketing is increasingly common in schools and educational programs across the country (Carr 2011; Simon 2009), as a solution to many of the same pressures (see also, e.g., Cucchiara et al. 2011; DiMartino and Jessen 2016; Jabbar 2015; Kasman and Loeb 2013; Lubienski 2005, 2007; Posey-Maddox 2014). For Fairview and Milltown leaders, marketing diversity helped them navigate the contradictions in the school system, and seemed to promise that they could recuperate the images of their school systems as positively diverse, and stave off transfer by middle- and upper-middle class white families.

But the move toward marketing and to marketing diversity in Milltown and Fairview demonstrates its limitations for upending negative perceptions and racist notions about multiracial and unequal school systems. Marketing diversity to appeal to white middle- and upper-middle-class families as "valued customers" reflected and reinforced the privileged status those families already held in those districts, and furthered the very raced and classed assumptions of good schools and bad schools that district leaders sought to disrupt.

The advantages of the IB program to low-income students and students of color in Milltown, or of the expansion of dual-language immersion that Julio and other Latinx community members advocated in Fairview, were secondary to meeting the desires of white teachers, district officials, and families. Inequity was perpetuated. The expansion of dual-language immersion programs, long sought by Latinx communities, only came about when they met the needs of white families and school district leaders.

To district leaders, the diversity discourse of global cosmopolitanism seemed like a way to challenge racist assumptions while attracting or retaining predominantly white middle-class families. To be sure, trying to overturn the inaccurate perceptions and racialized ideologies about schools with students of color is worthwhile and necessary. However, marketing diversity can exotify the languages, cultures, everyday interactions, and presence of students of color, positioning them as being for the instrumental benefit and educational advantage of upper- and middle-class white children. The danger is that identities and cultures of students of color become contained, co-opted, and commodified for others through the official antiracism of marketing.

But, by acknowledging and emphasizing how all students may gain from interracial and intercultural interactions and knowledge, the Fairview leaders' appeal to a thicker notion of diversity showed greater promise. Ben Sedlak discussed and promoted the cultural capital of the district's students and actual interaction across lines of race and class. In its focus on the benefits of diversity for all students, not just white-identified students, it was a more promising approach to conceptualizing diversity that had the potential to truly challenge the heightened value of white identification and demand the equal status of racialized children regardless of instrumental value. But it never was marketed officially. Although Fairview leaders did expand dual-language immersion, the plan to hire an outside firm to create a communications plan was axed in spring 2010 after a public outcry about spending forty thousand dollars when the district expected unprecedented budget shortfalls for the 2010–11 school year due to changes in anticipated state funding.

Fairview's experience underscores that, while the official antiracism focusing on the benefits of diversity may go part of the way toward racial justice, countering racial inequity with marketing is difficult if not impossible, because a color-blind approach will not address the problems of school funding and racial and class segregation, but will recreate the existing inequities of a racialized and classed school marketplace. While there are no easy solutions, awareness and confrontation of these contradictions and official antiracisms offers greater potential for addressing inequity in school districts, as I will discuss in the conclusion to this book.

"How Well Do We Live the Reality?" and How Do We Live the Reality Well?

A t the start of this book, Fairview superintendent Ben Sedlak asked: "How well do we live the reality?" This was a question weighing on the minds of Milltown and Fairview's district leaders as they considered their work and the ways their school districts were responding to the new reality: educating a more diverse and unequal student population while under the pressures of high-stakes accountability policies, heightened competition, and state disinvestment in schools. Under these conditions they were struggling, in particular, with imperatives to spur achievement and educational opportunity across lines of race, class, and language. But they did so in school systems that were developed to serve and respond to predominantly white middle-class majorities and elites who held the local reins of power but seemed to be only weakly committed to equitable education for low-income students of color. They were grappling with a difficult question about how to do their work well, and how to do it right.

Fairview and Milltown leaders were contending with a fundamental contradiction in the United States: that public schools must be sites to both transform and maintain social inequities (Blount 2005; Boyd 1976). The contradictions are particularly evident in public school districts, but all those involved in running public institutions—from classrooms to federal policy makers—confront some version of this contradiction in their work. The challenge that district leaders faced is one that will resonate particularly strongly in public school systems across the country. Scholars of educational policy and leadership, writing about other places and times in US history, have called the pressures to maintain status quo inequities "the privilege imperative" (Blount 2005) or "social justice for the advantaged" (Horsford 2016). How school district leaders deal with this contradiction and deal with their reality has important implications not just for the students they are expected to serve, but for the schools themselves and for democratic society. Indeed, public schools have been reshaped by efforts to deal with these fundamental contradictions (Blount 2005; Omi and Winant 2015).

In this conclusion, I consider how Milltown and Fairview leaders lived the contradicting realities of public schools, and what lessons we might take from these two cases about how to live the reality well. After reviewing what we learn from Milltown and Fairview about inequality in school districts, I revisit the concept of color-blind managerialism, and build on these insights to suggest ways forward, including identifying school district contradictions and taking action on those contradictions through intentional organizational work and collaborating with social movement actors to challenge the policies and broader inequities which sustain school inequities.

Lessons about School Districts and Racial Inequity

Previous scholars have pointed out patterns of inequality in school district policy making. In many ways their findings are similar to those described here: powerful constituencies limit educational policy and practice to what is acceptable to them; school district leaders are limited by these constituencies and typically capitulate to local pressures and the zones of acceptable change, leaving in place technical policy changes that fail to truly transform inequities in schools (Trujillo 2014). Though individual-level shortcomings may have been factors in creating these patterns in Milltown, Fairview and many other school districts, there is a danger in understanding these dynamics as explained simply by the biases of school district leaders, their failure to stand up for students marginalized by race and class, or their lack of preparation for political and normative challenges to their work. Furthermore, there is a tendency to see district decisions to forgo more equity-oriented policies and practices as the end of a story of school districts and racial inequity when school district policy and practice are constantly being made, challenged and remade in processes of policymaking and enactment. This study of Milltown and Fairview illuminates these lessons and several other key lessons about school districts and racial inequity.

First, Milltown and Fairview school district officials pursued new and increasingly common managerial policies and practices of marketing and data monitoring (e.g., DiMartino and Jessen 2018; Marsh 2012), which were an ostensible solution to the inequities in their schools, but which ultimately failed to remedy the disparities in those schools. In Milltown they created advertising plans; aired television spots promoting science and music offerings, International Baccalaureate programs, and language classes; and created school flyers touting the assets of individual schools. Aimed at predominantly white and middle-class families, these efforts reinforced inequity by centering these families and positioning "diversity" for the attraction and retention of these families, while offering little to students of color by way of programs or equal recognition of their cultures. In Fairview district leaders launched an eighty-five-page community-influenced strategic plan, and took initial steps to carry it out and monitor their progress in regular meetings, reports, and evaluations. Ostensibly an effort to address achievement gaps, strategic planning reinforced the use of high-stakes testing that persistently disadvantages low-income communities of color and legitimated the knowledge and control of white public officials. While these managerial efforts were aimed at helping to create solutions to inequities in each district, marketing and data monitoring approaches tended to reinforce the status and advantages of white and middle- or upper-middle classes in these two districts.

Second, the adoption of marketing and data monitoring developed not in a vacuum, but in the inequitable contexts in which district leaders worked. Color-blind managerialism was the Milltown and Fairview district officials' way to manage the contradictions they confronted. The district leaders advanced new managerial approaches as mechanisms of educational equity that would not unsettle white majorities or elites. They turned to data monitoring systems, in part to address NCLB pressures when test scores weren't sufficient to make yearly NCLB targets, and when teachers in their districts resisted further racial bias and cultural competency trainings. They proposed that data monitoring systems would achieve the official antiracisms of "raising test scores" and "narrowing achievement gaps." They marketed "diversity" as a selling point to attract predominantly white middle- and upper-middle-class families to Milltown and Fairview schools, and consequently to retain the state aid from their enrollment. Claims to value "diversity" and address the "achievement gap" were official antiracisms that painted a veneer of inclusion or concern over inequality onto these efforts, making them ways to navigate the contradictions brought out by the open enrollment system, fiscal austerity, and high-stakes testing.

We might have expected that Milltown, which was more conservative and working-class, and Fairview, which was more liberal and middle-class, would present very different cases of school districts navigating racial inequities, but the two school districts shared much in common in terms of the pressures and contradictions they faced, the policies and practices of marketing and data monitoring that they pursued, and the consequences of those actions. The overarching similarities between the two districts suggest the strength of the structures, ideologies, and pressures described here in organizing the particular kinds of responses that district leaders adopted.

The impulse of many readers will be to ask immediately about solutions and to insist that we judge which of the two districts' efforts was more successful. This eagerness to identify solutions is understandable, but it's necessary to pause to contemplate and appreciate the inherent contradictions in public schools, the significant pressures, and thus the formidable challenges Fairview and Milltown leaders confronted. Disinvestment in schools and social services and the press toward competition and test-based accountability, far from being neutral mechanisms, disadvantage school districts that serve students struggling in poverty and students of color as much as they harm those students. Until we truly grasp these circumstances and the broader, entrenched contexts of white supremacy and class inequality in schools and society, there is little chance of finding places and strategies for change.

Third, even as they worked under considerable structural limitations, district leaders played a crucial role in equity efforts. They attempted to merge imperatives to transform injustice with imperatives to maintain advantage. These efforts can be seen as examples of interest convergence (Bell 1980). From one view, this may have achieved improvements in their schools. In Fairview, for example, an effort to attract or retain enrollments with "diversity" led to interest convergence around the expansion of dual-language immersion schools that Latinx community members were advocating, and the marketing of diversity contributed to organizational-level structural change. But the official antiracism of these projects did not necessarily reassemble anything that local communities of color advocated, or even change the schools' practices, much less address the broader race and class structures that contributed to inequality. Moreover, in Milltown and Fairview, district leaders pursued color-blind managerialism with the aim of achieving a measure of seeming equity within the limits of what they believed would be acceptable to white majorities and elites they wished to mollify, and upon whom they were increasingly dependent. Much as Castagno (2014) found in her study of a Utah school district, they pursued equity when it conveniently converged with their interests. As critical race scholars have emphasized, to the degree that interest convergence occurred, it was limited by what those already in power believed to be acceptable (Alemán Jr. and Alemán 2010; see Capper 2015 for review). Though district leaders thought of the work they were doing as equity-oriented, it was subject to changes in those groups' whims, and it left power inequities in place.

While I have mainly emphasized the similarities between Milltown and Fairview in this book, there were differences in the ways their district leaders navigated contradictions. In Milltown, the more conservative and working-class town, diversity discourse was shallow, linked to practices only tangentially related to the inclusion of the actual communities of color in that city. In Fairview, on the other hand, the diversity discourse was thicker, suggesting reciprocal relationships between racialized groups, and contributing in part to interest convergence, however limited, in dual-language immersion programs. In terms of both meanings and practices, Fairview's approach still left in place overarching power relations, but seemed to offer a greater challenge to existing status inequities (Blackmore 2006). There were also notable differences in the districts' data monitoring approaches. The Milltown data-monitoring approach tended to be more narrowly centered on tested knowledge and test results, and involved only school and district educators. In Fairview, the foci of the strategic planning and evaluation were broader and more inclusive of the concerns of community members and families, including those who were typically more marginalized in formal policy processes. The Fairview approach still was limited by use of standardized testing and uneven political influence in the processes, but all other things being equal, it was a more promising approach to addressing systemic race and class inequities in schools. It is important to recognize these differences and their practical importance, even if the managerial policies of marketing and data monitoring did not fully disrupt school district inequity.

Finally, and most important, the results of color-blind managerialism strategies—and this way of navigating inequity—were not antiracist school districts. Color-blind managerialism contributed to remaking the *meaning and practice of inequity* in these districts, and *reshaped these public schools* in ways that perpetuated racial inequity. As their culture- and race-focused professional developments hit resistance from teaching staff, Milltown and Fairview district leaders focused more strongly on data-monitoring approaches to addressing "achievement gaps." The practices of the school districts changed to emphasize a plethora of reports, evaluations, new meetings, and conversations about standardized test data of various sorts. District leaders seemed to maintain a commitment to making their schools more equitable, but racial equity came to mean raising test scores, perhaps promoting "diversity," or keeping their school districts afloat rather than transforming inequities. A "back-to-basics" focus in Milltown was put forward as equitable. In Fairview, a focus on a notion of excellence for all (Schneider 2011) recast a capitulation to power as inclusion. Thus, not only was racial inequity maintained, albeit in new form, but the publicness of public schooling—that is, the commitment and design of democratic and equitable schools for the public, limited though those have been—was also diminished. For helping to make these shifts, district leaders were positioned as rational, diversity-appreciating, nonracist white people who were doing their jobs. Color-blind managerialism did not solve the problems of inequity. It created new forms of racism and undermined the public schools.

Revisiting Color-Blind Managerialism in School Districts

Color-blind managerialism as a racial project of school district leadership and policy is a conceptual tool to illuminate the linkages between racialized and classed structures or practices of new managerialism, and people's everyday color-blind meaning-making about race. This builds on Omi and Winant's (2015) concept of a racial project. Through the cases of Milltown and Fairview, I have tried to illuminate this racial project as it operates in school district officials' work, as well as the hows and whys of it.

In color-blind managerialism, policies and practices based in neo-liberal ideologies that prize an entrepreneurial spirit and free-market approaches are given the meaning of being against racism and of being good, appropriate, and equitable ways to lead schools. Practices of marketing "diversity" or raising test scores by examining data are defined as equitable, as are structures like accountability systems. Roles like data-wielding, diversity-appreciating school district leaders, and thin notions of diversity, choice, or achievement all become rearticulated as "equitable," or against racism. They are examples of official antiracism (Melamed 2011); they do little to challenge race and class inequities, and instead reformulate them in new ways. These new managerial approaches to school governance are posited as being against the very racism that the policies produce.

As a racial project of school governance, color-blind managerialism can be thought of as a strategy to navigate the contradictions in public schools—that is, to manage inequity. While public schools are expected to transform society, their ability to do so is often constrained by their dependence upon those who would like to maintain the status quo of color-blind racism and economic inequality. As a form of interest convergence (Bell 1980), we can expect that any advances to racial equity (or the appearances of such) only occur where white policy elites interpret their interests as being aligned with those of people of color. As a strategy for managing the contradictions of schools, color-blind managerialism is always on terms amenable to those in charge; it does not typically disrupt (and may obscure) the underlying power relations. Therefore, it cannot truly upset racial hierarchy. Color-blind managerialism may be an attractive way for school district leaders to navigate the contradictions of schooling, but it is a response that refracts rather than addresses, challenges, or reworks those contradictions.

To call color-blind managerialism a strategy is not to say that it reflects a conscious decision or strategic action. Certainly policymakers or policy advocates may strategically co-opt antiracist discourse to advance managerial or neoliberal goals, but color-blind managerialism may just as easily reflect the facile and largely unreflective ways in which people attempt to reconcile contradictory pressures to both advance equity and reproduce an unequal society, rather than be a strategic calculation to either undermine equity or cynically use equity language to advance new managerialism (Castagno 2014; Lewis and Diamond 2015). Indeed, support of neoliberal or new managerial approaches doesn't always reflect an acceptance of market goals for schooling (Apple 2006; Pedroni 2007). Whatever the intentions, these strategies are problematic.

Color-blind managerialism is flexible and malleable. There are variations in its meanings and practices across educational issues, policies or practices, and in places with people working in different historical, sociocultural, political, and economic conditions. These are reflective of district leaders' sense making and contexts, and what these afford and constrain. As noted earlier, discourses of diversity in education, for example, engage with power differentials in greater and lesser ways (Blackmore 2006), and can be linked to different practices or structures. Color-blind managerialism might be usefully seen as including a gamut of representational-material linkages that do more or less to further or challenge inequality. We can expect to see varieties of color-blind managerialism intervene to differing degrees into district inequities, and thus be more or less equitable, but without transforming the deep inequities in schools or society.

As I outline it here, the concept of color-blind managerialism and how it works is helpful for conceptualizing school district inequity. First, naming this as a broader phenomenon in education illuminates similarities across educational policies and practices in terms of their meaning and import, as well as how they come about. We can see marketing and accountability as being linked to a broader set of issues, and as an example of a broader phenomenon. The ways in which color-blind managerialism helps school district leaders navigate the contradictory terrain they confront helps to explain the phenomenon of people framing policies that do not intervene in racial inequity as being antiracist. Color-blind managerialism fills district leaders' political needs (Castagno 2014) and perhaps their professional aspirations, and suggests that noncontroversial techniques will be sufficient to alleviate the social inequities that play out in schools.

Second, color-blind managerialism as a racial project of school governance also allows us to see racial inequity as the product, in part, of school district officials' meanings and actions in everyday life. As public officials, school district leaders hold authority in formal decision making and in articulating official meaning in their school systems. They play a key role in mediating meanings of racism or inequity, particularly the ideologies of color blindness and whiteness that are so common and so interwoven in color-blind managerialism. Through the development of policies and practices, they are also centrally involved in mediating the experiences and structures of racism in schools and society, including rising inequality, disinvestment in public institutions, and market-based policies.

Third, understanding color-blind managerialism as a racial project links "micro" level practices and sensemaking of school district leaders with the macro structures and ideologies of color-blind racism, neoliberal political and economic transformation, and demographic change which shape and are shaped by district policymakers' actions. Demographic, economic, and political changes taking place at the current moment—all of which are intertwined with race—set the stage for color-blind managerialism.

Color-blind managerialism is evident in other studies in education. Discourses of racial equity have been marshaled by proponents of charter schools and high-stakes testing, market-based education policies that have negatively affected the poor and working classes and people of color (Au 2016; J. Scott 2013). At the state level, another example might be school finance laws that make claims of "redistribution" and "equal aid" but allow property-wealthy districts far greater levels of state aid than other districts, partly on the basis of laws that privilege debt financing (Alemán 2007). That these examples come from different levels of government and different sectors of education suggests the wider reach of the color-blind managerial racial project. To that end, a fourth point is that color-blind managerialism may be a useful concept for analyzing educational policy and governance more broadly.

Finally, while school district leaders may seem to have few alternatives to color-blind managerialism, that is not the case. Understanding this phenomenon as a racial project provides a lens for viewing color-blind managerialism, like all racial projects, as contested, subject to change over time, and not at all preordained (Omi and Winant 2015). That the racial project of color-blind managerialism is ubiquitous does not mean that it is inevitable. Lessons from this study also offer guidance and suggest possible ways forward.

How Do We Live the Reality Well?

Milltown and Fairview school district leaders confronted attacks on the public schools in the form of neoliberal policies—like state and federal limitations and cuts to education, high-stakes accountability, and

competition—that were rigged against these school districts and the minoritized and poor children they were ostensibly designed to serve, de-
pleting fiscal resources and narrowing the meaning and experience of
public schooling. But critics of the schools also cited school district inequities experienced by communities of color, especially including racism and inequality. Color-blind managerialism sustained these problems
rather than disrupting them. The way forward must address these issues
and contribute to an alternative racial project of school governance, one
that is more like the social justice project that educators and scholars
have been advocating.

The contradictions district leaders faced, which are a central focus
of this book, also provide a central starting point for intervention into
these issues (Omi and Winant 2015). As we have seen, many people believe that pursuing equity is incompatible with securing the support and
resources needed to sustain public schools. That belief was often the
logic behind color-blind managerialism. Indeed, if things are largely left
in place, the contradictions will likely continue. Equity and resources
can be at odds, but they need not be. For school district officials, public school supporters, and others who already are or are willing to become community leaders in public schooling, there are things that can
be done. In particular, two processes, described in greater detail below,
are needed to unlock the seeming conundrum here. The first is to identify and examine the contradictions at a particular site. The second is to
take action to change those contradictions, so that they become enabling
rather than limiting situations.

The participation of community members, particularly those from
minoritized and or marginalized positions, is essential to both understanding and acting on inequity in schools and communities. The *tes-
tamonios*, counternarratives, and counterstories of people of color can
provide a powerful critique of majoritarian discourses that perpetuate
racial inequity and power relations (Delgado and Stefancic 2001; Solórzano and Yosso 2002). In this book I provide examples of three people of color in Fairview, school district administrators Monica Collins
and Pakou Xiong, and community member Julio Garcia, who provided
knowledge and perspectives for critically examining color-blind managerialism. In Milltown, I described the work of Sedona Richards, the
Black mother and community advocate. There were others in both cities
whose voices and efforts would provide crucial knowledge, motivation,
and perspective on district inequities. However, the particular insights of

communities of color were not known to a wide range of district officials. Too often, in places like Milltown (where there were no people of color on the school board, or in executive or mid-level district administration), communities of color are not a central part of the conversation. Beyond critique, partnership and collaboration with community members, especially traditionally marginalized ones, is necessary to bring in alternative discourses, knowledge, and visions as well as resources and support for future action to address contradictions and inequities (Galloway and Ishimaru 2015; Khalifa et al. 2016; C. N. Stone et al. 2001). Parents and other residents hold key resources necessary for flourishing students and public schools. After years of growing poverty and defunding of public schools and other social services, many schools are underresourced and underprepared for the multiple roles they are being asked to fulfill. In short, this can't be done well if school districts try to go it alone.

Two additional points are in order. First, the ways forward will look different in different school districts, and places with greater inequality, fewer resources, or more deeply ingrained (or tightly held) racism will likely have more difficulty in making headway, just as the in-school strategies that district leaders developed have been shaped and limited by these same considerations. The specific discussions and actions must respond to the participants and resources unique to each site, and must address the particular economic, political, and demographic challenges in each locale, and the ways they are racialized. Second, there are many pitfalls and cautionary notes that could be given because of the way that color-blind managerialism can so easily and stealthily sneak into more emancipatory work, through the slow accretion of official antiracisms or the shifts and dilution of previously more emancipatory work over time. This is almost inevitable, and is certainly to be expected. The ubiquity and malleability of color-blind managerialism makes avoiding its trap difficult. Furthermore, because part of the strength of color-blind managerialism lies in marrying meanings about racial equity to managerial forms, it requires extra care and reflexivity to avoid it.

Examining School District Contradictions

The first move is to identify and understand key contradictions in a given school district. This requires examining both the equity issues and the dynamics and forces by which addressing them is unrecognized, ignored, or actively obstructed. School district leaders and educators across the country participate in formal and informal book clubs, shared readings, and book studies meant to stoke reflection and improvement in their practices. They often discuss books that describe how to improve professional development, or how to enact data-based decision making. There is certainly a place for this work. However, attention to the technical challenges of schooling rarely offers the insight necessary for equitable educational change (e.g. Holme et al. 2013; G. R. López 2003; Oakes et al. 1998). Having critical, reflective conversations and recognizing and critiquing the structural inequities and ideologies that (re)produce racial inequity and forms of oppression are essential steps toward further action advocated by critical race scholars of educational leadership (e.g., Anderson 2009; Capper 2015; Cooper 2009; Khalifa et al. 2016; Larson and Ovando 2001; Theoharis 2007; Welton et al. 2015) and are central to the social-justice racial project of school governance. Two possible approaches are book discussions and equity audits.

As a starting point, this book lays out some of the ideologies, practices, and structures of color-blind managerialism, as well as some of the sense making, contradictions, strategies, and identities that advance this racial project. A modest suggestion is to begin with the kinds of book conversations that already exist in schools, and to examine contradictions and questions raised in this book or others as an entry point to reflection and conversations that grapple with these tensions in one's own school districts.[1] Setting aside time to reflect on one's individual practice or dispositions is important, but the focus of these conversations should be on understanding the ideologies and practices that contribute to inequities, and the contradictions of schooling in one's district, and then identifying ways to change the conditions that create or exacerbate them. This information will come from reflecting on examples of contradiction in other sites (via the books chosen for discussion), and also from discussion within the school district.

For this process to generate new insights and be set up for further action, it must involve a diversity of people of color and other traditionally marginalized groups to surface the experiences and perspectives not already known to district leaders, and to serve as an accountability check on their work. A community-involved process will also be essential to further action. Thus, more privileged actors, including those without children, need to be involved in wrestling with these tensions and charting responses. However, it is a matter of not just getting involved, but also grappling with how to do so in a way that ameliorates rather than reproduces inequities (Anyon 2005b). So part of the intention of this work is to examine different notions of equity and inequity, as well as the common good, and to develop relationships, solidarities, and a sense of shared responsibility that will challenge privileged actors' resistance to equity-oriented change and will provoke action to address inequity.

Community-involved equity processes are another promising possibility for stoking reflexivity and action.[2] Equity audits have emerged as a way to encourage reflective conversations about inequity in schools and to take action. Equity audit approaches share an effort to examine root causes of "achievement gaps" and other educational disparities within schools (Capper and Young 2015; Skrla et al. 2004). However, some of these models give the sense that they could quickly become a part of the project of color-blind managerialism, and could easily be used more as audit than as equity tool, even if they were not designed or intended to be used that way.[3] A potential peril is that equity audits are used, as data monitoring techniques in Milltown were used, to push attention toward school-level actors in ways that obscure issues of power within and outside schools. Just as important is the lack of attention to outside-of-school factors on educational inequity. Green (2017) notes that traditional equity audits do not explicitly confront the political or normative challenges of equity-oriented change work, or the ways in which racial segregation and poverty limit or impact equity and equity-based change in schools. Without looking at those vexing problems, such audits will not be productive means of reflecting on and challenging inequities and contradictions in schools.

Community-involved equity audits can address these shortcomings. Green (2017) and Sanders (2008) have proposed ways to examine and address educational equity by using multiple forms of data and knowledge as part of a larger process of building relationships with families and community members. Green's "community-based equity audits model" emphasizes a commitment to inclusion of and partnership with diverse stakeholders and community members, especially those most underserved in schools. Such a process itself must be just. It cannot reflect or reproduce the maldistribution, malrecognition, and lack of representation of existing school systems. For example, a community-based equity audit must address community concerns and inequities, and not be driven purely or primarily by the concerns of school district officials. Both Green and Sanders require the use of diverse forms of data, including nonstandardized data generated by community members. Data that recognizes the histories and voices of marginalized communities is part of a process shift in how decisions get made and who makes them. Potentially, then, the process itself is an intervention in school district inequities as it shifts how governance and decision making are conducted and who gets to be involved in it.

In this approach, accountability is not to some higher level of bureaucracy, but to the very people whom the schools are expected to serve, particularly those who have been most marginalized historically in district policy making and decisions. In addition to the data monitoring that is undertaken to meet external demands of test-based accountability, in a community- and relational-centered approach data may also be used to "garner resources for growth and sustainability" (Sanders 2008), a way to intervene in structural inequity and support teachers and families rather than evaluate and punish them. In their strategic planning initiative, Fairview leaders went part of the way toward such an approach, relying on racial diversity (if not class representation) in community involvement and some inclusion of diverse knowledge and community accountability in the planning process, but continued use of high-stakes and standardized measures and limited community roles in ongoing change and accountability. While not fail-proof, in their attention to conditions in schools, resource issues, community-based knowledge, relationship building, and data use, these community-based audit models appear to have promise for reflecting on school district inequities and taking action.

The above approaches are promising because they are intended to counter or avoid falling into a trap of color-blind managerialism. They involve working with and being accountable to marginalized communities, recognizing and responding to structural problems of poverty and racism, and being oriented toward institutional and out-of-school structural changes. Whatever the method, the first step is to develop a deep understanding of contradictions in school districts, and of the relationships necessary to address political and cultural challenges of altering existing inequities.

Taking Action on School District Contradictions

The focus of this second set of processes is taking action to change practices and structures at institutional and societal levels. Changing specific racist practices or dispositions has a role, and may to a certain extent be a precursor to this work, but individual-level work can sometimes stall, derail, or distract from this structural-level work so that it never gets attempted (Welton, Owens, and Zamani-Gallaher 2018). As my research here has shown, however, state and federal policies, as well as broader political, social, and economic structures, were incredibly influential in shaping the uptake of color-blind managerialism. Shifting these limitations or constraints—which are themselves systems or structures of inequality—holds the promise for not only making district work easier but addressing the inequalities that limit the lives of students and the fortunes of schools. To address the contradictions that district leaders face in school districts, there will almost certainly be a need for changes within school district organizations and for broader social change outside of schools. The specific actions to be taken will depend upon what is learned though critical reflection at specific sites, and upon the shared decisions of community members and school district leaders to act. My intention here is to suggest some research-based directions and a framework for the kinds of organizational and social change that are necessary.

Welton and colleagues' (2018) antiracist change framework offers an approach that might guide action at the school-district or school level. Based on a synthesis of research on antiracism and on institutional change, Welton and colleagues outline elements of antiracism that must be addressed ("pedagogy and individual learning," "resistance to antiracism," and "systemic level commitment"), as well as elements of organizational change to be considered ("defining change," "context and conditions," "leadership," etc.). The framework helps educational leaders ensure that interventions attend to the political and normative challenges of antiracism work (such as whiteness), and that they do so in ways that are likely to change an institution with ingrained practices and taken-for-granted norms.

The antiracist change framework provides a process for planning change that can then be carried out at the organizational level. It takes into consideration resistance, such as that which Milltown district leaders perceived in Milltown's white teachers, and it provides guidance for addressing other common institutional inequities. It is a particularly good match with the findings suggested here, because it explicitly addresses issues of resistance and whiteness, but emphasizes institutional-level change over individual attitudes. One area of the framework that might be augmented is the inclusion of families and communities in the pro-

cesses Welton and colleagues describe. One remedy to this might be authentic partnership with community members to collaboratively codesign
changes in educational policy and practice (Ishimaru et al. 2018). As with
any such process, there are risks that such strategic planning and contin-
uous improvement can become an excuse to do nothing, a kind of color-
blind managerialism, as the authors acknowledge (Welton et al. 2018).

While school and district change is important, this study suggests that
poverty, policy, and racial inequity outside schools are at the heart of
the inequities that make their ways into schools (Berliner 2013; Ladson-
Billings 2006). District leaders need to be involved in recognizing and
acting on the broader issues. Raced and classed inequities are made visible and are counted in schools through the measuring of "achievement
gaps" and rising numbers of students in need of meals, but the root problems go beyond what can be counted in schools. Any focus on addressing poverty and inequality must attend to the racialized nature of both
of these. Racialized class structures—which have been fostered through
policy and practice since before the founding of the US government—
were part of what defined the marginalized from the privileged in these
cities, and thus were interwoven with the contradictions in the operation
of schools.

Although specific issues will vary by site, Anyon's (2005) "New Education Policy Paradigm" outlines some areas of intervention. Based on
an extensive review of research, Anyon (2005) argues that "urban poverty, low-wage work, and housing segregation . . . dwarf most curricular,
pedagogical, and other educational reforms" (p. 83) in their impact on
student achievement, and also matter for student well-being. She advocates policies to remove economic barriers to school quality (e.g., raising
the minimum wage, creating jobs, taxing corporations) and create access
to housing and job opportunities (e.g., enforcement of antidiscrimina-
tion laws, transportation). Furthermore, in Anyon's paradigm, education
policies would be linked to out-of-school policies that address barriers
to opportunity for students and their families. Thus, policy directions
suggested by the findings in Milltown and Fairview (such as fully funding schools and ending policies, like high-stakes accountability or school
choice, that created or exacerbated educational inequities) could be
linked to broader social policies that support families living in poverty,
end discriminatory barriers, affirmatively offer those families access to
opportunity, and so forth.

School district leaders obviously face limits here. Their jobs are already very demanding, they do not have particularly strong influence outside of schools, and schools cannot take on the full responsibility of these broader changes, past efforts to make schools the primary mechanism for social welfare notwithstanding (Kantor and Lowe 2016). Luckily, district leaders do not have to do this alone, nor be in charge of this work. Individuals and community groups involved in examining inequities in their schools can take roles here as well, if they feel they have a stake and voice in the process. Indeed, many organizations and groups are already doing relevant equity work. Teachers' unions and other unions, often those who have low-income people of color as their core leadership or membership, are engaged in challenging high-stakes testing and privatization in schools, and are linking demands for school resources and educators' living wages with other campaigns related to racism, poverty, and inequality (Schirmer 2019; Todd-Breland 2018). Involvement in cross-sector organizing might link vocational training in schools to advocacy for fair labor practices and living-wage jobs that impact students and their families, or link funding for health and social welfare programs in schools and communities to efforts to reduce racial disparities in school discipline and incarceration (interventions that Anyon would likely see as part of her "New Education Policy Paradigm").

Concluding Thoughts: Pursuing Racial Equity and Strengthening Public Schooling

The findings described here are of utmost importance as we close in on a "majority minority" society that is grappling with continued color-blind racism, resurgent explicit white supremacy, perilous levels of economic inequity (Wilkinson and Pickett 2011), and heightened questions about the erosion of public institutions and the roles they should play in ensuring a equitable and democratic society. The confluence of pressures that were playing out in Milltown and Fairview in 2009 and 2010 are part of larger demographic, economic, and political trajectories that remain relevant to school district equity today. Furthermore, NCLB is gone, but the Every Student Succeeds Act (ESSA) still carries on the mantle of high-stakes accountability. New mechanisms further market competition in schools, and state disinvestment in public education. And racism certainly has not disappeared. The resurgence of overt white supremacy joins, and gains strength from, the continued color-blind racism today.

In short, the Milltown and Fairview cases reflect many specificities of these two school districts at a particular interval in time, but the findings here have relevance and meaning for the ongoing and very pressing present challenges of eliminating white supremacy and restoring the *public* in public schools.

There is a crucial lesson here. District leaders saw color-blind managerialism as a solution to challenges they faced, and therefore as a way to sustain their districts, but it also undermined their school districts as *public* institutions. As part of the neoliberal push to reform the state, color-blind managerialism created new inequities and, through accountability and competition, and district data monitoring and marketing responses to those things, focused the district administrators and school board members on raising outputs and attracting customers, thus challenging their *public* mission. Furthermore, as we saw in chapter 1, the survival of public schools is challenged by neoliberal politics that seeks to cut public budgets, making it more and more difficult for schools to do their jobs. Though it is more politically palatable in the short term to embrace practices that continue racism in schools, and which themselves cannot be expected to address educational inequities, color-blind managerialism also undermines school districts as institutions that can educate children and address inequality in a democratic society. They will continue to be doubly delegitimated.

Through their racial sense-making and discourses, their strategies for managing contradictions, and their actions in schools, the Milltown and Fairview district leaders both navigated and made racial inequity through a racial project of color-blind managerialism. They pursued new managerial approaches not simply because maintaining the status quo benefited them psychologically or organizationally, though that may have played a role in their adoption of color-blind strategies (Shore and Wright 2000). The political and economic contexts in which they worked have profoundly shaped their approach to addressing school district inequities. Their efforts to navigate the contradictions of schooling—and to navigate the fact that those contradictions exist at all—have always taken place within a society deeply structured by race and class inequity. Those deeply structured inequities, in the form of color-blind managerialism and the perpetuation of racism, threaten racial equity *and* the public schools.

Methodological Appendix

The work on this book began in 2008 as I read a newspaper article about demographic changes occurring in school districts across the state of Wisconsin. In particular, I was interested in how school district officials in a "new immigrant destination" were responding to the growing numbers of immigrant students in their schools. Over time, I came to understand the study as about something different. It was not only a study of responses to immigrant students, but a study of racial change and of poverty—not only about people coming or going (or threatening to do so), but also about the intersecting social, economic, and political changes occurring across many parts of the United States, the ways that racial inequity was intertwined with these things, and the attendant struggles and inequities. The story grew richer at every turn. All along, it was guided by a consistent curiosity about how educational leaders made sense of the needs of marginalized students, how they responded with particular policies or practices, and how that response was shaped by the broader contexts in which they were embedded.

Design and Site Selection

I approached this question through a comparative case study of policy making and responses to demographic changes in two Wisconsin school districts. Qualitative case study methods call on us to examine "how" and "why" something happens in the real world, and how differences in context might matter to that (Yin 2003). I selected the sites for this study by examining US Census and school enrollment data to find school districts with enrollments between fifteen and twenty-five thousand students and growing immigrant and English-learner populations over the fifteen years leading up to the study (1994–2009). I used economic data (unemployment, poverty, household income), articles on immigration and demographic change from four newspapers (2006–9), and data on local immigration ordinances (e.g., "sanctuary" cities, English-only ordinances) to purposively sample (Patton 1990) for variation in local economic context and political orientation toward immigrants and people of color. In the end I selected Milltown and Fairview, both of which had increased immigrant populations (primarily Hmong refugees and Mexican immigrants), students of color, and students living in poverty over the previous decades. Milltown is a city with a struggling economy and a less inclusive attitude toward immigrants and people of color, whereas Fairview has a stronger economy and a more inclusive orientation.

Data and Analysis

I collected interviews, observations, and documentary materials primarily between the fall of 2009 and the spring of 2010. In focusing on words, actions, and artifacts, this kind of ethnographic data enlightens us to how particular groups or communities work, and allows us to explore beliefs, language, and behavior and issues such as power, resistance, and dominance—evidence that is virtually unobtainable through other methods (Quinn 2005).

A first source of data came from what a diverse range of district educational stakeholders (including school district administrators, school board members, school staff, parents, and community leaders) *say* about demographic change; the conditions, such as racial inequities, they confront in their work; the policies they adopt; and the decision-making processes behind these policies. I conducted semi-structured interviews with thirty-seven current and former Milltown and Fairview school district policy makers. They included former and current school board members (eight in Milltown and seven in Fairview); former and current superintendents (two in each district); other members of the superintendent's leadership teams, including assistant superintendents and directors of central office divisions such as curriculum, public relations, and special education (eleven in Milltown and nine in Fairview); and frontline administrators (six in Milltown and six in Fairview).

I consider the districts to be predominantly (Fairview) or entirely

(Milltown) white-led districts. However, I did not ask the respondents directly about their racial identifications. In the course of interviews, two Fairview respondents (12 percent) identified as persons of color, five (29 percent) identified as white, and ten (59 percent) offered no racial or ethnic identification. In Milltown, 40 percent of district policy makers indicated that they were white, and 60 percent offered no racial or ethnic identification. None explicitly identified as people of color. By the nature of their professional positions and educational backgrounds, I considered all school district participants to be middle-class or upper-middle-class.

Although these individuals' perspectives were not the focus of the study, I also interviewed nine school staff or community leaders with the purpose of gaining background on the cities and how the school systems fit into them, and the perspectives of people of color who had been involved in them. In Milltown, this included four advocates from communities of color and four school site staff members. In Fairview I interviewed eight community leaders or staff members, including three advocates from communities of color, and one school site staff member.

School-level staff, as well as students and parents, might have offered different views of how the schools were responding to demographic change, and different understandings of the effects of the policies and practices described here.[1] However, several excellent studies have already been conducted examining school leaders' roles in responding to demographic change or inequity in schools (e.g., Evans 2007b; Lewis and Diamond 2015). In this study, I was interested in "studying up" (Nader 1969). Due to my focus on understanding district-level sense making and response, and also the practical limits of data collection across two districts in different parts of the state, I did not attempt to widely interview school site staff or students and families.

A second source of data was the observations I conducted in school district board meetings, central office staff meetings, and public forums concerning what people, particularly school leaders, *do* to address demographic change, and how they reconcile tensions, respond to evidence of inequities, and prioritize work. I observed 107 hours of central office meetings, school board meetings, and public hearings, including events focused on marketing and data use as well as enrollment issues and curriculum and education for English learners.

A third source of data was more than 270 documentary materials such as newspaper reports, opinion pieces, blog posts, meeting agendas, school board minutes, marketing materials, school improvement plans, and district- or community-produced reports, as well as other artifacts that district leaders, school staff, families, and community leaders produced, used, referenced, and circulated in relation to policies responding to demographic change.

Finally, at the moment of site selection and as the study progressed in the years after the ethnographic data was collected, I expanded my research into the broader social, political, and economic contexts of the school districts. In addition to secondary sources, I searched out additional documents and data to develop and enrich that analysis. I assembled data on demographic change though decennial reports of the US Census and the three- to five-year estimates from the American Community Survey, school enrollment data from the Wisconsin Department of Public Instruction (DPI), local newspaper reports, reports from the UW–Madison Applied Population Lab, and community studies to describe the demographic changes underway in both districts. I used employment and unemployment data from the Bureau of Labor Statistics, median household income from the American Community Survey, local community reports, and homelessness data from DPI to capture economic conditions. I also drew from newspaper reporting, local laws, and election results to capture political attitudes or orientations in these communities.

I wrote analytic memos to capture insights and questions and to develop concepts and higher-level analysis while sticking close to the data (Corbin and Strauss 2008). Early reflection and preliminary data analysis were particularly valuable in developing two aspects of my study. First, through attending to and reflecting on the policies district leaders talked about, I could begin to identify and collect additional data on the focal policies related to demographic change in each district. In this way, I was able to enter my sites asking how districts construct the issues and challenges related to demographic change, rather than assuming that particular policies were the most important ones to follow. But I was also able to focus my data collection by paying attention to the policy responses district leaders most frequently mentioned in interviews and observations. Second, I began interviews by asking participants to define and characterize demographic changes in their own terms. I quickly noticed that rather than talking about "immigrants," the participants spoke of homelessness and the arrival of African Americans. It was clear that I needed to ground my inquiry by examining how school district and community members constructed and experienced the demographic changes going on in their districts.

I developed a code book from my original conceptual framework and the existing literature, and added inductively developed codes through my subsequent analysis. Then I systematically coded interview and observational data using NVivo 8 qualitative data analysis software, and a code book based on research, theory, and codes developed inductively through the method of constant comparison (Corbin and Strauss 2008). I constructed data displays (Miles and Huberman 1994) of participants' framing of demographic change, problems, and policy responses in order to analyze how they related these to each other. I examined this data for patterns, comparisons across districts, and disconfirming evidence.

Based on this analysis, I identified key ways of framing demographic change and the issues surrounding it (e.g., context, problems, policy responses, and educational goals) and traced the consequent policy trajectories and district decision making to show the ways in which performance monitoring and marketing strategies came about; the actors, messages, arguments, and debates that shaped policy over time; and the consequences of these issue frames on existing racial inequities in each district.

In presenting my data and findings here, I do not claim that the Milltown and Fairview districts are average, or that their experiences will be shared in every site. However, in shedding light on how these district leaders made sense of and responded to the changes occurring in their school districts, these particular cases embrace a degree of commonality (Erickson 1986, p. 130) and provide opportunities to reflect on and theorize the broader social, political, and economic trends in the Midwest and other places; the ways in which schools respond to these shifts, and the persistence of racial inequity under these conditions.

Acknowledgments

This book would not have been possible without the gracious participation of school district administrators, school board trustees, community members, and school staff in Milltown and Fairview. I thank all the people who took the time to speak with me and help me understand their work, their challenges, and their school systems. Everyone I met gave countless hours of their lives to serve children in the best way they knew how.

The work of many brilliant scholars at the University of California, Berkeley, has inspired this book: Cynthia Coburn, Margaret Weir, Dan Perlstein, Rick Mintrop, and Judith Warren-Little. They asked me good questions, gave me good answers, and have always offered impeccable advice.

I also wish to thank my colleagues at the University of Wisconsin who have offered support and inspiring scholarship. I thank Michael Fultz, Lesley Bartlett, Walter Stern, Michael Apple, Adam Nelson, Bill Reese, Gloria Ladson-Billings, Art Rainwater, and Diana Hess. Special appreciation goes to Nancy Kendall, Stacey Lee, and John Diamond, who read full drafts and provided guidance in the publishing process. For feedback and support in all ways big and small, I thank my colleagues and friends Linn Posey-Maddox, Bianca Baldridge, and Kathryn Moeller.

Writing can be a lonely process, but I have been fortunate to be a part of an amazing community of writers and academics. Whether for just a few weeks or over many years, I have greatly benefited from the companionship and wisdom of many brilliant and generous Black women scholars at the University of Wisconsin: Monica White (who helped me keep my eyes on the prize in Milwaukee), Linn Posey-Maddox, Christy Clark-Pujara, Rachelle Winkle-Wagner, Cherene Sherrod, Ethelene Whitmire,

Erica Bullock, Maxine McKinney de Royston, Bianca Baldridge, and Feneba Addo. Mindi Thompson invited me to my first writing group; I have been working with writing groups ever since.

This book has also benefited from the helpful feedback and insights of Angeline Spain, Elizabeth Blair, Nicole Breazeale, Rebecca Lowenhaupt, Willow Sussex, Laura Dresser, Kathy Cramer, and Carrie Sampson. Conversations with Tina Trujillo, Jeff Henig, Gary Anderson, Julie Marsh, Taylor Albright, Alison Mattheis, Lisa Dorner, Jenny Seelig, Maia Cucchiara, and Janelle Scott, as well as participants of the 2017 NAEd/Spencer Fall Retreat and comments from several anonymous reviewers, have also shaped my thinking about this project.

I am incredibly appreciative to the graduate students who have given their time and thought to this book. Lena Batt, Caitlin Brecklin, and Abby Beneke all helped with background research. I am especially grateful to Eleni Schirmer and Mai Neng Vang for their substantive feedback and editorial assistance. Their efforts have made this a better book.

For sharing their expertise in writing and publishing, I thank Cecelia Cancellaro, Judy Bridges, and especially Christopher Lura, whose many examples and kind guidance helped me at a critical time. Renaldo Migaldi offered expert editorial expertise. This *really* would not have been a book without Elizabeth Branch Dyson, whose books I have long admired, and who thought the project was interesting and never looked back.

The shortcomings remain my own.

Good meals, good discussions, good advice, and good laughs with good friends have sustained me over the years. In addition to those folks already listed above, I thank Leina Yamamoto, Andy Green, Ben Statz, Liz Blair and Dave Plante, Ila and Nate Deshmukh-Towery, Maiah Jaskoski, and John Kaltenstein. In my undergraduate years and in graduate school and beyond, a few folks reached out with kindness, enriched my learning and development as a scholar, showed me the generosity of academia, and have remained friends and mentors: Lisa Smulyan, Ariana Mangual Figueroa, Soung Bae, Jennifer Russell, Kenzo Sung, Rebecca Lowenhaupt, and Angeline Spain. Even when I did not want to reflect on my challenges and good fortune or take time to relax in the company of old friends, Nicole Breazeale, Casey Hanson, Chloe Dowley, Elisa Nigrini, Mandara Meyers, Elizabeth Blair, and Andrea Meller made me do it every single year for the last twenty, and I'm glad they did. My Milwaukee crew—Anne Getzin and Chris Burns, Kjersti Knox and Garrett Bucks, Emily Yu and Seth Bodden—offered friendship and food through the many years of this project, and new Madison friends and neighbors brought the champagne to celebrate when this was done.

Beth Tarasawa, Pamela Mather, and Daniel Mather offered shelter during research and writing. Terri Gifford came into our lives like Mary Poppins and made it possible for me to work in one city, live in another, and do research in a third while also raising two small children.

Chuck and Kathy Turner unknowingly started me on this path many years ago. My father, as a city planner and leader of a community-based organization, and my mother, as an advocate of public education and civil rights, were my first teachers of cities, schools, and social justice. Thank you to Christine Turner, Scott Sasso, and Carlito Turner for the moments of insight through the years and for being creative and inspiring in your own work, and to Angie Schiavoni, Sep Kamvar, Dario Kamvar and Vera Kamvar, and Claire Grimmet for being family. There are no more supportive in-laws than Mary Jo Schiavoni and Jim Sturm. Dante and Rocco Turner Sturm, with curious minds and loving hearts, made this work all the more meaningful.

Finally, I thank Tony Sturm. All I can say is: A true partner for more than half my life, he has been at my side from the start to the finish of this process, offering unconditional love, unwavering support, and occasionally some copyediting. I have much for which to be grateful.

* * *

The original work on which book is based was supported by the Mellon Mays Graduate Initiative Fund, the State Farm Companies Foundation, and the Dean's Normative Time Fund at the Graduate School of Education, University of California, Berkeley. The further development of the book into what it is today was made possible by an Anna Julia Cooper Postdoctoral Fellowship from the University of Wisconsin–Madison, the Department of Educational Policy Studies at the University of Wisconsin–Madison, the Wisconsin Center for Educational Research, the Wisconsin Alumni Research Foundation, a Vilas Lifecycle Professorship, and a 2017 National Academy of Education/Spencer Postdoctoral Fellowship.

Notes

Introduction

1. All names of people, districts, cities, and organizations given here are pseudonyms. I use the real names of state- and federal-level politicians. In previous scholarship I have used a different pseudonym for Milltown. I use the name "Milltown" here to clarify the distinction between the two study sites, and to avoid confusion that came from the previously similar-sounding district pseudonyms.

2. The term "Hispanic" was commonly used by study participants, and I retain that usage in quoting them. In my own writing, however, I use the term "Latinx" rather than "Hispanic," which denotes origins in Spain and is offensive to many people whose ancestors were colonized by the Spanish. "Latinx" refers to someone with origins or connection to Latin America, and is a more recently adopted gender-neutral alternative to "Latino."

3. The meanings we hold and the words we choose matter. As this book shows, the language we use is important because it shapes how we understand our world, reflects power relations in society, and can obscure what is really happening. For this reason, I have tried to use antiracist language throughout the book. For example, when possible I use the preferred terms of racially minoritized groups. I often describe the school districts as "racially diverse and unequal" to indicate that the school districts were attempting to serve students privileged by racism as well as those oppressed by it, and to serve students living in poverty as well as those whose families held substantial wealth. In both cases I want to recognize that underlying racial diversity and poverty are power dynamics that cannot be ignored. The language of "inequality" rather than "poverty" signals this underlying power relation.

4. This is the espoused ethos; however, the term "public" has historically excluded women and people of color in the United States, and it continues to do so.

Chapter One

1. Though it might be celebrated or framed as an example of the United States becoming more welcoming or inclusive of the Global South, the unprecedented growth in immigration from Asia, as well as from Africa and South America, was in fact an outcome that the bill's sponsors had neither anticipated nor intended (Ngai 2004).

2. The bracero program highlights the long history of Mexico-to-US migration to serve US labor needs, a history that extends back to before the 1900s. The end of the bracero program followed about a decade of efforts by the Department of Labor to tighten labor protections and address concerns that the bracero program harmed US farmworkers. These moves made the program less financially lucrative for employers, and led to its decline (Bracero Program 2003).

3. Though such comments were less common in Milltown, I found that white residents there made similar statements about African American migration to their city; see, for example, chapter 2. In research on the "welfare magnet" claim, Corbett (1991) reviewed evidence specifically about Wisconsin, pointing to the lack of evidence that welfare benefits affect migration decisions, and findings that were mixed at best. The economists Philip Levine and David Zimmerman (1999) and James Walker (1994) later took different approaches to investigating the "welfare magnet" hypothesis, but came to similar conclusions. Poor female-headed households tend to migrate to places with more jobs, mirroring overall migration trends (Schram and Krueger 1994) and women most likely to be welfare candidates were no more likely to move from states that offer low benefits than were other poor women who were not candidates for welfare (i.e., the Aid to Families with Dependent Children program; Levine and Zimmerman 1999). The welfare-magnet argument, then, is more likely to reflect racialized stereotypes than evidence. As Walker (1994) wrote: "The longevity of this issue in public debates owes more to voter perceptions than to migration flows observable in the census" (p. 48).

4. Given the national depression of wages amid increased productivity, even keeping pace with the national average would reflect a decline (Bivens et al. 2014).

5. Based on 2005–9 five-year estimates of poverty status for families in the past twelve months, from the American Community Survey.

6. It is interesting to note that the Earned Income Tax Credit is an antipoverty program in the form of a tax credit, and the ACA is a health care program in the form of a controlled market-based system. So both programs do take market-based forms. It is also of note that the ACA has already seen some rollback of its provisions.

7. In 2010, for example, a report from the Council on Foreign Relations, au-

thored by former New York Schools Chancellor Joel Klein and former Secretary of State Condoleezza Rice, echoed *A Nation at Risk*, claiming that the schools were widely seen as failing, while noting achievement gaps, improving but low graduation rates, and business' struggle to find qualified employees (Klein and Rice 2010).

8. Specifically, QEO allowed a school district to avoid arbitration with a teachers' union over compensation disputes, so long as it made a "qualified economic offer" to the teachers' union. An offer was considered a QEO if it provided for a combined 3.8 percent increase in salary and benefit costs over the previous year (made up of an at least 1.7 percent increase in benefit costs and at least a 2.1 percent increase in wages, including step increases for length of service) (Lund and Maranto 1996).

9. The revenue caps, originally only passed for a five-year time period, were made permanent in 1995 (Kava and Olin 2005).

10. Austerity politics in Wisconsin has been a bipartisan effort. Walker's proposals were of a greater magnitude, but not substantively different from what Democrats had been carrying out in the state. For example, Governor Jim Doyle, Walker's Democratic predecessor, had issued cost controls on public sector employees and corporate tax cuts (Davidoff 2010; Kertscher 2011).

Chapter Two

1. Terms like "inner city" or "ghetto," like the word "urban," are often used in pejorative ways, as described in this chapter. For that reason, I only include this language when quoting from individuals or in scare quotes, as a way to indicate that common meanings associated with that language should be questioned rather than taken for granted.

2. City residents and school district staff frequently positioned minoritized groups as additions to a white, middle-class norm in their cities.

Chapter Four

1. Net open enrollment loss was approximately 1.7 percent of the student body in Fairview, and approximately 3.11 percent of the student body in Milltown.

2. Data existed on the racial identification of transfers. For example, state reports on the open enrollment program indicated that white families were most likely to use the program (Cleaver and Eagleburger 2007; Kava 2011). At the time of the study, however, district leaders did not report this data or report having it, and I was not able to obtain it, so I cannot be certain whether they knew

the racial breakdown of those transferring from the district, or if they were infer-ring this based on other information or assumptions. Either way, they expressed their beliefs with certainty.

3. Given the small overall number of transfers relative to total student enroll-ment, it is unlikely that transfers greatly shifted the demographic composition of the Milltown and Fairview districts between 2004 and 2009. Open enrollment may have contributed to declining percentages of white students in each city to some degree, but the overall picture is more likely related to declining birth rates of white populations, the growth of the suburbs and movement of white families (who on average were more likely to be able to afford to move), the in-migration of families of color, and the higher birth rate for women of color.

4. There was some variation in the demographics of the neighboring school districts in Milltown and Fairview counties, but nonetheless, *every single* neigh-boring school district was less racially diverse, more economically advantaged, and less likely to serve English learners than were their city counterparts. Ac-cording to the Wisconsin Information System for Education Data Dashboard, all seven of the other school districts in Milltown County were substantially less diverse than Milltown (ranging from 84 to 95 percent white in the neighboring districts) and substantially less economically disadvantaged (ranging from 9 to 21 percent economically disadvantaged in the neighboring districts), and served substantially smaller percentages of English learners (ranging from 1 to 3 per-cent English learners in the neighboring districts). In Fairview the fifteen neigh-boring districts were more varied, but were still all less racially diverse (ranging from 72 to 95 percent white in the neighboring districts) and more economically advantaged (ranging from 7 to 26 percent economically disadvantaged in the neighboring districts), and served smaller percentages of English learners (rang-ing from 0 to 13 percent in the neighboring districts).

Conclusion

1. Recent examples of books that might be useful for this exercise include Castagno (2014) and Cucchiara (2013) at the school and district level. Also at the school level, see Lewis and Diamond (2015). For community-based spaces, see Baldridge (2019). These books do not use the language of contradictions, but they offer examples, analysis, and many important insights for discussion.

2. The language of equity audits is now fairly common in the field of edu-cational leadership, so I use it here with caveats. In doing so, I hope to make it recognizable to scholars and practitioners in that field. However, the language of audits is problematic, both because such language—echoing the high-stakes accountability movement—now carries negative associations for many educat-

ors, and because spread of the language itself can contribute legitimacy to the broader "audit" culture in the United States. However, as Strathern (2000) argues, audit cultures are always being made. My hope is that a community-involved form of equity audit, as I describe here, will contribute to a new kind of audit culture.

3. Data processes and interventions do not operate on their own. They must be put into practice by people. The ways in which data use is enacted may differ from the imagined ideal. An equity audit process might easily become something more like a high-stakes monitoring process. See Coburn and Turner (2011, 2012) for additional reviews and conceptualizations of work on data *use*.

Methodological Appendix

1. And some of the community and district respondents were parents.

References

Adams, D. W. 1995. *Education for Extinction: American Indians and the Boarding School Experience, 1875–1928*, 3rd ed. Lawrence: University Press of Kansas.

Alemán, E. 2007. "Situating Texas School Finance Policy in a CRT Framework: How 'Substantially Equal' Yields Racial Inequity." *Educational Administration Quarterly* 43(5), 525–58. https://doi.org/10.1177/0013161X07303276.

Alemán, E., Jr., and S. M. Alemán. 2010. "'Do Latin@ Interests Always Have to "Converge" with White Interests?' (Re)claiming Racial Realism and Interest-Convergence in Critical Race Theory Praxis." *Race Ethnicity and Education* 13(1), 1–21. https://doi.org/10.1080/13613320903549644.

Anderson, G. L. 2009. *Advocacy Leadership: Toward a Post-Reform Agenda in Education*. New York: Routledge. Retrieved from http://site.ebrary.com/id/10282389.

Anderson, G. L., and K. Herr. 2015. "New Public Management and the New Professionalism in Education: Framing the Issue." Education Policy Analysis Archives, 23, 84. https://doi.org/10.14507/epaa.v23.2222.

Anyon, J. 1997. *Ghetto Schooling: A Political Economy of Urban Educational Reform*. New York: Teachers College Press.

———. 2005a. *Radical Possibilities: Public Policy, Urban Education, and a New Social Movement*. New York: Routledge.

———. 2005b. "What 'counts' as Educational Policy? Notes toward a New Paradigm." *Harvard Educational Review* 75(1), 65–88.

Apple, M. W. 2005. "Audit Cultures, Commodification, and Class and Race Strategies in Education." *Policy Futures in Education* 3(4), 379–99. https://doi.org/10.2304/pfie.2005.3.4.378.

———. 2006. *Educating the Right Way: Markets, Standards, God, and Inequality*. New York: Routledge.

Applied Population Lab. 2007, December. "A Look at Wisconsin's Foreign Born Population Through Time." *Population Notes* 2, 1–3.

Au, W. 2007. "High-Stakes Testing and Curricular Control: A Qualitative Meta-synthesis." *Educational Researcher* 36(5), 258–67. https://doi.org/10.3102/0013189X07306523.

———. 2009a. "High-Stakes Testing and Discursive Control: The Triple Bind for Non-Standard Student Identities." *Multicultural Perspectives* 11(2), 65–71.

———. 2009b. *Unequal by Design: High-Stakes Testing and the Standardization of Inequality*. New York : London: Routledge.

———. 2016. "Meritocracy 2.0: High-Stakes, Standardized Testing as a Racial Project of Neoliberal Multiculturalism." *Educational Policy* 30(1), 39–62. https://doi.org/10.1177/0895904815614916.

Baldridge, B. J. 2014. "Relocating the Deficit: Reimagining Black Youth in Neoliberal Times." *American Educational Research Journal* 51(3), 440–72. https://doi.org/10.3102/0002831214532514.

———. 2019. *Reclaiming Community: Race, Politics, and the Uncertain Future of Youth Work*. Stanford, CA: Stanford University Press.

Beauregard, R. A. 2002. *Voices of Decline: The Postwar Fate of US Cities*, 2nd ed. New York: Routledge.

Bell, D. A. 1980. "Comment: Brown v. Board of Education and the Interest-Convergence Dilemma." *Harvard Law Review* 93(3), 518.

Berkman, M. B., and E. Plutzer. 2005. *Ten Thousand Democracies: Politics and Public Opinion in America's School Districts*. Washington: Georgetown University Press.

Berliner, D. C. 2013. "Effects of Inequality and Poverty vs. Teachers and Schooling on America's Youth. *Teachers College Record* 115(12), 1–26.

Berliner, D. C., and B. J. Biddle. 1995. *The Manufactured Crisis: Myths, Fraud, and the Attack on America's Public Schools*. Reading, MA: Basic Books.

Berrey, E. C. 2005. "Divided over Diversity: Political Discourse in a Chicago Neighborhood." *City & Community* 4(2), 143–170. https://doi.org/10.1111/j .1540-6040.2005.00109.

Bezruki, D., D. Varana, M. Gustafson, J. Lathrup, and R. Sommerfeld. 2002. *An Evaluation: Open Enrollment Program*. Madison: Wisconsin Legislative Audit Bureau.

Bieder, R. E. 1995. *Native American Communities in Wisconsin 1600–1960: A Study of Tradition and Change*. Madison: University of Wisconsin Press.

Binder, A. J. 2002. *Contentious Curricula: Afrocentrism and Creationism in American Public Schools*. Princeton, NJ: Princeton University Press.

Bivens, J., E. Gould, L. R. Mishel, and H. Shierholz. 2014. "Raising America's Pay: Why It's Our Central Economic Policy Challenge." Economic Policy Institute. Retrieved from https://www.epi.org/publication/raising-americas -pay/.

Blackmore, J. 2006. "Deconstructing Diversity Discourses in the Field of Educational Management and Leadership." *Educational Management Administration & Leadership* 34(2), 181–99.

Blount, J. 2005. "Educational Leadership through Equity, Diversity, and Social Justice and Educational Leadership for the Privilege Imperative: The Historical Dialectic." In L. C. Tillman and J. J. Scheurich, eds., *Handbook of Research on Educational Leadership for Equity and Diversity*, pp. 7–21. New York: Routledge.

Bonilla-Silva, E. 2003. *Racism without Racists: Color-Blind Racism and the Persistence of Racial Inequality in the United States.* New York: Rowman & Littlefield.

Booher-Jennings, J. 2005. "Below the Bubble: "Educational Triage" and the Texas Accountability System." *American Educational Research Journal* 42(2), 231–68.

Boris, E., and J. Klein. 2012. *Caring for America: Home Health Workers in the Shadow of the Welfare State.* New York: Oxford University Press.

Boustan, L. 2017. "The Culprits behind White Flight." *New York Times*, May 15. Retrieved from https://www.nytimes.com/2017/05/15/opinion/white-flight .html.

Boyd, W. L. 1976. "The Public, the Professionals, and Educational Policy Making: Who Governs?" *Teachers College Record* 77(4), 539–78.

———. 2003. "Public Education's Crisis of Performance and Legitimacy: Introduction and Overview of the Yearbook." In W. L. Boyd and D. Miretzky, eds., *American Educational Governance on Trial: Change and Challenges*, pp. 1–19. Chicago: University of Chicago Press.

Bracero Program. 2003. *Rural Migration News* 9(2). Retrieved from https:// migration.ucdavis.edu/rmn/more.php?id=10.

Buendía, E., N. Ares, B. G. Juarez, and M. Peercy. 2004. "The Geographies of Difference: The Production of the East Side, West Side, and Central City School." *American Educational Research Journal* 41(4), 833–63.

Burch, P. 2009. *Hidden Markets: The New Education Privatization.* New York: Routledge.

Burke, M. A. 2017. "Racing Left and Right: Color-Blind Racism's Dominance across the US Political Spectrum." *Sociological Quarterly* 58(2), 277–94. https://doi.org/10.1080/00380253.2017.1296335.

Capper, C. A. 2015. "The 20th-Year Anniversary of Critical Race Theory in Education: Implications for Leading to Eliminate Racism." *Educational Administration Quarterly* 51(5), 791–833.

Capper, C. A., and M. D. Young. 2015. "The Equity Audit as the Core of Leading Increasingly Diverse Schools and Districts." In G. Theoharis and M. Scanlan, eds., *Leadership for Increasingly Diverse Schools*, pp. 186–97. New York: Routledge.

Carlson, D., G. D. Borman, and M. Robinson 2011. "A Multistate District-Level Cluster Randomized Trial of the Impact of Data-Driven Reform on Reading and Mathematics Achievement." *Educational Evaluation and Policy Analysis* 33(3), 378–98. https://doi.org/10.3102/0162373711412765.

Carr, N. 2006. "Courting the Middle Class: What Can Schools Do to Keep Parents from Going Private, or Moving to the Suburbs?" *American School Board Journal* 193(12), 46–49.

———. 2011. *Telling Your Story: A Toolkit for Marketing Urban Education.* Alexandria, VA: National School Boards Association Council of Urban Boards of Education. Retrieved from http://nvasb.org/assets/telling_your_story2.pdf.

Carter, P. L., and K. G. Welner, K. G. 2013. *Closing the Opportunity Gap: What America Must Do to Give Every Child an Even Chance.* New York: Oxford University Press.

Castagno, A. E. 2014. *Educated in Whiteness: Good Intentions and Diversity in Schools.* Minneapolis: University of Minnesota Press.

———. 2017. "Liberal Ideologies and Federal School Reform: Following Individualism, Meliorism, and Neutrality through SIG Policy to Adelante Alternative School." *Urban Education*: 0042085916685762.

Chubb, J. E., and T. M. Moe. 1990. *Politics, Markets, and America's Schools.* Washington: Brookings Institution.

Clarke, J., and J. Newman. 1997. *The Managerial State: Power, Politics and Ideology in the Remaking of Social Welfare.* Thousand Oaks, CA: SAGE Publications.

Clarke, S. E., R. Hero, M. S. Sidney, L. R. Fraga, and B. A. Erlichson. 2006. *Multiethnic Moments: The Politics of Urban Education Reform.* Philadelphia: Temple University Press.

Clark-Pujara, C. 2017. "Contested: Black Suffrage in Early Wisconsin." *Wisconsin Magazine of History*, 21–27.

Cleaver, M., and S. Eagleburger. 2007. *The Wisconsin Inter-District Public School Open Enrollment Program, 2003–04 and 2004–05.* Madison: Division of Finance and Management, Wisconsin.

Coburn, C. E., S. Bae, and E. O. Turner. 2008. "Authority, Status, and the Dynamics of Insider–Outsider Partnerships at the District Level." *Peabody Journal of Education* 83(3), 364–99. https://doi.org/10.1080/01619560802222350.

Coburn, C. E., J. Toure, and M. Yamashita. 2009. "Evidence, Interpretation, and Persuasion: Instructional Decision Making at the District Central Office." *Teachers College Record* 111(4), 1115–61.

Coburn, C. E., and E. O. Turner. 2011. "Research on Data Use: A Framework and Analysis." *Measurement* 9(4), 173–206. https://doi.org/10.1080/15366367.2011.626729.

———. 2012. "The Practice of Data Use: An Introduction." *American Journal of Education* 118(2), 99–111.

Cole, T. 2012. "The White-Savior Industrial Complex." *Atlantic*, March 21. Retrieved from https://www.theatlantic.com/international/archive/2012/03/the-white-savior-industrial-complex/254843/.

Collins, J. L., and V. Mayer. 2010. *Both Hands Tied: Welfare Reform and the Race to the Bottom in the Low-Wage Labor Market.* Chicago: University Of Chicago Press.

Committee on Incentives and Test-based Accountability in Public Education. 2011. *Incentives and Test-Based Accountability in Public Education,* M. Hout and S. W. Elliot, eds.). Washington: National Academies Press. Retrieved from https://ebookcentral.proquest.com/lib/wisc/detail.action?docID=3378909.

Conley, D. 2010. *Being Black, Living in the Red: Race, Wealth, and Social Policy in America,* 2nd ed. Berkeley: University of California Press.

Cooper, C. W. 2009. "Performing Cultural Work in Demographically Changing Schools: Implications for Expanding Transformative Leadership Frameworks." *Educational Administration Quarterly* 45(5), 694–724. https://doi.org/10.1177/0013161X09341639.

Corbett, T. 1991. "The Wisconsin Welfare Magnet Debate: What Is an Ordinary Member of the Tribe to Do When the Witch Doctors Disagree?" *Focus* 13(3), 19–27.

Corbin, J., and A. L. Strauss. 2008. *Basics of Qualitative Research: Techniques and Procedures for Developing Grounded Theory.* Thousand Oaks, CA: Sage.

Cramer, K. J. 2016. *The Politics of Resentment: Rural Consciousness in Wisconsin and the Rise of Scott Walker.* Chicago: University of Chicago Press.

Cucchiara, M. 2008. "Re-Branding Urban Schools: Urban Revitalization, Social Status, and Marketing Public Schools to the Upper Middle Class." *Journal of Education Policy* 23(2), 165–79. https://doi.org/10.1080/02680930701853088.

———. 2013. *Marketing Schools, Marketing Cities: Who Wins and Who Loses When Schools Become Urban Amenities.* Chicago: University of Chicago Press.

Cucchiara, M., E. Gold, and E. Simon. 2011. "Contracts, Choice, and Customer Service: Marketization and Public Engagement in Education." *Teachers College Record* 113(11), 2460–2502.

Curtis, K. J., and S. E. Lessem. 2014. *2010 Census Chartbook: Demographic Trends in Wisconsin.* Madison: Board of Regents of the University of Wisconsin. Retrieved from https://apl.wisc.edu/publications/2010_census_chartbook_wi.pdf.

Darling-Hammond, L. 2010. "Doing What Matters Most: Developing Competent Teaching." In L. Darling-Hammond and R. Rothman, eds., *Teaching in the Flat World: Learning from High-Performing Systems.* New York: Teachers College Press.

Davidoff, J. 2010. "Jim Doyle's Final Report Card." *Capitol Times*, October 13. Retrieved from https://madison.com/ct/news/local/govt-and
-politics/jim-doyle-s-final-report-card/article_0c7079a6-d642-11df-9ccd
-001cc4c03286.html.

Davis, B. W., M. A. Gooden, and D. J. Micheaux. 2015. "Color-Blind Leadership: A Critical Race Theory Analysis of the ISLLC and ELCC Standards." *Educational Administration Quarterly* 51(3), 335–71.

DeBray, E. H. 2006. *Politics, Ideology, and Education*. New York: Teachers College Press.

Delgado, R., and J. Stefancic. 2001. *Critical Race Theory: An Introduction*. New York: NYU Press.

Dentler, R. A., and A. L. Hafner. 1997. *Hosting Newcomers: Structuring Educational Opportunities for Immigrant Children*. New York: Teachers College Press.

Deschenes, S., L. Cuban, and D. Tyack. 2001. "Mismatch: Historical Perspectives on Schools and Students Who Don't Fit Them." *Teachers College Record* 103(4), 525–47.

Diamond, J. B. 2007. "Where the Rubber Meets the Road: Rethinking the Connection Between High-Stakes Testing Policy and Classroom Instruction." *Sociology of Education* 80(4), 285–313.

———. 2018. "Race and White Supremacy in the Sociology of Education: Shifting the Intellectual Gaze." In J. Mehta and S. Davies, eds. *Education in a New Society: Renewing the Sociology of Education*. Chicago: University of Chicago Press.

Diamond, J. B., and J. P. Spillane. 2004. "High-stakes Accountability in Urban Elementary Schools: Challenging or Reproducing Inequality?" *Teachers College Record* 106(6), 1145–76.

DiAngelo, R. 2011. "White Fragility." *International Journal of Critical Pedagogy* 3(3).

Diem, S., E. Frankenberg, C. Cleary, and N. Ali. 2014. "The Politics of Maintaining Diversity Policies in Demographically Changing Urban-Suburban School Districts." *American Journal of Education* 120(3), 351–89. https://doi
.org/10.1086/675532.

DiMartino, C., and S. B. Jessen. 2016. "School Brand Management: The Policies, Practices, and Perceptions of Branding and Marketing in New York City's Public High Schools." *Urban Education* 51(5), 447–475. https://doi
.org/10.1177/0042085914543112.

———. 2018. *Selling School: The Marketing of Public Education*. New York: Teachers College Press.

Dorner, L. 2015. "From Global Jobs to Safe Spaces: The Diverse Discourses that Sell Multilingual Schooling in the USA." *Current Issues in Language Planning* 16(1–2), 114–31.

Dresser, L. and J. S. Rodriguez. 2017. *Wisconsin's Extreme Racial Disparity: Vast Chasm Separates Whites and African Americans in the State*. Madison, WI: COWS, University of Wisconsin–Madison. Retrieved from https://www.cows.org/_data/documents/1816.pdf.

Edsall, T. B., and M. D. Edsall. 1991. *Chain Reaction: The Impact of Race, Rights, and Taxes on American Politics*. New York: W. W. Norton.

Education Commission of the States. 2017. "Open Enrollment: 50-State Report." Retrieved from http://ecs.force.com/mbdata/MBQuestNB2n?rep=OE1701.

Engel, E., and S. Longworth. 2012. *Industrial Cities Initiatives*. Chicago: Federal Reserve Bank of Chicago.

Erickson, F. 1986. "Qualitative Methods in Research on Teaching." In M. C. Wittrock, ed., *Handbook of Research on Teaching*. New York: Macmillan.

Espeland, W. N., and M. Sauder. 2007. "Rankings and Reactivity: How Public Measures Recreate Social Worlds." *American Journal of Sociology* 113(1), 1–40.

Evans, A. E. 2007. "School Leaders and Their Sensemaking about Race and Demographic Change." *Educational Administration Quarterly* 43(2), 159–88.

Ewing, E. L. 2018. *Ghosts in the Schoolyard: Racism and School Closings on Chicago's South Side*. Chicago: University of Chicago Press.

Fink, D. 1998. *Cutting into the Meatpacking Line: Workers and Change in the Rural Midwest*. Chapel Hill: University of North Carolina Press.

Fischer, C. S., and M. Hout. 2006. *Century of Difference: How America Changed in the Last One Hundred Years*. New York: Russell Sage Foundation.

Flores, N. 2016. "A Tale of Two Visions: Hegemonic Whiteness and Bilingual Education." *Educational Policy* 30(1), 13–38.

Frankenberg, E., and G. Orfield, eds. 2012. *The Resegregation of Suburban Schools: A Hidden Crisis in American Education*. Cambridge, MA: Harvard Education Press.

Frey, W. H. 2014. Diversity Explosion: *How New Racial Demographics Are Remaking America*. Washington: Brookings Institution Press.

Galloway, M. K., and A. M. Ishimaru. 2017. "Equitable Leadership on the Ground: Converging on High-Leverage Practices." *Education Policy Analysis Archives* 25(2). http://dx.doi.org/10.14507/epaa.24.2205.

Gamson, D. A., and E. M. Hodge. 2016. *The Shifting Landscape of the American School District: Race, Class, Geography, and the Perpetual Reform of Local Control, 1935–2015*. New York: Peter Lang.

Gewirtz, S. 2002. *The Managerial School: Post-Welfarism and Social Justice in Education*. London: Routledge.

Glickman, L. B. 2018. "The Racist Politics of the English Language." *Boston Review*, November 26. Retrieved from http://bostonreview.net/race/lawrence-glickman-racially-tinged.

Goldstein, A. 2018. *Janesville: An American Story*. New York: Simon and Schuster.

Goldstein, D. 2014. *The Teacher Wars: A History of America's Most Embattled Profession.* New York: Doubleday.

Gonzales, R. G. 2015. *Lives in Limbo: Undocumented and Coming of Age in America.* Berkeley: University of California Press.

Green, T. L. 2017. "Community-Based Equity Audits: A Practical Approach for Educational Leaders to Support Equitable Community-School Improvements." *Educational Administration Quarterly* 53(1), 3–39.

Grubb, W. N., and M. Lazerson. 2004. *The Education Gospel: The Economic Power of Schooling.* Cambridge, MA: Harvard University Press.

Hacker, J. S. 2006. *The Great Risk Shift: The New Economic Insecurity and the Decline of the American Dream.* Oxford, UK: Oxford University Press.

Hall, A. 2007. "Schools and Fiscal Angst; on the Question of School Funding in Wisconsin, There Is an Increased Sense of Urgency. *Wisconsin State Journal,* January 30, p. 1A.

Hamann, E. T. 2003. *The Educational Welcome of Latinos in the New South.* Westport, CT: Praeger.

Harris, C. I. 1995. "Whiteness as Property." In K. Crenshaw, N. Gotanda, G. Peller, and K. Thomas, eds., *Critical Race Theory: The Key Writings That Formed the Movement,* pp. 276–91. New York: The New Press.

Harrison, J. L., and S. E. Lloyd. 2013. "New Jobs, New Workers, and New Inequalities: Explaining Employers' Roles in Occupational Segregation by Nativity and Race." *Social Problems* 60(3), 281–301. https://doi.org/10.1525/sp .2013.60.3.281.

Henig, J. R. 1995. *Rethinking School Choice: Limits of the Market Metaphor.* Princeton, NJ: Princeton University Press.

——. 2009. "The New York Times/AFT Charter School Controversy." In *Spin Cycle: How Research Is Used in Policy Debates: The Case of Charter Schools.* New York: Russell Sage Foundation.

Henig, J. R., R. C. Hula, M. Orr, and D. S. Pedescleaux. 1999. *The Color of School Reform: Race, Politics and the Challenge of Urban Education.* Princeton, NJ: Princeton University Press.

Hernández, L. E. 2016. "Race and Racelessness in CMO Marketing: Exploring Charter Management Organizations' Racial Construction and its Implications." *Peabody Journal of Education* 91(1), 47–63. https://doi.org/10.1080/0 161956X.2016.1119566.

Hochschild, J. L. 2005. "What Boards Can and Cannot (or Will Not) Accomplish." In W. G. Howell, ed., *Besieged School Boards and the Future of Education Politics.* Washington: Brookings Institution Press.

Hochschild, J. L., and N. Scovronick. 2003. *The American Dream and the Public Schools.* New York: Oxford University Press. Retrieved from http://public .eblib.com/choice/publicfullrecord.aspx?p=272798.

Holme, J. J., S. Diem, and A. Welton. 2014. "Suburban School Districts and

Demographic Change: The Technical, Normative, and Political Dimensions of Response." *Educational Administration Quarterly* 50(1), 34–66. https://doi.org/10.1177/0013161X13484038.

Honig, M. I. 2006. "Street-Level Bureaucracy Revisited: Frontline District Central-Office Administrators as Boundary Spanners in Education Policy Implementation." *Educational Evaluation and Policy Analysis* 28(4), 357–83.

———. 2008. "District Central Offices as Learning Organizations: How Sociocultural and Organizational Learning Theories Elaborate District Central Office Administrators' Participation in Teaching and Learning Improvement Efforts." *American Journal of Education* 114(4), 627–664. https://doi.org/10.1086/589317.

Horsford, S. D. 2016. "Social Justice for the Advantaged: Freedom from Racial Equality Post-Milliken." *Teachers College Record* 118(3), 1–18.

Horsford, S. D., and C. Sampson. 2014. "Promise Neighborhoods: The Promise and Politics of Community Capacity Building as Urban School Reform." *Urban Education* 49(8), 955–91. https://doi.org/10.1177/0042085914557645.

Horsford, S. D., C. Sampson, and F. Forletta. 2013. "School Resegregation in the Mississippi of the West: Community Counternarratives on the Return to Neighborhood Schools in Las Vegas, 1968–1994." *Teachers College Record* 115(11), 1–28.

Howard, C. 2008. *The Welfare State Nobody Knows: Debunking Myths about U.S. Social Policy.* Princeton, NJ: Princeton University Press.

Ishimaru, A. M., A. Rajendran, C. M. Nolan, and M. Bang. 2018. "Community Design Circles: Co-designing Justice and Wellbeing in Family-Community-Research Partnerships." *Journal of Family Diversity in Education* 3(2), 38–63.

Jabbar, H. 2015. "'Every Kid Is Money': Market-Like Competition and School Leader Strategies in New Orleans." *Educational Evaluation and Policy Analysis* 37(4), 638–59. https://doi.org/10.3102/0162373715577447.

———. 2016. "Selling Schools: Marketing and Recruitment Strategies in New Orleans." *Peabody Journal of Education* 91(1), 4–23. https://doi.org/10.1080/0161956X.2016.1119554.

Kalleberg, A. L. 2011. *Good Jobs, Bad Jobs: The Rise of Polarized and Precarious Employment Systems in the United States, 1970s to 2000s.* New York: Russell Sage Foundation.

Kane, T. J., and D. O. Staiger. 2002. "The Promise and Pitfalls of Using Imprecise School Accountability Measures." *Journal of Economic Perspectives* 16(4), 91–114.

Kantor, H., and R. Lowe. 2006. "From New Deal to No Deal: No Child Left Behind and the Devolution of Responsibility for Equal Opportunity." *Harvard Educational Review* 76(4), 474–502.

———. 2013. "Educationalizing the Welfare State and Privatizing Education." In

P. L. Carter, ed., *Closing the Opportunity Gap: What America Must Do to Give Every Child an Even Chance*, pp. 25–39. New York: Oxford University Press.

Kasman, M., and S. Loeb. 2013. "Principals' Perceptions of Competition for Students in Milwaukee Schools." *Education Finance and Policy* 8(1), 43–73.

Katznelson, I. 2006. *When Affirmative Action Was White: An Untold History of Racial Inequality in Twentieth-Century America*. New York: W. W. Norton.

Katznelson, I., and M. Weir. 1985. *Schooling for All: Class, Race, and the Decline of the Democratic Ideal*. New York: Basic Books.

Kava, R. 2011. "Interdistrict Public School Open Enrollment." Informational paper no. 30, Madison: Wisconsin Legislative Fiscal Bureau. Retrieved from http://docs.legis.wisconsin.gov/misc/lfb/informational_papers/january_2011/0029_interdi strict_public_school_open_enrollment_informational_paper_29.pdf.

Kava, R., and R. Olin, R. 2005. "Local Government Expenditure and Revenue Limits." Informational paper no. 12. Madison: Wisconsin Legislative Fiscal Bureau.

Kertscher, T. 2011. "Former Wisconsin Gov. Jim Doyle Says He Imposed Tougher Cost Controls on State Employees Than Any Previous Governor." *Politifact Wisconsin*, January 11. Retrieved from https://www.politifact.com/wisconsin/statements/2011/jan/11/jim-doyle/former-wisconsin-gov-jim-doyle-says-he-imposed-tou/.

Khalifa, M. A., M. A. Gooden, and J. E. Davis. 2016. "Culturally Responsive School Leadership: A Synthesis of the Literature." *Review of Educational Research* 86(4), 1272–1311.

Kober, N. 2012. *A Public Education Primer: Basic (and Sometimes Surprising) Facts about the U.S. Educational System*. Washington: Center on Education Policy.

Kozol, J. 1991. *Savage Inequalities: Children in America's Schools*. New York: Crown Publishers.

Kumashiro, K. K. 2012. *Bad Teacher!: How Blaming Teachers Distorts the Bigger Picture*. New York: Teachers College Press.

Labaree, D. F. 1997. "Public Goods, Private Goods: The American Struggle over Educational Goals." *American Educational Research Journal* 34(1), 39–81. https://doi.org/10.3102/00028312034001039.

Lacy, K. 2016. "The New Sociology of Suburbs: A Research Agenda for Analysis of Emerging Trends." *Annual Review of Sociology* 42(1), 369–384. https://doi.org/10.1146/annurev-soc-071312-145657.

Ladson-Billings, G. 2006. "From Achievement Gap to the Education Debt: Understanding Achievement in US Schools." *Educational Researcher* 35(7), 3–12.

Ladson-Billings, G., and W. Tate IV. 1995. "Toward a Critical Race Theory of Education." *Teachers College Record* 97(1), 47–68.

Larson, C. L., and C. J. Ovando. 2001. *The Color of Bureaucracy: The Politics of Equity in Multicultural School Communities.* New York: Taylor and Francis Group.

Leachman, M., K. Masterson, and E. Figueroa. 2017. *A Punishing Decade for School Funding (Policy Report).* Washington: Center on Budget and Policy Priorities. Retrieved from https://www.cbpp.org/sites/default/files/atoms/files/11-29-17sfp.pdf.

Lee, S. J. 2005. *Up against Whiteness: Race, School, and Immigrant Youth.* New York: Teachers College Press.

———. 2008. "The Ideological Blackening of Hmong American Youth." In L. Weis, ed., *The Way Class Works: Readings on School, Family, and the Economy*, pp. 305–14. New York: Routledge.

Lee, S. J., and M. R. Hawkins. 2015. "Policy, Context and Schooling: The Education of English Learners in Rural New Destinations." *Global Education Review* 2(4), 40–59.

Leonardo, Z. 2007. "The War on Schools: NCLB, Nation Creation and the Educational Construction of Whiteness." *Race Ethnicity and Education* 10(3), 261–78. https://doi.org/10.1080/13613320701503249.

———. 2013. *Race Frameworks: A Multidimensional Theory of Racism and Education.* New York: Teachers College Press.

Leonardo, Z., and M. Hunter. 2007. "Imagining the Urban: The Politics of Race, Class, and Schooling." In W. Pink & G. Noblit, eds., *International Handbook of Urban Education.* Dordrecht, Netherlands: Springer.

Leong, N. 2013. "Racial Capitalism." *Harvard Law Review* 126(8), 2151–2226.

Levine, P. B., and D. J. Zimmerman. 1999. "An Empirical Analysis of the Welfare Magnet Debate Using the NLSY." *Journal of Population Economics* 12(3), 391–409.

Lewis, A. E., and J. B. Diamond. 2015. *Despite the Best Intentions: How Racial Inequality Thrives in Good Schools.* New York: Oxford University Press.

Lewis-McCoy, R. H. 2014. *Inequality in the Promised Land: Race, Resources, and Suburban Schooling.* Stanford, CA: Stanford University Press.

Light, I. 2006. *Deflecting Immigration: Networks, Markets, and Regulation in Los Angeles.* New York: Russell Sage Foundation.

Lipman, P. 2004. *High Stakes Education: Inequality, Globalization, and Urban School Reform.* New York: Routledge Falmer.

———. 2011. *The New Political Economy of Urban Education: Neoliberalism, Race, and the Right to the City.* New York: Routledge.

Livingston, M., and S. Porter. 2014. "The Great Chicago Migration Myth." *Journal and Courier*, October 18. Retrieved from http://www.jconline.com/story/news/2014/10/17/truth-black-white/17293817/.

Loew, P. 2013. *Indian Nations of Wisconsin: Histories of Endurance and Renewal*, 2nd ed. Madison: Wisconsin Historical Society Press.

López, G. R. 2003. "The (Racially Neutral) Politics of Education: A Critical Race Theory Perspective." *Educational Administration Quarterly* 39(1), 68–94. https://doi.org/10.1177/0013161X02239761.

López, I. H. 2014. *Dog Whistle Politics: How Coded Racial Appeals Have Reinvented Racism and Wrecked the Middle Class*. Oxford, UK, and New York: Oxford University Press.

López, M. P., and G. R. López. 2010. *Persistent Inequality: Contemporary Realities in the Education of Undocumented Latina/o Students*. New York: Routledge.

Lubienski, C. 2005. "Public Schools in Marketized Environments: Shifting Incentives and Unintended Consequences of Competition-Based Educational Reforms." *American Journal of Education* 111(4), 464–86.

———. 2007. "Marketing Schools: Consumer Goods and Competitive Incentives for Consumer Information." *Education and Urban Society* 40(1), 118–41. https://doi.org/10.1177/0013124507303994.

Lund, J., and C. Maranto. 1996. "Public Sector Labor Law: An Update." In D. Belman, M. Gunderson, and D. Hyatt, eds., *Public Sector Employment in a Time of Transition*, pp. 21–58. Ithaca, NY: Cornell University Press.

Lynch, K. 2014. "New Managerialism: The Impact on Education." *Concept* 5(3), 11.

Macek, S. 2006. *Urban Nightmares: The Media, the Right, and the Moral Panic over the City*. Minneapolis: University of Minnesota Press.

MacGillis, A. 2014. "The Unelectable Whiteness of Scott Walker." *New Republic*, June 15. Retrieved from https://newrepublic.com/article/118145/scott-walkers-toxic-racial-politics.

MacQueen, K. M., E. McLellan, K. Kay, and B. Milstein. 1998. "Codebook Development for Team-Based Qualitative Analysis." *Cultural Anthropology Methods* 10(2), 31–36.

Madison, J. 1787. "The Utility of the Union as a Safeguard against Domestic Faction and Insurrection (*The Federalist Papers*, no. 10)." Retrieved from http://avalon.law.yale.edu/18th_century/fed10.asp.

Marrow, H. B. 2005. "New Destinations and Immigrant Incorporation." *Perspectives on Politics* 3(4), 781–99.

Marsh, J. A. 2007. *Democratic Dilemmas: Joint Work, Education Politics, and Community*. Albany, NY: SUNY Press.

———. 2012. "Interventions Promoting Educators' Use of Data: Research Insights and Gaps." *Teachers College Record* 114(110303), 1–48.

Massey, D. S., ed. 2008. *New Faces in New Places: The Changing Geography of American Immigration*. New York: Russell Sage Foundation.

Massey, D. S., and N. A. Denton. 1993. *American Apartheid: Segregation and the Making of the Underclass.* Cambridge, MA: Harvard University Press.

Massey, D. S., J. Durand, and N. J. Malone. 2002. *Beyond Smoke and Mirrors: Mexican Immigration in an Era of Economic Integration.* New York: Russell Sage Foundation.

Massey, D. S., and K. A. Pren. 2012. "Unintended Consequences of US Immigration Policy: Explaining the Post-1965 Surge from Latin America." *Population and Development Review* 38(1), 1–29.

Maxwell, L. A. 2014. "U.S. School Enrollment Hits Majority-Minority Milestone." *Education Week*, August 19. Retrieved from http://www.edweek.org/ew/articles/2014/08/20/01demographics.h34.html.

McDermott, K. A. 1999. *Controlling Public Education: Localism versus Equity.* Lawrence: University Press of Kansas.

McGinnis, E., and A. L. Palos. 2011. *Precious Knowledge.* Dos Vatos Productions.

McNeil, L. 2000. *Contradictions of School Reform: Educational Costs of Standardized Testing.* New York: Routledge.

Mehta, J. 2015. "Escaping the Shadow: A Nation at Risk and Its Far-Reaching Influence." *American Educator* 39(2), 20–26.

Meier, D. 1995. *The Power of Their Ideas: Lessons for America from a Small School in Harlem.* Boston: Beacon Press.

Melamed, J. 2006. "The Spirit of Neoliberalism: From Racial Liberalism to Neoliberal Multiculturalism." *Social Text* 89, 24(4), 1–24.

———. 2011. *Represent and Destroy: Rationalizing Violence in the New Racial Capitalism.* Minneapolis: University of Minnesota Press.

Menken, K., and C. Solorza. 2014. "No Child Left Bilingual: Accountability and the Elimination of Bilingual Education Programs in New York City Schools." *Educational Policy* 28(1), 96–125. https://doi.org/10.1177/0895904812468228.

Mickelson, R. A., M. Bottia, and S. Southworth. 2012. "School Choice and Segregation by Race, Ethnicity, Class, and Achievement." In G. Miron, K. G. Welner, and P. H. Hinchey, eds., *Exploring the School Choice Universe: Evidence and Recommendations*, pp. 167–92. Charlotte, NC: Information Age Publishing.

Miles, M. B., and A. M. Huberman. 1994. *Qualitative Data Analysis: An Expanded Sourcebook.* Thousand Oaks, CA: Sage Publications.

Mollenkopf, J. H., and M. Castells. 1991. *Dual City: Restructuring New York.* New York: Russell Sage Foundation.

Moses, M. S., and M. J. Chang. 2006. "Toward a Deeper Understanding of the Diversity Rationale." *Educational Researcher*, 35(1), 6–11. https://doi.org/10.3102/0013189X035001006.

Mulcahy, C. C., and M. E. Mulcahy. 1995. "Innovation as the Key to a Redesigned and Cost Effective Local Government." *Marquette Law Review*, 78(3), 549–82.

Nader, L. 1969. "Up the Anthropologist: Perspectives Gained from 'Studying Up.'" In D. Hymes, ed. *Reinventing Anthropology*, pp. 284–311. New York: Pantheon Books.

National Center for Education Statistics. n.d. "Back to School Statistics for 2017." Retrieved May 23, 2018, from https://nces.ed.gov/fastfacts/display .asp?id=372.

National Commission on Excellence in Education. 1983. "A Nation at Risk: The Imperative for Educational Reform." *Elementary School Journal*, 84(2), 113–30.

National Research Council. 2011. "Incentives and Test-Based Accountability in Education," M. Hout and S. W. Elliott, eds. Washington: National Academies Press. Retrieved from http://0-site.ebrary.com.fama.us.es/lib/unisev/ Doc?id=10520719.

Ngai, M. M. 2004. *Impossible Subjects: Illegal Aliens and the Making of Modern America*. Princeton, NJ: Princeton University Press.

Ngo, B., and S. J. Lee. 2007. "Complicating the Image of Model Minority Success: A Review of Southeast Asian American Education." *Review of Educational Research* 77(4), 415–53. https://doi.org/10.3102/0034654307309918.

Noguera, P. 2003. *City Schools and the American Dream: Reclaiming the Promise of Public Education*. New York: Teachers College Press.

Novak, J. R., and B. Fuller. 2003. *Penalizing Diverse Schools?: Similar Test Scores, but Different Students, Bring Federal Sanctions* (Policy Brief 03-4). Berkeley: Policy Analysis for California Education.

Oakes, J. 1985. *Keeping Track: How Schools Structure Inequality*. New Haven: Yale University Press.

Oakes, J., A. S. Wells, and M. Jones. 1997. "Detracking: The Social Construction of Ability, Cultural Politics, and Resistance to Reform." *Teachers College Record* 98(3), 482–510.

Oakes, J., K. Welner, S. Yonezawa, and R. L. Allen. 1998. "Norms and Politics of Equity-Minded Change: Researching the "Zone of Mediation." In A. Hargreaves, A. Lieberman, M. Fullan, & D. W. Hopkins, eds., *International Handbook of Educational Change*, pp. 952–75. Dordrecht, Netherlands, and Boston: Springer.

Office for Civil Rights. 2012. 2011–2012 *Civil Rights Data Collection*. Retrieved March 28, 2018, from https://ocrdata.ed.gov/DistrictSchoolSearch.

Oliver, M., and T. M. Shapiro, eds. 2005. *Black Wealth / White Wealth: A New Perspective on Racial Inequality, 2nd Edition*. New York: Routledge.

Omi, M., and H. Winant. 2015. *Racial Formation in the United States*, 3rd ed. New York: Routledge.

Orfield, G., E. Frankenberg, J. Ee, and J. Kuscera. 2014. *Brown at 60: Great*

Progress, a Long Retreat and an Uncertain Future. Los Angeles: Civil Rights Project, University of California, Los Angeles.

Orfield, G., J. Kucsera, and G. Siegel-Hawley. 2012. *E Pluribus . . . Separation: Deepening Double Segregation for More Students*. Los Angeles: Civil Rights Project, University of California, Los Angeles.

Palmer, D. 2010. "Race, Power, and Equity in a Multiethnic Urban Elementary School with a Dual-Language 'Strand' Program." *Anthropology & Education Quarterly* 41(1), 94–114. https://doi.org/10.1111/j.1548-1492.2010.01069.x.

Parents Involved in Community Schools v. Seattle School District, no. 1 127 S.Ct. 2738, 168 L.Ed.2d. 508 (Supreme Court 2007).

Patton, M. Q. 1990. *Qualitative Evaluation and Research Methods*. Thousand Oaks, CA: Sage Publications.

Payne, C. M. 2008. *So Much Reform, So Little Change: Building-Level Obstacles to Urban School Reform*. Cambridge, MA: Harvard Education Press.

Pedroni, T. 2007. *Market Movements: African American Involvement in School Voucher Reform*. Hoboken, NJ: Routledge.

Peterson, P. E. 1981. *City Limits*. Chicago: University of Chicago Press.

Pew Research Center. 2016. *America's Shrinking Middle Class: A Close Look at Changes within Metropolitan Areas*, pp. 1–74. Washington: Pew Research Center. Retrieved from http://www.pewsocialtrends.org/2016/05/11/americas -shrinking-middle-class-a-close-look-at-changes-within-metropolitan-areas/.

Pierson, P. 1995. *Dismantling the Welfare State? Reagan, Thatcher and the Politics of Retrenchment*. Cambridge: Cambridge University Press.

Pollock, M. 2004. *Colormute: Race Talk Dilemmas in an American School*. Princeton, NJ: Princeton University Press.

Posey-Maddox, L. 2014. *When Middle-Class Parents Choose Urban Schools: Class, Race, and the Challenge of Equity in Public Education*. Chicago and London: University of Chicago Press.

———. 2017. "Schooling in Suburbia: The Intersections of Race, Class, Gender, and Place in Black Fathers' Engagement and Family-School Relationships." *Gender and Education* 29(5), 577–93. https://doi.org/10.1080/09540253.2016. 1274389.

Prier, D. D. 2015. "The Racial Politics of Leadership, Culture, and Community." *Urban Education*, 1–29. https://doi.org/10.1177/0042085915618719.

Quinn, N. 2005. Introduction to N. Quinn, ed., *Finding Culture in Talk: A Collection of Methods*, pp. 1–34.

Ray, V. 2019. "A Theory of Racialized Organizations." *American Sociological Review* 84(1), 26–53.

Reay, D., S. Hollingworth, K. Williams, G. Crozier, F. Jamieson, D. James, and P. Beedell. 2007. "'A Darker Shade of Pale?' Whiteness, the Middle Classes and Multi-Ethnic Inner City Schooling." *Sociology* 41(6), 1041–60.

Refugee Processing Center. 2018. "Department of State Bureau of Population,

Refugees, and Migration Office of Admissions – Refugee Processing Center: Refugee Arrivals Calendar Year as of 31 December 2010." Retrieved from http://ireports.wrapsnet.org/.

Rigby, J. G. 2014. "Three Logics of Instructional Leadership." *Educational Administration Quarterly* 50(4), 610–44.

Roda, A., and A. S. Wells. 2013. "School Choice Policies and Racial Segregation: Where White Parents' Good Intentions, Anxiety, and Privilege Collide." *American Journal of Education* 119(2), 261–93. https://doi.org/10.1086/668753.

Romell, R. 2016. "Wisconsin Has the Nation's Three Most Middle-Class Metro Areas." *Milwaukee Journal Sentinel*, May 11. Retrieved from http://www.jsonline.com/business/wisconsin-has-the-nations-three-most-middle-class-metro-areas-b99723702z1-379043181.html.

Rothstein, R. 2017. *The Color of Law: A Forgotten History of How Our Country Segregated America.* New York: Liveright.

Sanders, M. G. 2008. "Using Diverse Data to Develop and Sustain School, Family and Community Partnerships: A District Case Study." *Educational Management Administration & Leadership* 36(4), 530–45. https://doi.org/10.1177/1741143208095792.

Schirmer, E. 2019. "After Act 10: How Milwaukee Teachers Fought Back." *Dissent* 66(2), 48–56.

Schneider, J. 2011. *Excellence for All: How a New Breed of Reformers is Transforming America's Public Schools.* Nashville: Vanderbilt University Press.

Schram, S., and G. Krueger. 1994. Interstate Variation in Welfare Benefits and the Migration of the Poor: Substantive Concerns and Symbolic Responses. Institute for Research on Poverty, discussion paper no. 1032-94. University of Wisconsin–Madison.

Scott, J. 2013. "School Choice and the Empowerment Imperative." *Peabody Journal of Education* 88(1), 60–73. https://doi.org/10.1080/0161956X.2013.752635.

Scott, J., and J. J. Holme. 2016. "The Political Economy of Market-Based Educational Policies: Race and Reform in Urban School Districts, 1915 to 2016." *Review of Research in Education* 40(1), 250–97.

Scott, J. T. 2005. *School Choice and Diversity: What the Evidence Says.* New York: Teachers College Press.

Seligman, A. I. 2005. *Block by Block: Neighborhoods and Public Policy on Chicago's West Side.* Chicago: University of Chicago Press.

Shaefer, L. H., and K. Edin. 2018. "Welfare Reform and the Families It Left Behind." *Pathways*, 22–27.

Shipps, D. 2006. *School Reform, Corporate Style: Chicago, 1880–2000.* Lawrence: University of Kansas Press.

Shore, C., and S. Wright. 2000. "Coercive Accountability: The Rise of Audit Culture in Higher Education." In M. Strathern, ed., *Audit Cultures: Anthro-*

pological Studies in Accountability, Ethics and the Academy, pp. 57–89. New York: Routledge.

Simon, S. 2009. "Hard-Hit Schools Try Public-Relations Push." *Wall Street Journal*, August 17. Retrieved from https://www.wsj.com/articles/SB12504653075 3735355.

Sirin, S. R. 2005. "Socioeconomic Status and Academic Achievement: A Meta-Analytic Review of Research." *Review of Educational Research* 75(3), 417–53. https://doi.org/10.3102/00346543075003417.

Skrla, L., J. J. Scheurich, J. Garcia, and G. Nolly. 2004. "Equity Audits: A Practical Leadership Tool for Developing Equitable and Excellent Schools." *Educational Administration Quarterly* 40(1), 133–61. https://doi.org/10.1177/0013161X03259148.

Solórzano, D. G., and T. J. Yosso. 2002. "Critical Race Methodology: Counter-Storytelling as an Analytical Framework for Education Research." *Qualitative Inquiry* 8(1), 23–44.

Spicuzza, M. 2010. "Governor Leaves Mixed Legacy; Outgoing Leader Will End His Second Term in Much Different Climate Than the One He Entered in 2003; End of an Era." *Wisconsin State Journal*, December 19, p. 1A.

Spicuzza, M., and C. Barbour. 2010. "Education Funding a Touchy Subject. *Wisconsin State Journal*, July 24. Retrieved from http://host.madison.com/news/local/education/local_schools/education-funding-a-touchy-subject/article_bod53e22-4d53-5a77-ac71-19a160bdeaaf.html.

Spillane, J. P. 1996. "School Districts Matter: Local Educational Authorities and State Instructional Policy." *Educational Policy* 10(1), 63–87.

——. 1998. "State Policy and the Non-Monolithic Nature of the Local School District: Organizational and Professional Considerations." *American Educational Research Journal* 35(1), 33–63. https://doi.org/10.3102/00028312 035001033.

Staats, C., K. Capatosto, R. A. Wright, and D. Contractor. 2015. "State of the Science: Implicit Bias Review 2015." Kirwan Institute for the Study of Race and Ethnicity. Retrieved from http://kirwaninstitute.osu.edu/wp-content/uploads/2015/05/2015-kirwan-implicit-bias.pdf.

Stack, C. 1996. *Call to Home: African Americans Reclaim the Rural South*. New York: Basic Books.

Stone, C. N. 1998. *Changing Urban Education*. Lawrence: University Press of Kansas.

Stone, C. N., J. R. Henig, B. D. Jones, and C. Pierannunzi. 2001. *Building Civic Capacity: The Politics of Reforming Urban Schools*. Lawrence: University Press of Kansas.

Stone, D. A. 2002. *Policy Paradox: The Art of Political Decision Making*. New York: W. W. Norton.

Strathern, M., ed. 2000. "Introduction: New Accountabilities: Anthropological

Studies in Audit, Ethics and the Academy." In *Audit Cultures: Anthropological Studies in Accountability, Ethics, and the Academy*, pp. 13–30. New York: Routledge Press.

Suitts, S. 2015. *A New Majority: Low Income Students Now a Majority in the Nation's Public Schools*. Atlanta: Southern Education Foundation. Retrieved from http://www.southerneducation.org/Our-Strategies/Research-and-Publications/New-Majority-Diverse-Majority-Report-Series/A-New-Majority-2015-Update-Low-Income-Students-Now.

Sung, K. K. 2015. "Hella Ghetto!": (Dis)locating Race and Class Consciousness in Youth Discourses of Ghetto Spaces, Subjects and Schools." *Race, Ethnicity and Education* 18(3), 363–95. https://doi.org/10.1080/13613324.2013.792799.

Taylor, K. 2014. *Race for Results: Wisconsin's Need to Reduce Racial Disparities*. Madison: Wisconsin Council on Children and Families.

Theoharis, G. 2007. "Social Justice Educational Leaders and Resistance: Toward a Theory of Social Justice Leadership." *Educational Administration Quarterly* 43(2), 221–58. https://doi.org/10.1177/0013161X06293717.

Tienken, C. H., and Y. Zhao. 2013. "How Common Standards and Standardized Testing Widen the Opportunity Gap." In P. L. Carter and K. G. Weiner, eds., *Closing the Opportunity Gap: What America Must Do to Give Every Child an Even Chance*, 113–22. Oxford, UK: Oxford University Press.

Todd-Breland, E. 2018. "Serving the Public: Black Woman at the Center of Labor Struggle," the Gender Policy Report. Retrieved at https://genderpolicyreport.umn.edu/serving-the-public-black-women-at-the-center-of-labor-struggle/.

Trujillo, T. 2013. "The Politics of District Instructional Policy Formation: Compromising Equity and Rigor." *Educational Policy* 27(3), 531–59. https://doi.org/10.1177/0895904812454000.

———. 2014. "The Modern Cult of Efficiency: Intermediary Organizations and the New Scientific Management." *Educational Policy* 28(2), 207–32.

Turner, E. O. 2015. "Districts' Responses to Demographic Change: Making Sense of Race, Class, and Immigration in Political and Organizational Context." *American Educational Research Journal* 52(1), 4–39. https://doi.org/10.3102/0002831214561469.

———. 2018. "Market Diversity: Selling School Districts in a Racialized Marketplace." *Journal of Education Policy* 33(6), 793–817.

Turner, E. O., and A. K. Spain. 2016. "The Multiple Meanings of (In)equity: Remaking School District Tracking Policy in an Era of Budget Cuts and Accountability." *Urban Education*, 1–30. https://doi.org/10.1177/0042085916674060.

Tyack, D. 1974. *The One Best System: A History of American Urban Education*. Cambridge, MA: Harvard University Press.

Tyson, K. 2011. *Integration Interrupted: Tracking, Black Students, and Acting White after Brown*. New York: Oxford University Press.

US Bureau of Labor Statistics. 2011. "Local Unemployment Data: Wisconsin." Retrieved from http://data.bls.gov/.

US Census Bureau. 2009a. "2005–2009 American Community Survey 5-Year Estimates, S1702 Poverty Status in the Past 12 Months of Families." Retrieved from https://www.socialexplorer.com/.

———. 2009b. "State and County QuickFacts." Retrieved from http://quickfacts .census.gov/qfd/index.html.

———. 2011. "County-to-County Migration Flows: 2006–2010 ACS." Retrieved from https://www.census.gov/data/tables/2010/demo/geographic-mobility/ county-to-county-migration-2006-2010.html.

———. 2017a. "Profile of General Population and Housing Characteristics. 2010 Demographic Profile Data." Retrieved from https://factfinder.census.gov/ faces/nav/jsf/pages/community_facts.xhtml.

———. 2017b. "Small Area Income & Poverty Estimates (SAIPE) main page." Retrieved from https://www.census.gov/data-tools/demo/saipe/saipe.html?s_ appName=saipe&map_yearSelector=2016&map_geoSelector=aa_c.

———. N.d. "Decennial Census Data." Retrieved from https://www.census.gov/ programs-surveys/decennial-census/data.html.

US Department of Education. 2013. "Digest of Education Statistics, 2013." Retrieved from https://nces.ed.gov/programs/digest/d13/tables/dt13_203.50.asp.

Valdés, G. 1996. *Con Respeto: Bridging the Distances between Culturally Diverse Families and Schools: An Ethnographic Portrait.* New York: Teachers College Press.

Valencia, R. R. 1997. *The Evolution of Deficit Thinking: Educational Thought and Practice.* London: Falmer Press.

Valencia, R. R., and L. A. Suzuki. 2000. *Intelligence Testing and Minority Students Foundations, Performance Factors, and Assessment Issues.* Thousand Oaks, CA: Sage Publications.

Valenzuela, A. 1999. *Subtractive Schooling: U.S.-Mexican Youth and the Politics of Caring.* Albany: SUNY Press.

Varsanyi, M. 2010. *Taking Local Control: Immigration Policy Activism in U.S. Cities and States.* Stanford, CA: Stanford University Press.

Walker, J. R. 1994. Migration among Low-Income Households: Helping the Witch Doctors Reach Consensus. Institute for Research on Poverty, discussion paper no. 1031-94, University of Wisconsin–Madison.

Wells, A. S., and I. Serna. 1996. "The Politics of Culture: Understanding Local Political Resistance to Detracking in Racially Mixed Schools." *Harvard Educational Review* 66(1), 93–118.

Welton, A. D., S. Diem, and J. J. Holme. 2015. "Color Conscious, Cultural Blindness: Suburban School Districts and Demographic Change." *Education and Urban Society* 47(6), 695–722. https://doi.org/10.1177/0013124513510734.

Welton, A. D., D. R. Owens, and E. M. Zamani-Gallaher. 2018. "Anti-Racist

Change: A Conceptual Framework for Educational Institutions to Take Systemic Action." *Teachers College Record* 120(14).

Wheeler-Bell, Q. 2016. "Bring the State Back into Focus: Civic Society, the State, and Education." *Philosophy of Education*, 126–34.

Wilkinson, R., and K. Pickett. 2011. *The Spirit Level: Why Greater Equality Makes Societies Stronger.* New York: Bloomsbury Press.

Wilson, T. S., and R. L. Carlsen. 2016. "School Marketing as a Sorting Mechanism: A Critical Discourse Analysis of Charter School Websites." *Peabody Journal of Education* 91(1), 24–46. https://doi.org/10.1080/0161956X.2016.1119564.

Wisconsin Department of Children and Families. 2016. "15-year refugee Arrivals in Wisconsin by Destination County, Calendar Year 2001–2015." Retrieved from https://dcf.wisconsin.gov/refugee/statistics-population.

Wisconsin Department of Public Instruction. 2010. "2009–2010 Open Enrollment and Tuition Waiver Aid Adjustments and Open Enrollment Transfers by District." Retrieved from https://dpi.wi.gov/open-enrollment/data/aid-adjustments.

———. 2011. "Wisconsin Information System for Education: Data Dashboard." Retrieved from http://wisedash.dpi.wi.gov/Dashboard/portalHome.jsp.

———. 2013. "WINNS Historical Data Files." Retrieved from https://dpi.wi.gov/wisedash/download-files/type.

———. 2017. "Wisconsin Homeless Student Enrollment by Public School District." Retrieved from https://dpi.wi.gov/homeless/data.

———. 2018. "Wisconsin School District Performance Reports." Retrieved from https://apps2.dpi.wi.gov/sdpr/home.

———. N.d. "School Financing Reporting Portal (Custom Referenda Reports)." Retrieved from https://apps4.dpi.wi.gov/referendum/customreporting.aspx.

Witte, J. F., P. A. Schlomer, and A. F. Shober 2007. "Going Charter? A Study of School District Competition in Wisconsin." *Peabody Journal of Education* 82(2–3), 410–439. https://doi.org/10.1080/01619560701313051.

Wittkopf, S., and M. Robinson. 2014. *Segregation of Opportunity: Education Funding.* Madison, WI: Forward Institute.

Wortham, S., E. G. Murrillo Jr., and E. T. Hamann, eds. 2002. *Education in the New Latino Diaspora: Policy and the Politics of Identity*, Vol. 2. Westport, CT: Ablex.

Wright, W. E., and D. Choi. 2006. "The Impact of Language and High-Stakes Testing Policies on Elementary School English Language Learners in Arizona." *Education Policy Analysis Archives* 14(13), 1–58. https://doi.org/10.14507/epaa.v14n13.2006.

Yanow, D. 1996. *How Does a Policy Mean? Interpreting Policy and Organizational Actions.* Washington: Georgetown University Press.

Yin, R. K. 2003. *Case Study Research: Design and Methods.* Thousand Oaks, CA: Sage Publications.

Zaniewski, K. J. 2004. "Population Change in Wisconsin, 1990–2000." *Wisconsin Geographer* 20: 23–28, 35–38.

Zaniewski, K. J., and C. J. Rosen. 1998. *The Atlas of Ethnic Diversity in Wisconsin.* Madison: University of Wisconsin Press.

Zimmerman, J. 2000. "'Each "Race" Could Have Its Heroes Sung': Ethnicity and the History Wars in the 1920s." *Journal of American History* 87(1), 92–111.

Index